Praise for *The New Marketing P*

'There are theoretical books on marketing, and there are practical books on marketing. This is a great combination of them both! The frameworks, exercises and templates will enable you to work through any marketing challenge or opportunity and help you deliver impact and value. A must buy!'

Keith Weed, non-executive director, Sainsbury's and WPP

'This book is a great read that will help you add value to your business, customers and partners like no other. It guides you through the latest tools and techniques and breaks them down into simple to use templates that you can apply to your marketing activities.'

Margaret Jobling, Chief Marketing Officer, NatWest Group

'A must-have book for anyone interested in marketing to learn, step by step, how marketing is actually done.'

Jaideep Prabhu, Professor of Marketing, the Cambridge Judge Business School, Cambridge University

'This book is a very digestible and actionable playbook for the latest marketing tools and techniques. It's one of those books that you are glad you came across but wish you had discovered earlier.'

Mark Evans, Managing Director of Marketing and Digital, Direct Line Group

'A much needed book that demystifies how marketing can be used to generate business and societal value.'

Paul Polman, Chairman, Imagine and ex-CEO, Unilever

'The fundamentals of marketing haven't changed but the tools of execution are very different. The *New Marketing Playbook* captures this perfectly offering you fresh thinking on the basics and actionable insight into what's new.'

Russell Parsons, Editor in Chief, *Marketing Week*

The New Marketing Playbook

The New Marketing Playbook

The latest tools and techniques to grow your business

Ritchie Mehta

Pearson

Harlow, England • London • New York • Boston • San Francisco • Toronto • Sydney
Dubai • Singapore • Hong Kong • Tokyo • Seoul • Taipei • New Delhi
Cape Town • São Paulo • Mexico City • Madrid • Amsterdam • Munich • Paris • Milan

PEARSON EDUCATION LIMITED
KAO Two
KAO Park
Harlow CM17 9NA
United Kingdom
Tel: +44 (0)1279 623623
Web: www.pearson.com/uk

First edition published 2021 (print and electronic)

ISBN: 978-1-292-37380-5 (print)
978-1-292-37379-9 (PDF)
978-1-292-37378-2 (ePub)

British Library Cataloguing-in-Publication Data
A catalogue record for the print edition is available from the British Library

Library of Congress Cataloging-in-Publication Data
A catalog record for the print edition is available from the Library of Congress

10 9 8 7 6 5 4 3 2 1
25 24 23 22 21

Cover design by Two Associates

Print edition typeset in 10/14pt Charter ITC Pro by SPi Global
Printed by Ashford Colour Press Ltd, Gosport

NOTE THAT ANY PAGE CROSS REFERENCES REFER TO THE PRINT EDITION

To Deeya, Sophia and Evaan for all your support

Contents

Contents

About the author

Ritchie Mehta is the CEO of the School of Marketing (www.schoolofmarketing. co), an award winning, internationally recognised marketing skills and capability training organisation. The organisation helps upskill marketers and executive teams from leading Fortune 500 and FTSE 100 companies.

Ritchie is a globally sought-after consultant who has worked with some of the leading chief marketing officers and executive leadership teams on the development of their marketing approaches and strategies. He is also a regular speaker and lecturer at international conferences and renowned business schools. He was listed as one of the Change Makers of 2020 by *Marketing Week*, for his contribution to widening accessibility of marketing within the industry. He is also named in the BIMA100 list as a Champion of Change.

He is the founder of a number of investment-backed digital marketing agencies and consultancies. Prior to this, he was an Honorary Fellow of Marketing at the Cambridge Judge Business School, Adjunct Professor of Marketing at the Hult International Business School and Lecturer at Pearson Business School. He has also had a professional marketing career, having worked with a number of leading organisations including HSBC, RBS, Direct Line Group, Toyota and Pearson plc.

Ritchie earned an MBA (Distinction) from Warwick Business School (Warwick University), MPhil in Innovation, Organisation and Strategy from the Cambridge Judge Business School (University of Cambridge), MA (Hons) in Business (1st class) from University of Edinburgh and BSc in Financial Management from Manchester Business School (University of Manchester).

Publisher's acknowledgements

Text credits:

15 Living Media India Limited: Smitha Verma (2019), Potpourri of the real and the imagined world, India Today; **15 Penguin Random House:** Mark Reiter (2007), What Got You Here Won't Get You There: How Successful People Become Even More Successful, Random House Audio; Abridged edition; **7 eMarketer inc:** How Marketers Are Using Social Listening Right Now, eMarketer Editors, Jul 16, 2020; **19 Google LLC:** Optimize Help Center; **22 Jeff Bezos:** Dennis Green (2019), Jeff Bezos has said that Amazon has had failures worth billions of dollars — here are some of the biggest ones; **23 LexisClick Growth Consultancy:** Stephen Bavister (2019), Customer Obsession: The secret to Amazon's success, LexisClick; **33 Matt Francois:** How to build your SaaS platform prototype in 1 week, Matt Francois – MarketPlace Consultant; **47 Harvard Business Publishing:** Bruce Jones, Senior Programming Director, Disney Institute (2018), '3 Principles Disney Uses to Enhance Customer Experience', Harvard Business Review; **48 Qualtrics:** Diana Kaemingk (2018), 6 Ways Disney World delivers top customer experiences, Qualtrics; **51 Business 2 Community:** Harry Buckle (2019), The Relentless Pursuit of the Perfect Customer Experience: A Netflix Story, Business 2 Community; **55 Built for Mars Ltd:** The UX of banking, What the challenger banks did differently: a study into the UX of banking, Built for Mars; **69 Simon & Schuster:** Seth Godin (2007), Permission Marketing: Turning Strangers Into Friends And Friends Into Customers, Simon & Schuster UK; **72 Chipotle Mexican Grill:** Adapted from Values-Chipotle Mexican Grill; **88 Haymarket Media Group:** Emmet McGonagle (2020), Why Just Eat waited five weeks to unleash its Snoop, Campaign UK; **89 Rory Sutherland:** Rory Sutherland, Vice Chairman of Ogilvy; **90 Gordon Stanley:** Used with permission from Gordon Stanley, Director of

Commercial & Digital Practice at Leathwaite; **91 Alan Jope:** Quote by Alan Jope, the CEO of Unilever; **101 Haymarket Media Group:** Raja Rajamannar (2020), Marketing in times of crisis: Mastercard's global CMO shares 4 common traps and how to do better, Campaign US; **102 UGLY BRANDS INC:** Tagline from UGLY BRANDS INC; **103 Benjamin Braun:** Benjamin Braun, Chief Marketing Officer at Samsung Europe; **137 Penguin Random House:** Good To Great: Why Some Companies Make the Leap. . . and Others Don't, Hardcover – 4 Oct. 2001 by Jim Collins; **137 Clive Woodward:** Time to Reset: How businesses can accelerate out of the pandemic, Published on May 27, 2020; **137 The One Club for Creativity:** Fernando Machado (2020), WHAT DOES IT TAKE?, The One Club; **138 Harvard Business Publishing:** Michael Mankins and Eric Garton (2017), How Spotify Balances Employee Autonomy and Accountability, Harvard Business Review; **139 Alex Stephany:** Alex Stephany, one of the UK's leading social entrepreneurs; **141 JobAdder:** Stuart Read (2020), "Marketing is no longer about the stuff you make, but the stories you tell" – Seth Godin, JobAdder; **144 Ascential Events (Europe) Limited:** Fluent Devices and the forgotten art of memorability, WARC; **169 Google:** Google, Google Ads Help; **203 Kevin Johnson:** Quoted by Kevin Johnson; **207 John Esprian:** Tagline from John Esprian; **254 MindSea Team:** MindSea Team, 28 Mobile App Statistics To Know In 2020; **266 Foundation Inc:** The Canva Backlink Empire: How SEO, Outreach & Content Led To A $6B Valuation, Used with permission. https://foundationinc.co/lab/canva-seo; **276 Built for Mars:** Built for Mars. The UX of banking. Retrieved from https://builtformars.com/banks/; **284 John Wanamaker:** Quoted by John Wanamaker; **285 Institute of Practitioners in Advertising:** Adapted from Media in Focus, Marketing effectiveness in digital era.

Photo credits:

11 Shutterstock: chuckstock/Shutterstock; **11 Shutterstock:** Anastasia_Panait/Shutterstock; **11 Pearson Education:** Coleman Yuen/Pearson Education Asia Ltd; **11 123RF:** andyfletch/123rf.com.

Screenshots:

5, 6, 87, 165, 166, 167, 183 Google: Screenshot of Google adword tool © Google LLC; **8 BuzzSumo Ltd:** Adapted from Buzzsumo social listening tool – vegan recipes, BuzzSumo Ltd, Buzzsumo social listening tool–vegan recipes, BuzzSumo Ltd, https://app.buzzsumo.com/content/web?q=vegan%20

recipe&search=true&begin_date=Feb%2001%202020&end_date=Aug%2001%202020&result_type=total&language=en&range=P6M; **9 Sparktoro:** Sparktoro competitor and social analysis tool, Used with permission from Sparktoro; **16 Facebook:** Screenshot of Facebook audience selection tool, Facebook; **18 Google:** Screenshot of Google optimize research © Google LLC; **92 Unilever UK:** The three big goals, The Unilever Sustainable Living Plan 2010-2020, Used with permission from Unilever, https://www.unilever.co.uk/sustainable-living/the-unilever-sustainable-living-plan/; **123 DreamGrow:** Content Marketing Strategy: Getting Results Online and Offline, FEBRUARY 16, 2018, Dreamgrow; **126 School Of Marketing:** Screenshot of School of Marketing Sign up page, Used with permission from School Of Marketing; **174 Facebook:** Screenshot of Facebook ad manager, Facebook; **175 Facebook:** Screenshot of Facebook's audience selection tool, Facebook; **175 Facebook:** Screenshot of Facebook detailed targeting tool, Facebook; **176 Linkedin:** Screenshot of LinkedIn ad formats, Linkedin; **177 Linkedin:** Screenshot of Forecasted Results, Linkedin.

Introduction

The world of marketing is transforming at an ever-increasing rate. There are new disruptive innovations, tools, techniques and platforms coming into the market on an almost daily basis in a bid to grab, excite and engage customers. This is compounded by the fact that what we are witnessing is an intense and prolonged period categorised as being volatile, uncertain, complex and ambiguous (VUCA for short), or put simply in the words of Salman Rushdie: "We are living in the age of anything can happen."[1]

So with this level of change firmly upon us, it begs the question: What are you doing to keep yourself and your organisation at the top of your marketing game?

Increasingly, organisations are turning to marketers[2] to help interpret and make sense of this ambiguity and carve out the path less, or rather not, travelled before. This is because marketing has one very significant advantage over all other functions, which is its fundamental role as the customer champion and voice in the organisation. Its relentless focus on understanding the customer and anticipating and delivering to their constantly evolving needs and wants is the single greatest offence and defence an organisation has during these times.

It certainly feels like the time has come when all the training, experience, marketing models and previously relied upon wisdoms are not sufficient to help navigate this new reality. So in the famous words of Marshall Goldsmith: "What got you here, won't get you there."[3]

This is where this playbook comes in. It is your personal and practical guide to help you learn and apply all of the latest marketing tools and techniques, so you can not only navigate this new reality but also be a disruptive force, driving change within your organisation.

Using this playbook you will be able transform your marketing activities by unearthing undiscovered insights about your customers, developing new propositions and customer experiences to meet their needs, create compelling communication and engagement strategies integrating the latest tools, and finally provide you with new ways to iterate and improve your marketing.

At each point along the way you will find relevant frameworks, tables, exercises, activities and case studies. These are aimed at getting you to think differently about your current marketing challenges and provide you with a roadmap on how to deal with even the most complex situations. This playbook, therefore, becomes an essential and invaluable resource that you can keep coming back to over time, when faced with pivotal decision points in your career.

It is intended to be an interactive, thought-provoking experience where you can use the templates, figures and tables to make notes, highlight things, draw your own analysis and create your marketing blueprint. Above all it is intended to be your catalyst to taking action in a structured and strategic way to maximise your marketing potential.

To help you get the most out of this playbook, I have broken it down into five parts of the marketing process:

Part 1: How to understand your customers and deliver to their needs

You will use the latest market research tools and techniques to generate insights in order to create new propositions and customer experiences.

Part 2: How to build your brand

You will craft a brand that resonates with your target audience and determines how to create a strong connection with them.

Part 3: How to scale your marketing

You will use the latest digital tools and techniques to reach new audiences and amplify your message in cost-effective ways.

Part 4: How to engage your customers

You will engage and delight your customers and turn them into advocates of your brand.

Part 5: How to check your marketing is working

You will be able to measure and iterate your marketing activities to continually improve your results.

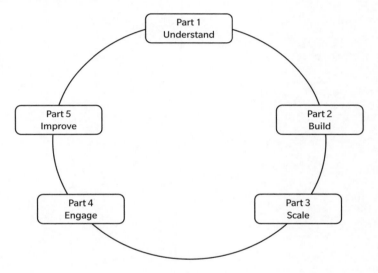

Who is this playbook for?

This playbook is for those who want to use the power of marketing to get ahead. It is likely that you are or aspire to be a change-maker, an out-of-box thinker, an innovator, an instigator or even a rainmaker in your chosen organisation. It is ideal for anyone who is both strategic and action-oriented, regardless of your role, level or industry, and will give you the edge to be able to create real tangible change, even if you do not have 'marketing' in your job title.

A key thread flowing through this playbook is the need to be entrepreneurial (or intrapreneurial), actively experiment and see the process as being an iterative one. Therefore, you need to be the type of person who wants to break away from the norm, put yourself out there and achieve significant results. This does require a certain entrepreneurial mindset to stand out from the crowd, to challenge the status quo and think differently, perhaps even irrationally, so when everyone else zigs, you zag. It takes a combination of bravery, creativity, strategy, collaboration and innovation to achieve this, which you will develop as you go through the process in this playbook.

It is also relevant for anyone who is looking to forge a career in marketing and wants to learn about the latest ways to use marketing to generate significant value for any organisation. This playbook will help springboard you into the role that you want by demonstrating your ability to apply the tools, techniques and platforms outlined in any organisational context.

Why now?

This book certainly couldn't come at a better time as even companies that were seemingly on the cutting edge of innovation, where they themselves were disrupting industries, are on the brink of collapse. For instance, evidence shows that the lifespan of a company in the S&P 500 has decreased from around 25 years at the turn of the century to around 17 years twenty years later[4] (by the way it was around 60 years in the 1960s).[5] This is largely due to the pace of disruption and transformation that has accelerated over recent years, exacerbated further by the recent global pandemic. So much so that Satya Nadella, CEO of Microsoft, was quoted as saying that in today's environment companies had undergone two years' worth of digital transformation in two months.[6]

This reveals two important lessons for organisations. The first is that no company is immune from the risk of extinction, as business models change at a rapid pace. The second, perhaps more encouraging, is that in the face of such disruption organisations are able to achieve things they may have thought impossible before. It's abundantly clear that in the face of adversity the single most important ingredient that separates the winners and losers is the pursuit of customer obsession.

This is where organisations foster a deep appreciation and empathy for what the customer is going through and adapts the way it operates to align to their new customer reality quickly. The way they achieve this is by going through the marketing process and by leveraging the full spectrum of the marketers' toolkit to pivot their way to success.

Perhaps mostly interestingly, many of these actions involved no additional (marketing) budget. In fact, counterintuitively quite the opposite – they relied purely on creativity, a shift in mindset and a desire to use new tools and techniques to meet wider societal needs.

By using this playbook, you will be able to achieve this too, so you can tackle the many challenges that your organisation will face in the future.

— Change promotional materials from appreciation of business to empathy / understanding of what the client is going through & how we can help

part 1

How to understand your customers and deliver to their needs

chapter 1

Know what your customers really want

At the centre of every marketing strategy lies a research process that helps you understand your customer's needs and wants. It forms the very basis from which you can then build compelling propositions, experiences and communications to satisfy and exceed expectations. It is therefore an appropriate place for you to start on your marketing journey, and so this chapter will help you to determine how to combine some of the latest research tools and techniques to unearth new and interesting insights about your customers.

Today, there is a sophisticated range of data-driven tools and techniques that you can use to gain an in-depth understanding of your customer's needs, behaviours and even emotions. Increasingly, these are becoming more digitally oriented, from social media listening tools to automation and AI platforms that present new ways of conducting market research.

Despite the many advantages that these new and streamlined approaches present, it would be foolish to underestimate the task at hand. There are seemingly an ever-growing number of tools and techniques available that can make it confusing for you to know even where to begin. And when combined with the sheer amount of information that you need to analyse, it becomes a complex task for even the seasoned professional.

So to keep you on track, let me help create a logical order and process for you to use these tools and demonstrate the types of ways you can use a range of them to get the most out of your research. You will need to contextualise the approach for your brand, but this should give you a good structure to use.

This process consists of four key stages.

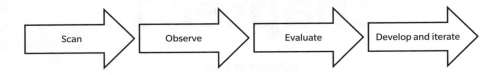

Scan → Observe → Evaluate → Develop and iterate

Stage 1: Scan

The first stage in the process is to scan your audience's context and environment. Bear in mind that it is constantly shifting and evolving in subtle ways and therefore tracking the ebbs and flows over time is essential.

Setting up the right tools to help automate this process will not only save time but actually lead to a more accurate understanding. Let's start with one of the best resources you have at your fingertips – Google. Although I'm sure you will be familiar with this tool, here are three handy techniques to optimise the platform for trend analysis.

First, setting up Google Alerts on key topics of interest can really help you keep up to date with trends in real time. I recommend you track your key customers, companies, industries, local news and any other areas you think would be relevant to your audience. I have found that this is not only incredibly insightful but often is a great reason to connect with potential customers to learn more from them first hand.

Write down the topics you think will be most relevant in the template below:

Customers/companies
- caregivers
- other agencies
- facilities

Industries
- staffing
- travel
- aL/MC

Other relevant topics
- pay

Second, the importance of generating longitudinal data about your customers is key, which is where Google Trends (https://trends.google.com/) can be very useful. To help illustrate, let's say we are interested in starting or expanding into a vegan product line. Type in the term 'vegan' into Google Trends. You will see over a number of years the popularity of the search term 'vegan' has consistently risen, suggesting an increasing interest in this topic.

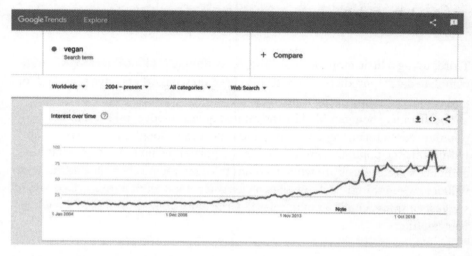

Google Trends: Vegan search term

Once you have understood the high-level trend, your next step is to dig a little deeper. Scroll down in Google Trends and take a look at the related queries. This will give you an indication of the type of things that sit under the broad trend.

You will see top searches related to 'vegan recipes' and various specific foods. This is helping to narrow down 'what' people are interested in, which is useful on our path to determine their 'why'.

Related queries	Top		Related queries	Top
1 vegan recipe	100		6 vegetarian	48
2 vegan recipes	98		7 vegan chocolate	42
3 vegan food	90		8 vegan near me	41
4 vegan diet	55		9 vegan cake	40
5 vegan restaurants	55		10 vegan cheese	39

Google top search results – vegan recipes

Jot down a number of related searches for the trends that are relevant for you:

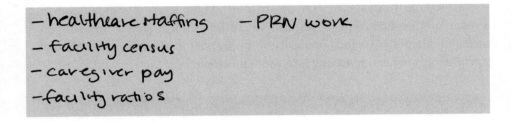

— healthcare staffing   — PRN work
— facility census
— caregiver pay
—facility ratios

Third, to dig a little more, another simple technique is to look at Google's auto-complete data. It predicts search terms based on what others have searched for and what is trending at the time.

For instance, being guided by the related queries above, take the most popular search term, 'vegan recipe', and type it into Google. You can see that within this the popular searches in this category show up indicating what our audience's preferences are when it comes to vegan recipes. Simple and yet very valuable when thinking about what a customer could want in this area. I would suggest running a number of queries like this with your keywords to see what you can find.

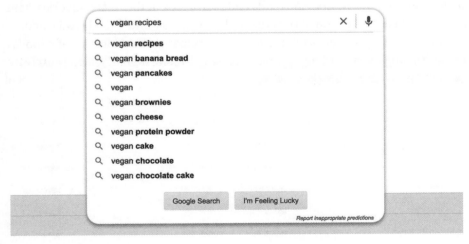

Google autocomplete

Now, if you want a more in-depth understanding of these autocomplete terms here is a little tip. There is a great tool called Answerthepublic.com that uses many thousands of these data points and generates a mind map for you to easily visualise the responses. Go to the site and check out the feature.

Let's consolidate your understanding so far. In the box, write down some of the key trends you have uncovered and the keyword search terms that are most relevant.

Hear it from them

Let's turn to automated social media listening tools in order to generate a more holistic understanding of consumer sentiment. In fact, these tools are famously said to be "the world's largest and most open focus group".[1]

These platforms allow you to scan and analyse consumer conversations, posts, comments, shares and likes that can be very useful in explaining some of the high-level trends identified above. There are a range of great tools out there to achieve this, including Buzzsumo, Hootsuite and Sprout Social to name a few.

Let's stick with the vegan theme and use the most searched term under the vegan category 'vegan recipes' to illustrate how you can use these tools effectively. Using the tool you are able to determine the 'buzz' over time and assess the level of engagement of the audience.

In most social listening tools you will be able to analyse around a six-month view of the top engagement posts which gives you great insights into both the types of vegan recipes that are most popular as well as the influencers in this area. In addition, they will also give you a breakdown of where these conversations are happening, which could be very useful later on when determining where the target audience is, as it's a strong indicator of age, location and other demographic and attitudinal characteristics. Run a similar analysis with what is relevant to you and see what comes up.

Social Feeds and Key Topics	Social Media Channels and Levels of Engagement						Engagement Score
	Faceboo k Shares	Instagram Shares	Tik Tok Shares	LinkedIn Shares	Pinterest Shares	YouTube Shares	
Vegan recipe goes viral after celeb chef shares his secret	1,679	3,234	6,325	328	45	65	73
Latest vegan health trends and recipes revealed with much acclaim from the vegan community	890	1,357	3,754	890	9,864	167	79
Debate breaks out on the health benefits of certain vegan recipes that contain a range of different ingredients	765	1,234	9,876	6,543	1,543	56	65
The latest gameshow on who can make the best vegan desserts is back across primetime TV	5,789	2,765	908	435	1,865	982	80

Buzzsumo social listening tool – vegan recipes

Competitor scanning

To this point you have focussed on scanning the search trends and the customer conversation. However, you must also look at your competitors and wider norms of the industry to determine the various styles, tone and offerings. To achieve this, let's turn to an evolving area of digital semiotics. This is where you observe a range of digital assets, such as websites, podcasts, social media pages and customer journeys, to identify standards and commonalities that form customer expectations.

You can conduct your own analysis in this area by deciding on the most popular competitor websites and podcasts to analyse. Alternatively, you can use a range of tools to generate this level of information. The tool that I find most helpful is Sparktoro (https://sparktoro.com/) to identify the digital assets to analyse further, as shown below when searching for vegan recipes. Head over to the platform and see what you can find out about your competitors and market position. Alternatively, you can use Semrush to analyse your competitors' digital footprint.

Now you can investigate how your key competitors design, talk about, write about, share content and monetise. You are also able to generate a comparison of the popularity of the various digital assets and thereby judge what is working and what is not.

Here is the Sparktoro competitor and social analysis tool.

① job title that is common among the audience you want to research

② popular hashtags in industry

③ a source of influence our audience already pays attention to

You should now have a good understanding of the key trends, people conversations and how the industry and competitors are approaching the situation. This should start to reveal potential gaps. Here is a simple model you can use to summarise your thoughts.

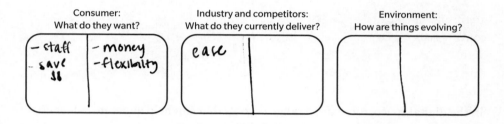

Stage 2: Observe

There are a range of tools and techniques that enable you to gain a first-hand account of how people behave in their natural environment.

Customer journey analysis

First, you need to conduct a customer journey analysis as it can really help to determine the behaviours of your audience in their natural setting.

At a practical level, the most useful technique I have seen is to ask a sample of your audience to walk through the experience, physically or digitally, when looking to buy a certain product, while being observed in person or remotely. This is a guided form of ethnographic research where an observer takes notes while watching and listening to the person, looking out for key insights into 'why' they are making certain decisions along the way. Try it!

Go into your local supermarket or screenshare with a sample of your audience and observe the process as they make a purchase, looking for both overt as well as subtle things they do.

Note that most people get hung up on trying to identify and define the ideal journey, where in most instances there isn't one. In fact, Google conducted an experiment of thousands of users and found that no two journeys were exactly the same.[2] Rather, what you should be trying to observe is specific pain points in the journey and consider ways to make it more seamless and frictionless for your customers.

Write down some of your observations, particularly the pain points in the journey here.

In the digital space, there are a range of tools that can help generate a deeper level of understanding such as Crazyegg (www.crazyegg.com), Hotjar (www. hot- jar.com), Cool Tool (https://cooltool.com) and Element Human (https:// www.elementhuman.com).

Let's discuss four of the key techniques these tools allow you to do.

Session recordings	Heat maps	Eye tracking analysis	Emotion tracking
This is where you can actually record the screen and your customer's voice as they go through the end-to-end journey.	This is very useful to understand where on the page and journey is receiving the most clicks and engagement. It helps you determine the area in the journey where customers are drawn to including, areas, words, pictures, videos, offers etc.	Although this requires some set up it provides an extra layer of insight into how your customers view and interact online. Using motion sensors it tracks eye movement which helps you understand what your customers are most attracted to across the digital journey.	Combining advanced AI with techniques such as voice and facial analysis, human language usage and gesture recognition to enable an accurate understanding of consumer emotions during a process.

I would recommend checking these out and seeing if they are relevant to use in your context.

Shopper preferences

You are beginning to determine key behaviours and are gaining an understanding as to why your audience takes certain action over others. One of the most powerful indicators of your customer's intent is to look at their purchasing habits. To achieve this, a useful technique is to research shopper data, including ratings and reviews. Let's head over to a leading e-commerce platform to see what we can learn. There are two easy steps here.

Step 1: Identify relevant items

You need to determine the type of products that are relevant to you and search for them. Let me illustrate. Continuing with the vegan theme, let's say you wanted to learn more about vegan banana bread, since it's the most popular searched item within vegan recipes. When I type 'vegan banana bread' into the e-commerce site, a vast array of items comes up. The first thing to do is to choose items that have a significant number of reviews to make it reliable.

Here is an example I found where you can see a huge variation in the number of reviews. The second option has the largest sample size and overall it has good reviews, although it has a number of 3-star reviews and below we can learn from as well.

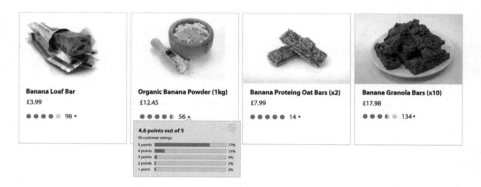

Vegan banana bread search on a leading e-commerce website

Step 2: Investigate ratings and reviews

Let's dig deeper into the ratings and reviews to see if we can gain some very valuable insights into 'why' it does or does not appeal. In the example below, we can see that the 5-star review highlights that it appeals to busy mums while on the go as an indulgent snack rather than chocolate when doing activities with their toddler. This one review has provided invaluable insights into the type of customer it appeals to, when it appeals to them and why they choose it over something else. On the other hand, the 1-star review is very revealing about the attitudes of this type of individual in that they are likely to have a heightened ethical stance.

★★★★★ **Busy Working Mum**
A handbag must for mums constantly on the go

I really wouldn't go anywhere without these bites in my bag - they come in handy and often a life saver when I'm out with my infant like taking him swimming. I love the taste and at only 140 calories I feel good about snacking on them. It's a much better alternative than chocolate. Great price as well!

★☆☆☆☆ **Scott D**.
Contains Palm Oil - a no go for me!

Ah although it's technically still vegan it still contains palm oil. It does taste good but really disappointing that it has ingredients like palm oil, especially as the branding is trying to portray a more environmentally conscious snack!

Banana bread reviews from a leading e-commerce website

Now have a go at doing this investigative work yourself on an e-commerce platform and record your findings here.

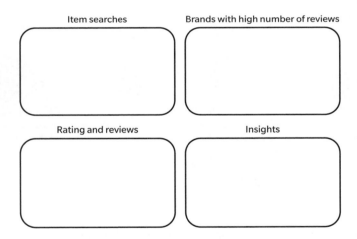

Mobile interactions and geolocation

It's important to note that people tend to act differently depending on the context they are in. So if we can understand the where and when they do something we can more accurately predict behaviours, needs and wants. This is where mobile data is invaluable. For example, Google reports that 48% of experience bookings are happening once people arrive at a destination. The choice of which restaurant to eat at or hotel to stay at would therefore be vastly different depending on when and where the person is at the time they made the booking.

So how can you use mobile interactions and geolocation to your advantage?

Here are a number of ways you can use these techniques to understand more about your target customer.

- **Audience identification**: You can find new audiences based on location tracking and interactions. Knowing when someone is near you and has expressed an interest in your product or service creates an increased likelihood that they could be a potential customer of yours. Using services like Foursquare (https://foursquare.com) you can achieve this type of data in real time.

- **Real-time research**: Using the power of social media or within your own app you have the ability to service a push notification, offer or even a polling question to someone who 'checks-in' to a location. This gives you an additional layer of insight into where and when someone is interacting with you.

- **Understand broad location trends**: Using mobile location data you have the ability to develop macro and micro-level insights on your audience. For instance, services like Foursquare provide macro trends on your typical audience's location footprint. This gives you vital information on what to offer them at different times and locations. At the same time, you can achieve this level of information even in a store using beacons to determine how your customers are browsing, which can help with product placement and overall customer experience.

Through this observation of specific behaviours we are able to generate an understanding of how your audience is likely to act. Capture your key observations here.

Customer experience: How do you create a frictionless journey?	Product preferences: What do they love and hate about current offerings?	Location and moment to engage: When and where is the optimal time for them to engage?

Stage 3: Evaluate

Sense-check and validate

By this point, you have generated a significant amount of information about your customers and through the process understood their wider context, preferences, views, opinions, attitudes and behaviours. You have used multiple data sources through this process that you can cross-reference against, which will help increase the accuracy of results.

The next step, to add an extra layer of assurance and give you the opportunity to clarify any potential misunderstandings, is worth carrying out some form of validation research. You can use techniques you may already be familiar with including (online) polling, (virtual) in-depth interviews or even conducting data analysis using existing datasets you may have. This is a form of triangulation, where you pay particular attention to where any potential bias or inaccuracies may have crept into your research.

Write down your thoughts on what research techniques you intend on using for this validation and exactly what you are looking to clarify.

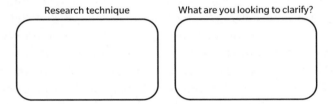

Let's now take some time to reflect and evaluate what you have learned about your customers. This involves three steps: the first is to develop a consolidated view of our ideal target audience by creating a customer persona; the second is to determine the addressable market size; and the third is to put together some initial marketing goals and objectives.

Step 1: Developing a customer persona

A customer persona is a caricature of your ideal target customer based on all the information you have including demographic, geographic, psychographic, attitudinal and behavioural factors. There are plenty of templates you can use for this, but it comes down to a few killer questions. In the template below I have given you an example using the insights revealed from the vegan example, and left space for you to follow suit using your own context.

Who are they/where do they go/what do they do?

Example	Your customer
Jen is in her late 30s and is a mum. She is time poor and finds juggling a career with her responsibilities as a parent tiring but rewarding. She is health conscious and looking at ways to improve her family's diet, which is why she started following a range of vegan bloggers and websites.	All ages in a healthcare role. Crave flexibility and money to support families and school costs.

What motivates/interests them?

Example	Your customer
She is an energetic person that tries to fill her day to the brim. She is interested in swimming and spending time with her child. She is also ethically conscious and currently considering both the health and moral benefits of veganism.	Money, making a difference in patients' lives

What are their current pain points?

Example	Your customer
She finds it difficult to figure out ways to make her diet healthier, yet interesting particularly as she is constantly on the go and hence is constantly researching on social media and other websites. She is unsure of the different vegan food options available particularly as she eats out regularly and would like to know what is in her local area that will cater for her.	

What will overcome the pain points?

Example	Your customer
She would be happy if she could find a wide variety of vegan options to prepare herself and in her local area. She would also like help to determine healthier options for her family both at meal time and as a snack on the go. She would want to have continued support on her mobile and just make it so easy that it fits into her life.	

Step 2: Finding and sizing these audiences

Now that you have a clear idea of who your target customer is and what moti-
vates them, it's important to translate this persona into real life and identify
where these customers are. This will not only help you with your targeting
approach but also allows you to create realistic goals for you to achieve. There
are numerous ways to determine this total addressable market, but I prefer an
approach that is tangible and linked to our ability to target them.

This is where you can effectively use social media platforms to conduct
this market sizing exercise. Let me show you how this is done using Facebook
(although it works similarly across most social media platforms).

Let's head over to the Facebook Ad Centre. You can customise the targeting
approach across demographics, interests and behaviours based on the customer
persona you have put together. As you narrow down your target audience in the
Facebook tool you will see the impact that has on the total addressable market.

For instance I have narrowed down the criteria for the vegan example and
found that the potential market opportunity is around 14 million people.

Facebook audience selection tool:

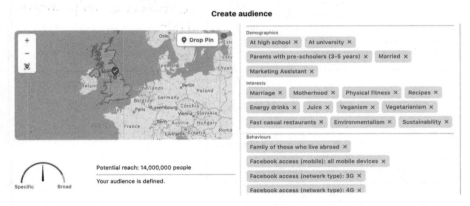

Source: https://www.facebook.com/ad_center/create/websitead/?entry_point=www_
pages_product_picker&page_id=648613898536257

Have a go at doing this yourself and see what you come up with. This will feed
into how we create tangible customer goals and objectives to meet those needs
later on.

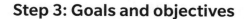

Step 3: Goals and objectives

Based on all this information, you are now in the position to develop customer goals and objectives. It's important to set realistic but ambitious targets. There is a simple acronym to use here, SMART.

Specific	A very well-defined, clear and unambiguous goal
Measurable	Has specific criteria that you measure against toward the accomplishment of the goal
Achievable	Attainable yet not impossible to achieve
Realistic	A goal that is within reach and realistic
Timely	Has a very clearly defined timeline, including a start and end date

Here is a list of some of the types of key performance indicators goals you should consider. On the right-hand side consider reasonable targets that are achievable for you.

Awareness/salience	Target to achieve	Digital KPIs	Target to achieve
Growth in organic traffic Brand recall Brand satisfaction		Traffic volume Average time on site Subscribers, likes and shares	
Commercial KPIs		**Customer KPIs**	
Sales Profit Cost per acquisition		Average customer value % of repeat purchases % of recommendations	

It is worth considering the SMART acronym when developing your KPIs.

Stage 4: Develop and iterate

In this last section, we will look at a number of tests you can run to understand how your customers are responding to the product or service that you have developed. It is important that you constantly test and iterate your approach based on feedback and monitoring.

Active experimentation

So let's assume you launch a beta version of your product or service. To achieve optimal results you must adopt the mindset of 'active experimentation', where you constantly make tweaks to see how it impacts on performance. I recommend carrying out three different types of testing that can be carried out using Google Optimise (https://marketingplatform.google.com/):

- **A/B testing:** This is very straightforward where you test one item against another to see which is preferred by the audience. For example, it was famously known that Google conducted 41 A/B tests on different variations of blue in their logo. This can extend to product, content, placement comparisons as well.

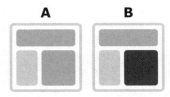

- **Redirect testing:** This is a variant on A/B testing but allows you to test one website against each other. It is useful if you are trying to determine which overall experience appeals more to a customer. Google Optimise will direct certain traffic to one versus another automatically based on volumes to give you an accurate assessment of your customer's preferences.

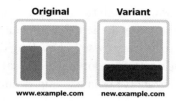

- **Multivariate testing:** This is where you test two or more variants simultaneously to assess which combination works best. Again, Google Optimise will conduct the test for you and direct customers to the different variants in a way that delivers you robust results.

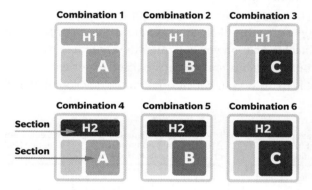

Source: https://support.google.com/optimize/topic/9340207?hl=en&ref_topic=6197429

Go on to the platform and conduct some of the tests recommended above, write down any key observations here.

Active engagement and listening

As customers go through your journey you want to review how they engage with you and take on board their feedback. Let's go through a number of ways you can achieve this.

First, you need to set up Google Analytics (analytics.google.com) to understand if you are attracting the target audiences you want, and it also gives you traffic trends – what pages they are browsing, how long they are staying, what they are purchasing and even cart abandonment. You can use this information to iterate our targeting strategy and make improvements to the customer journey.

Second, you need to implement feedback tools into the platform to understand how people are reacting. In a similar way to Amazon's rating system, you can implement your own using tools such as Feefo (www.feefo.com/) or Gong (www.gong.io/) to monitor real-time customer service conversations. This will give you real-time feedback on what is most important to your customers in order to make improvements.

Finally, you can use mobile app location data as a way to determine when and where people are most likely to view your different products and services. Armed with this information you can tailor the content to these times and contexts to give your customers a more personalised experience.

Here is a table to draw your conclusions on the development and iterate stage.

Co-creation: Tight alignment to customer expectations	Active experimentation: To continually optimise the product and customer journey	Active engagement and listening: Generate feedback and make improvements

chapter 2

Create an innovative value proposition

We are now going to focus on how to determine the key features and benefits of a proposition that are not only valued by the audience but also highly differentiated.

Now that you have uncovered how to understand what your customers are looking for through the research process, I will now help you to build a value proposition to meet their needs. Truly remarkable value propositions are those that understand the intrinsic nature of going beyond the core features and benefits of a product and look at crafting a compelling experience that influences someone at an emotional level.

Take, for example, a new pair of Apple Airpods. It has a compelling set of features such as its world-class ergonomic design, surround-sound quality and market-leading noise-cancelling technology. All of these features together deliver the 'rational' benefit of a superior listening experience to the customer. However, in addition to this, and perhaps the reason why people choose this device over competitors (and even pay a premium), is the way it makes them feel. The emotional benefit of being part of the 'Apple experience' from the moment they research the Airpods, to the service in-store and the status they feel when walking around with them, all form an important part of what makes up the value proposition.

To this end, a value proposition can be said to have two distinct dimensions that we need to tap into, summarised in the model below. Part 1 is the rational dimension of a value proposition and focuses on the features and benefits and how these are differentiated from competitor offerings (which we will cover in this chapter). Part 2 is the emotional dimension where we look to develop a customer experience that evokes an emotional response from our audience, which we will cover in the next chapter.

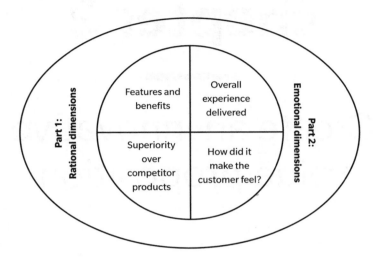

Proposition development is a risky business

Before we begin, it's worth acknowledging that value proposition development is in itself a risky business. The reality is the majority of launches fail to make any impact, largely due to poor product/market fit, inadequate marketing and a proposition not delivering on its promises.[1] The market is littered with the gravestones of such products that failed to achieve traction and success from even some of the most iconic companies.

What sets the companies that do this well apart is not just their process but attitude. For instance, where failure is seen as part of the process rather than an end in itself. A good example of this is Amazon where Jeff Bezos often remarks that the company is one of "the best places in the world to fail" and cites that they have spent billions on product failures.[2] Despite setbacks, what they do extremely well is foster a culture of 'fail fast and fail small', which allows them to embrace failure and learn from their mistakes till eventually they succeed.

In a similar way we will look at the process and identify the type of mindset at different stages you should adopt when putting together a value proposition. Let's get started.

We are going to follow a simple three-stage process.

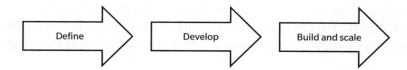

Stage 1: Define

When defining a value proposition, we always start with the customer and build around their needs. For instance, Amazon talks about having a customer-obsessed culture that in turn creates the best environment for value proposition development. At the heart of this it suggests "experiment patiently, accept failures, plant seeds, protect saplings, and double down when you see customer delight. A customer-obsessed culture best creates the conditions where all of that can happen".[3]

To achieve this, a useful first step is to define the current customer problem that the intended proposition looks to solve.

Defining a problem statement

It begins with what is known as a problem statement. This is a sentence or two that identifies the issue or gap the customer is currently experiencing (use the Customer Persona you developed in the previous chapter as a starting point). It's important when carrying out this exercise to put yourself in the shoes of the customer and try not to think about the problem from your perspective but rather from theirs. To help create this statement just look to answer the following 'killer questions'.

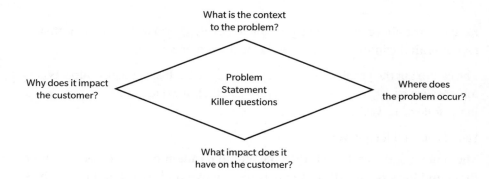

Let's turn to another industry that has seen exponential growth on the back of delivering to a customer's need: the virtual video conferencing industry. The industry is estimated to become a $50 billion industry by 2026, largely accelerated by the change in customer demand at the hands of the recent COVID pandemic.[4] Here is an example summary of the response to the killer questions.

What is the context to the problem?	Where does the problem occur?
More customers were looking for alternative ways to communicate to reduce the need to travel due to environmental and other concerns. This trend moved from a 'nice to have' to compulsory in the early part of 2020 due to a global COVID pandemic. We saw the swift 'lockdown' of companies and country borders that created a significant need to quickly implement remote working video communication tools.	The acceleration of the issue occurred in a rapid and unprecedented way across the globe and particularly due to the grounding of flights and halting of transportation. This left people with no ability to carry on their normal working, home or social lives and therefore they had to quickly revert to more remote tools and ways of working.
What impact does it have on the customer?	**Why does it impact the customer?**
Severely impacts on people's daily work and personal life, being unable to have normal face-to-face interactions and carry on normal business activities. This impacts them on a number of levels such as economically, socially and health wise. It is likely that over the long term this event will cause a shift in the way people work.	People are not able to carry on with their routines, business, education, socialising and a threat of an impact on their health. It also has a dramatic impact on the way people live and view their lives. Therefore, they need a solution that allows them to still engage in these activities without the preceding health threat.

Based on the above, we are in a position to develop a problem statement that captures all the information, using the below sentence:

The context of the problem is _____. It specifically impacts customers such as _____ due to their need to _____ in the following ways _____.

Here is our model answer:

The context of the problem is **that the global pandemic has created an immediate and long-term shift in the way people live their work and home lives,**

causing an economic, social and health impact. It specifically impacts customers like **business customers** due to their need to **constantly interact with different stakeholders** in the following ways: **face-to-face meetings and international travel to conferences**.

The importance of this problem statement cannot be underestimated as it's what you refer back to at each stage of the process to ensure the solution is actually meeting that customer need.

So, following the same process as above, have a go. Here is a 'Killer question' blank template for you to use for your proposition:

What is the context to the problem?

Where does the problem occur?

What impact does it have on the customer?

Why does it impact the customer?

Based on your answers, fill in your problem statement.

The context of the problem is _____

It specifically impacts customers such as _____

due to _____

in the following ways _____

Which customers to focus on?

After reading our example problem statement above, you may be thinking that this particular problem could relate to a number of different people such as business people, teachers or those who just miss their friends and families. This 'catch-all' situation is true and fairly typical of many problems, but the very best solutions are those that actually solve the problem for a specific audience or set of individuals. So it's your job to narrow this down and determine which group of people you are focussing on.

Take for instance the video conferencing platform industry, where there are multiple brands each delivering very similar core functionality of video calls. However, interestingly they almost entirely focus on different customer groups. Let me show you a method to identify which customer groups your competitors are focussed on, which is an important insight to determine the 'gap' for your proposition.

You should conduct a competitor keyword analysis, using tools such as Spy Fu (www.spyfu.com/). This tool allows you to identify where your competitors are targeting their proposition based on the keywords that they are using. All you need to do is type in the competitor's URL and it will bring up the keywords they are using. Try it for yourself. Here is a simple template that you can use to fill in your competitor propositions keywords.

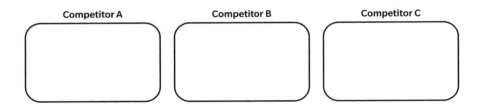

Once you have done this you can then identify patterns and determine who they are trying to attract by using certain keywords. For instance, a business video conferencing tool such as Microsoft Teams, focuses on phrases such as team-work, collaboration and sharing. On the other hand, more personal video conferencing tools like Houseparty focus on phrases such as chat with friends, meet people virtually and have fun together virtually.

Based on your analysis, you can create a perceptual map where you divide the market according to key characteristics. For instance, in the map below you will see I have divided the video conferencing market into internal collaboration/external engagement and business/personal. This is not only useful in creating a visual representation of where each company operates but also in identifying potential gaps in the market.

Perceptual map of video conferencing industry:

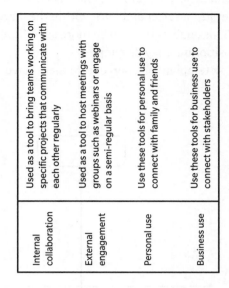

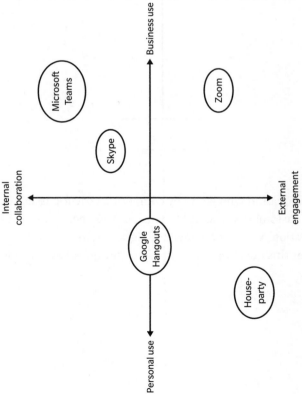

As you can see, these companies make an active choice to not solve everyone's problem – rather just a select audience within the larger space of those who need their services. This enables them to be more specific about the types of features, benefits and positioning they develop.

Here is a blank template of a perceptual map. Have a go at creating one for your industry.

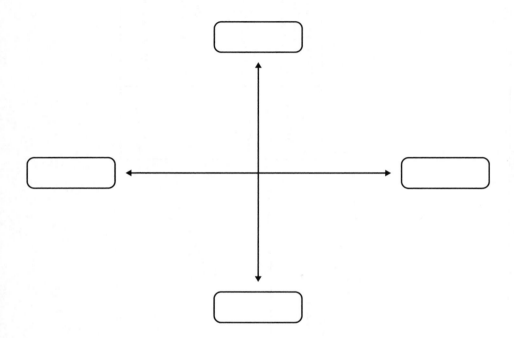

Now that you understand who your key competitors are focussed on, you need to decide which customers you should focus on. You need to ask yourself one overarching question: Where do I have the right to win?

To help answer this question, there are four sub-questions to consider:

Which capabilities are most demanded by our customers?

With whom does our existing brand have most resonance?

Right to win

Where do we have the most advantages relative to the competition?

Where is our distribution and reach the strongest?

The right-to-win mindmap

Let's take an example of how Houseparty, the youth-based video conferencing app, would possibly answer these questions.

Questions	Description
With whom does our existing brand have most resonance?	Our brand is most popular with young people in their late teens to early twenties, who enjoy socialising and having fun with their friends on mobile.
Where is our distribution and reach the strongest?	We have a very strong following on Instagram and reach across the US and other markets such as the UK. We are very well penetrated in the youth segment who are active across social media and engage with digital platforms predominantly on mobile devices, which is great as that's the only channel we are in via our app.
Where do we have the most advantages relative to the competition?	Our app is full of fun which is our big advantage over the competition. For example, our audience loves the fact that anyone in the list can join at any time bringing the element of surprise onto this mobile experience.
What capabilities are most demanded by these customers?	The mobile-only version is not an issue for this segment and they really enjoy the quizzes and games that they can play with their friends on the app.

Fill in this template with your own thoughts for your proposition here:

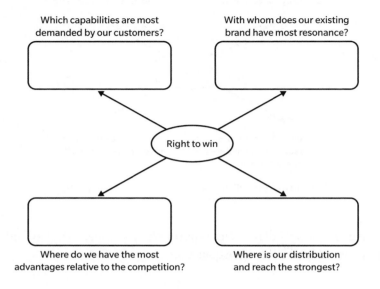

Initial hypothesis

Based on the problem statement and target audience, you now need to develop an initial proposition hypothesis that you believe solves the problem you have defined. The key mindset to adopt here is not to dwell on this for too long as the reality is it will likely change as you go through the process. Use a 'best guess' approach that acts as a starting point to validate and iterate upon.

There is a simple new technique you can use to develop your hypothesis known as the XYZ hypothesis developed by Alberto Savoia.[5] You need to fill in the blanks to the formula that goes like this:

X% of **Y** target market will buy/subscribe to **Z** proposition **IF**...

Let's break this down. First, you need to make an assumption about the **X**% of your target market who would likely use the solution that you propose. At this stage this is your best guess based on what you know about the market. The next step is to define your target market or **Y**, considering the above. Third, **Z** is a summary of our features and benefits of the proposition. Finally, the **IF** element taps into the rational, emotional and experiential elements of the proposition that provides clear differentiation from other things available on the market.

Here is an example I have put together for the Houseparty app.

An additional 7% of young people between the ages of 18 to 20 who are at university (target market) will buy/subscribe to **the Houseparty app proposition if we create a new section for young people to go on virtual dates on the app.**

Have a go at developing an initial hypothesis for your proposition here.

Before you go into testing, it would be beneficial to expand on the **Z** aspect of the proposition and more accurately define the key features and benefits. There are four key elements to consider that sit within the features and benefits pyramid:

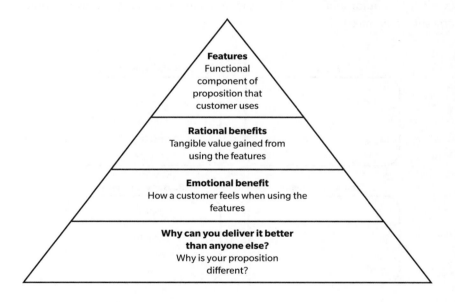

To illustrate, let me take a hypothetical example where I propose to extend Houseparty's current offer and add a new 'virtual dating' proposition, based on some of the trends we have seen earlier in relation to the need for video conferencing tools to help connect people virtually.

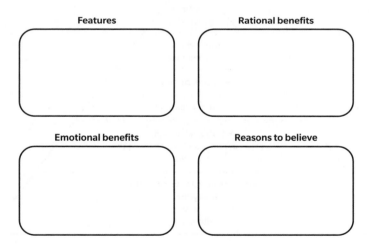

Features

A virtual dating section where we add in fun, surprises and games into the virtual dating experience.

Rational benefits

Reduces the need to have a physical date and overcomes the awkward moments while on a date by introducing activities and things to talk about.

Emotional benefits

Most people are quite nervous on a first date as they are worried about striking up a conversation with a complete stranger. This helps calm their nerves and makes it a less pressured situation.

Reasons to believe

Houseparty is a leading app where thousands of young people meet new people already and enjoy their virtual experiences. This service is an extension of this.

Virtual dating proposition for the Houseparty app

Now using a similar method, fill out the template below for your proposition using this template.

Features

Rational benefits

Emotional benefits

Reasons to believe

Testing the hypothesis

Once you have developed a hypothesis, it's time to test it out on your target audience.

According to Savoia, there are three broad principles to adhere to:

Distance to data	Time to data	Expense to generate data
It would be easy to create an elaborate testing plan at this stage but, given you are testing a hypothesis, simplicity is key. Therefore, find the most convenient place where your target audience is and get feedback on each aspect of the proposition in the table you have developed.	Immediacy is of the essence here as we are looking for quick validation of the hypothesis and whether it would work for your audience. So consider where and how this can be done quickly. For instance, can you set up a virtual conference call this evening with a group of people who fit the target audience?	It may be tempting to spend money to get validation here, but resist. It is likely with a little effort you can actually generate initial data from your target audience at little expense. Trust me, you will need the money later down the line!

Based on the feedback you receive, you need to iterate your original hypothesis and then move on to the next stage. For instance, I found that the audience loved the idea of a virtual dating service for Houseparty, but despite it being virtual they only want to meet people in their local area to ensure they didn't get into long-distance relationships. So I needed to amend the feature to incorporate this geo-location element. Bear in mind that when making adjustments it's worth ensuring that all other aspects – the rational, emotional and reasons to believe – still remain relevant.

Stage 2: Develop

You are at a stage where you have a defined proposition that has been through some initial validation. Now you need to actually create an early version of what the end proposition could look like. This is called a minimum viable product (MVP) or prototype. It is important, as we have identified in Chapter 1, that there can be vast differences between what someone says versus actually does. Remember, since you are not yet convinced that there is a viable market you need to take a very cautious approach to the development. On the one hand, it must be realistic enough to generate some real consumer feedback, while on the other hand it needs to be as cost-effective and as quick to market as possible to minimise wasted effort. After all, you may find that it's not viable after this stage.

When developing your proposition further, it's worth adopting a certain mentality which is the willingness to trade-off 'the perfect solution' for the 'workable one'. Or in the words of Y Combinator co-founder Paul Graham, rather counterintuitively build something that is "not meant to scale".[6] No doubt you will have a moonshot or ambitious vision for the proposition and what it can become, but at this stage you only want to create an accurate representation of that vision to test it out on real customers. I call this the 'hackathon mentality', as this is where a group of people come together and go from a process of proposition ideation to prototype in a weekend. No pressure! It's likely that your MVP may take a little more time than that, but it's the sense of urgency and frugality that are important attributes to adopt.

You may be wondering how you are going to pack all the aspects of your proposition into a quick, cost-effective MVP. Here is where using substitute 'off-the-shelf' tools can be very useful, some examples of which are here.

End proposition	Prototype
Membership app	Prototype software such as proto.io (https://proto.io/)
Bespoke membership/ subscription platform	Off-the-shelf website from Wix or Shopify Developing wireframes using Sketch or Adobe XD
Community pages with chat function and sharing tools	Create a social media group on Facebook or LinkedIn
Native app	App wrapper using Good Barber

Off-the-shelf tools to consider for your MVP

There are clearly too many off-the-shelf tools to mention and they are very dependent on the type of proposition you are launching. My starting point for digital propositions would be to either wireframe the solution using software like Sketch or Adobe XD or build a prototype using Proto.io (https://proto.io/). For more physical products, using 3D printing options to create a mock version of your proposition may be a good route to go down. Whatever the proposition, the important point is the process in your mind about developing a prototype to represent the idea but using very quick and cost-effective alternatives.

There will inevitably be a number of compromises, such as a scaled-down version and requiring more manual intervention. Substituting effort for money at this stage is worth the trade-off and allows you to 'fail fast' but more importantly 'fail cheap'. A good example of this is when Joe Gebbia and Brian Chesky, the founders of Airbnb, in a bid to pay their rent decided to rent three air mattresses on their floor to determine whether there was in fact any demand for their idea.[7]

Testing the prototype

Remember that, unlike in the hypothesis stage, we need to test the prototype across a larger segment of the target market. We need to be very clear at this stage about the outcomes of success we are looking for, of which there should be three to achieve a 'proof of concept'.

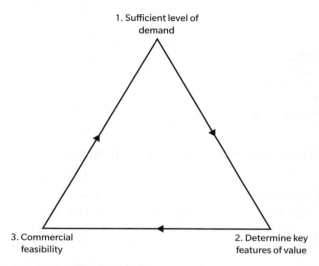

Proof of concept threshold

The aim of this is to identify the level of demand and key features of value for the proposed proposition in the market that then allows us to determine if the proposition 'has legs' and whether it can be commercially viable. There will inevitably be both a minimum threshold of revenue that the proposition needs to achieve to be viable, and certain features that are more desirable than others. It's critical that we figure the answer to both these points at this stage.

To help, let's carry out what I call a 'demand generation and features' test. There are several methods to achieve this. All involve making the prototype live 'in-market', placing adverts using channels such as social media, search engines, push notifications or email lists, and assessing the response. I'm going to demonstrate how to do this using Google Sponsored Ads. For this specific test you will need a website or at least a landing page for your proposition. It will work regardless of whether your offering is physical or digital.

Using Google Ads will give you an immediate 'litmus test' of the level of interest or demand both for search terms linked to your proposition, as well as whether people find it appealing enough to make a purchase. This will also allow you to make a financial assessment of the necessary marketing spend required to achieve a critical mass and if it's commercially viable. Let me walk you through the three steps in this process.

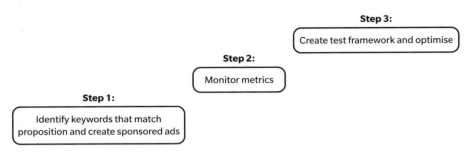

Key steps in demand generation and features test

Step 1: Identify keywords and create sponsored ads

In the Google Ads console you are able to set up a campaign by adding specific keywords and search terms, which – depending on a number of factors (such as bidding price, relevance and targeting) – come up as a sponsored ad for people to click on.

The key is to use similar terms you have outlined in the proposition features and benefits section in order to create a good match between what people search for and what your proposition delivers. Furthermore, you should try to avoid key phrases competitors are using (you know how to determine this through competitor keyword analysis, discussed earlier) in order to try and differentiate your proposition. Once you are happy with this it's time to make the ads live. Write your keywords here.

Step 2: Monitor metrics

As part of the test, there are a range of metrics you can monitor but for this purpose the two most helpful are click-throughs and conversions. Click-throughs are the number of people who visit our proposition based on the spend limit we set, while conversions is the number of people going on to purchase the prototype once on the site.

Think of it like a funnel where you are testing at each stage.

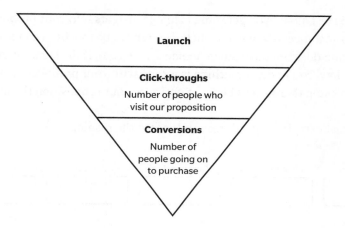

As you carry out your test there are three things you are looking for:

1 Identify the number of products sold at a particular *daily spending limit.*

2 *Click-through data* reveals level of demand for the offering based on keywords aligned to your proposition.

3 *Conversions* show us if the proposition is actually appealing enough for those that have a need to purchase it over alternatives available.

Let's take an example using the illustrations below. Let's say you spend £1,000 per day in order to achieve 2,000 click-throughs and ten conversions for a particular proposition. In Illustration 1, below, you can see that the cost to you is 50p per click and £100 per conversion. You now know that if you increased spend, it's likely – notwithstanding at some point you would see diminishing returns – that you could increase conversions by a similar amount, as you see in Illustration 2.

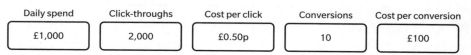

Daily spend	Click-throughs	Cost per click	Conversions	Cost per conversion
£1,000	2,000	£0.50p	10	£100

Demand generation – Illustration 1

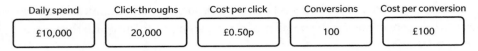

Daily spend	Click-throughs	Cost per click	Conversions	Cost per conversion
£10,000	20,000	£0.50p	100	£100

Demand generation – Illustration 2

Based on this test alone, you get some valuable insights into your proposition's viability. For instance, if you deem click-throughs to be too low, then it's possible the proposition does not have much demand. However, if the clicks are high but conversions low, you know something is wrong with your product/market fit. But you won't stop there – let's begin to optimise your proposition through this method.

Have a go at carrying out this test and record the results here.

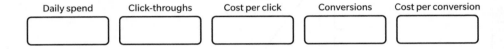

Daily spend	Click-throughs	Cost per click	Conversions	Cost per conversion

Step 3: Create test framework and optimise

Based on your initial results, you are able to tweak your approach in order to derive the most appealing version of the proposition (considering keywords and proposition features). To help, we can use a testing matrix to determine how different combinations perform across these metrics.

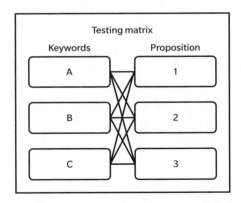

Here is a template you can use to test different variations of your proposition.

	Daily spend	Click-throughs	Cost per click	Conversions	Cost per conversion
A1					
A2					
A3					
B1					
B2					
B3					
C1					
C2					
C3					

Over a period of time, you will be able to determine the best cost per click and conversion rate for the best combination of keywords and proposition features. At this point you will know the following:

- The optimal cost of conversion for the proposition, allowing you to estimate volumes required to make it commercially viable.

- The best performing keywords to give you a strong indication of the type of features that resonate most with the target audience.

- The optimal keywords to use to market the proposition effectively to build traction.

- The most desired proposition features for you to make decisions on which ones to keep and what to lose.

Jot down some of your findings here.

Now you have generated the optimal version of the proposition and what works best to generate demand at a certain cost, you can assess whether it's going to be commercially viable.

Commercial feasibility

Before you can take the proposition any further, you need to understand if it is commercially feasible to deliver while making a profit. Based on the above information, you should carry out a break-even analysis that will allow you to understand the minimum number of products you need to sell and at what cost in order to break even and thereafter begin to make a profit.

To calculate this, there is a simple formula to consider. Let me use an example to illustrate.

Let's return to the earlier example of the Apple Airpods, only this time we will be an innovative competitor that wants to launch a new style earphone. We are intending to sell the product for £150 per unit and have fixed costs of £300,000 that cover the initial development plus ongoing costs such as rent, computers and software. We have been able to reach the optimal cost per conversion of £45 per unit, using the test matrix above, to which we need to add another £25 per unit to cover other variable costs such as salaries, bringing the total variable cost to £70 per unit.

We are ready to conduct our break-even analysis using the formula:

Fixed costs ÷ (revenue per unit − variable cost per unit) = break-even point (units)

So in our example, this is the breakdown:

£300,000 ÷ (£80) = 3,750 units

Now that we know we need to sell 3,750 units to make it viable, the next step is to determine the marketing budget we need to achieve this, using the following formula:

Total number of units × total variable costs per unit.

Once again it breaks down to this in our example:

3,750 × £70 = £262,500

Therefore, the total variable spend we need to achieve break even is £262,500. In order to determine total costs to break even, we add fixed and variable costs which is equal to £562,500. In other words, this is the total amount we have spent in order to sell the 3,750 units in order to break even.

By conducting this analysis, you can determine the commercial feasibility of your proposition based on the amount you would have to spend to make it viable. Questions you need to consider are whether the proposition is worth investing in, whether you can increase revenue per product and whether you can reduce fixed and variable costs. If any of these factors change, you need to redo the analysis and determine the new point of break even and re-assess if it's achievable.

Calculate your break-even point here.

Stage 3: Build and scale

You are now at a point where you have validated the prototype, assessed its commercial feasibility and are ready to build and scale. Let's go through how you do this.

Proposition trade-off triangle

During this phase, it may seem like you need to build each element from scratch, but, as you have learned from the previous stage, this clearly isn't the case. In fact, adopting a 'flexible mindset' to tap into a variety of different ways to deliver each element of the proposition is vital and will help vastly reduce time, costs and even improve the quality of the proposition.

There are broadly three choices you have to consider when developing each element, categorised by what I call the 'proposition trade-off triangle'.

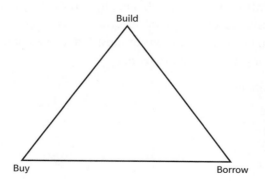

When building your proposition, consider these different elements and determine what parts of the proposition could benefit from each.

Build	Buy	Borrow
When you need something highly bespoke e.g. custom platform	When there is strategic value of acquiring an asset that exists which is worth owning, such as to extend reach or to gain intellectual property, for example brand assets.	Non-core 'enablers' that would be expensive to build or acquire and where you can access 'best-in-class' tools to use at low cost, such as, email, analytics or CRM software

Build, buy and borrow considerations

Write down what aspects of your proposition you think you would build, buy and borrow.

Considering how to scale the proposition

Often companies build propositions that could have significant appeal to a large group of customers, but they are not able to realise the potential since they can't scale. You need to bear this risk in mind. To overcome this requires you to understand the economic concept of 'elasticity in demand' and how you use a variety of marketing tools and techniques to your advantage. The premise is based on the fact that companies suffer two primary problems. The first is that they scale too fast and their infrastructure can't handle it, or they scale too slow and have built too much infrastructure they can't afford.

Let me show you how you build your proposition to overcome this fundamental problem, breaking it down into two areas:

- Dynamic components
- Demand control

Dynamic components

To be able to scale with the ebbs and flows of demand, your proposition should incorporate four key components of elasticity. The template below highlights each element and also allows for you to consider how you would apply it to your proposition.

Components of elasticity	Description	How would you apply it to your proposition?
Technological	This is where you use technology that has the ability to dynamically adapt in real-time based on demand. For instance, using elastic cloud-based servers to ensure platform performance is always at the optimal level, balancing costs and reliability.	
Process/ production	To maximise efficiencies while delivering to the customer need it would be useful to look at combining in-house and out-sourced approaches to ensure we can service core and spill-over demand easily. You can also leverage the role of partners and partnerships to be able to deliver certain aspects of the proposition. It's based on the premise that there are likely to be specialised providers that do certain aspects of what your provide, possibly better than you can.	
People	People are often the largest expense and therefore having many people getting compensated on a variable basis is certainly advantageous as the proposition scales. The principles and advantages of a core team remain true here as well, usually consisting of the founding team who live and breathe the vision. However, without these individuals you can opt to use a variety of freelancers (from platforms such as https://www.upwork.com/ and https://fiverr.com/) or agencies.	
Reach	A good way to extend reach is to use partners that have an established network and infrastructure that can deal with the peaks and troughs of demand. Good examples of such services include Deliveroo for food delivery and Stuart (https://stuart.com/) for other types of items.	

Demand control

As you develop your proposition, and despite putting the infrastructure in place to scale with demand, there is no doubt at times you will need to control the floodgates of customers. This could be to smooth out the demand cycle to maintain the operation more efficiently, increase traffic during quiet periods or due to an issue where we need to temporarily lighten the load on our proposition due to a technical glitch.

To help with this you can use the marketing mix, or in this context I call them the 'levers of demand control'. Let's consider how each of them work using the template below and consider how you would apply them to your proposition.

Levers of demand	Description	Example	How would you apply it to your proposition?
Promotion	As we have seen at the prototype stage, you have an ability to adjust marketing spend that in turn increases and decreases customer click-throughs and conversion. Since you have already established the cost of conversion, you can reasonably accurately forecast demand based on the amount of money you use for promotions of this nature.	Sponsored adverts on Google or other search platforms Paid advertising on social media platforms such as Facebook or LinkedIn Affiliate network advertising using Google AdSense Video advertising on YouTube	
Pricing	In line with the concept of elasticity of demand (with a few notable exceptions) at a general level, raising or reducing prices for a period of time will in turn decrease or increase conversion levels.	Using special offers or promotions to reduce price Reducing the term of subscriptions to decrease pricing Increase prices of packages or subscriptions	

Levers of demand	Description	Example	How would you apply it to your proposition?
Place	You have the ability to adjust your distribution strategy by either expanding or contracting the number of places that offer the proposition. Often, companies turn off certain distribution channels at different times to manage the demand flow.	Increase or decrease the number of distribution channels Turn on or off certain distribution channels depending on time of day or levels of demand Use a variety of partnerships to expand reach cost effectively	
Product	You can adjust the product to offer different aspects of things at different times to help control demand. For instance, you could add or remove popular features that you know will increase or decrease demand for a period of time.	Add or remove certain features Offer free trials of the product Offer limited additional features Partner with others to add to the proposition	

Levers of demand control

chapter 3

Design a compelling customer experience

I'm now going to demonstrate how you can create a customer experience that makes a positive emotional impact on your customers, increasing satisfaction, loyalty, advocacy and profit.

At the heart of any proposition lies a customer experience, or CX for short, that enables customers to seamlessly navigate their way through the offering. Most of these experiences are actually rather functional in nature, used simply as a way to get customers to the checkout with as many things in their basket as possible. Creating a simple-to-use navigational experience is important – in fact, it forms the baseline in delivering to a customer's expectation; I cover more on this in Chapter 15. However, in line with part 2 of our proposition dimensions framework (seen in the previous chapter), it's those few companies that use their customer experience journey to bring their brand to life, create moments of connection with their audience and spark an emotional response that leaves a lasting impression, that are the real winners.

This is important as we are increasingly seeing a trend where "companies compete as much on customer experience as they do on product and price".[1] Take, for example, one of the most iconic companies in the world, Disney, that has been able to achieve a 70% return rate of first-time visitors to its parks[2] due to the world-class customer experience approach centred around the concept of 'creating happiness' at each touch-point. Bruce Jones, Senior Director, Disney Institute, said "When our cast members know their primary goal is to create happiness, they are empowered to create what we like to call magical moments. From our park greeters to our attraction attendants, every employee makes decisions regarding a guest interaction centered on this key theme of 'creating happiness.'"[3]

The experience triangle

To begin with, it's worth considering that there are three key dimensions to consider, what I call the 'experience triangle'.

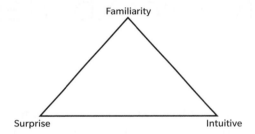

Familiarity

When designing your customer experience, it's important to bear in mind that it needs to have a familiarity to it so the customer recognises and relates to the journey. It must reflect your brand values, tone, style and design at each touch-point so with each step the customer experiences a comfort factor as they know what they are getting each and every time. This consistency builds memory structures in the mind of your customers where over a period of time they develop trust due to the familiarity of the journey they go on. It's just like their favourite song – it gets better the more they listen to it.

Disney, for instance, uses this concept to a tee in its parks as every aspect of its CX, from rides to restaurants, is based on existing iconic characters and contexts that people would have seen time and time again across TV and stores. It goes the extra mile in the parks to bring these to life where visitors, for example, can meet and interact in-person with characters and immerse themselves into the sets of their favourite show, providing that once in a lifetime sense of excitement, yet with a remarkable sense of familiarity.

Surprise

Embedded with this familiarity you need to create real moments of surprise that make the customer feel special and valued. Often, these do not need to be large things but rather actively demonstrate that you care about them. Surprising moments can also come in the form of empathy, where you either recognise a customer's circumstances or appreciate where you may not have delivered to their expectations. In these 'moments of truth' you really can create lasting impressions and loyalty by going above and beyond, especially when the customer has no expectation of you doing so.

This is an aspect where Disney really excels, not just for the kids but adults too. It adds little touches to the journey such as your favourite Disney character handing out free gifts and goodies for everyone to enjoy. Key to this is that it instils an 'experience mentality' rather than a 'task mentality' in the staff, as it sees great experiences as an asset rather than an expense.[4] This highlights the importance of, even at this stage, adopting the right mindset that we touched on throughout the previous chapter.

Intuitive

The end-to-end journey needs to anticipate how a customer would ideally want to go through it and then remove all barriers and friction points for them to achieve this. Removing steps in the way and making it as simple as possible demonstrates to customers you value their time and effort, and makes it more likely that will complete their journey with you.

One way that Disney achieves this is through its app that helps visitors navigate their way through the park seamlessly. By being GSP-enabled, it also delivers an unparalleled level of personalisation and becomes their 'at your side' helper guiding them and providing them with information like showtimes, wait times for rides and pre-ordering food. This gives visitors a comfort factor with their surroundings that puts them at ease and removes ambiguity from their experience.[5]

Gather some initial thoughts on these dimensions and how they may apply to your customer experience approach here.

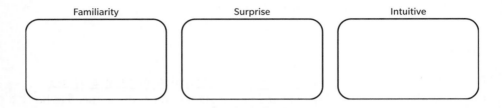

Familiarity　　　　　Surprise　　　　　Intuitive

OK, let's now put these dimensions into practice and begin to design, test and iterate the customer experience for your proposition. There are three stages to the process we will cover.

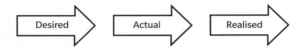

Desired　　Actual　　Realised

Stage 1: Desired

To this point, you have understood who you're targeting and developed the rational dimensions of the proposition that meets their needs. Now, you need to create an experience to delight your customers at each step. To achieve this let's first break down the journey into four steps. These steps also form what is known as the 'Customer Lifecycle' and can be applied it a number of ways. including communications and media planning.

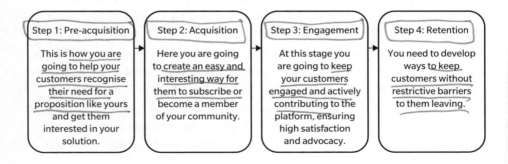

Step 1: Pre-acquisition	Step 2: Acquisition	Step 3: Engagement	Step 4: Retention
This is how you are going to help your customers recognise their need for a proposition like yours and get them interested in your solution.	Here you are going to create an easy and interesting way for them to subscribe or become a member of your community.	At this stage you are going to keep your customers engaged and actively contributing to the platform, ensuring high satisfaction and advocacy.	You need to develop ways to keep customers without restrictive barriers to them leaving.

Gather some of your thoughts on how you plan to tailor the experience at each stage.

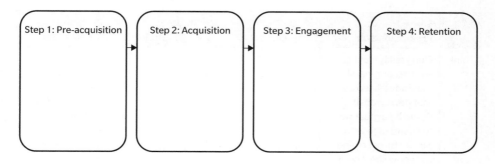

At each stage, you need to define the desired effect that you would like to have on your customers. To achieve this, you first need to put yourself in your customer's shoes and consider how they would ideally like to go through each of the four stages outlined.

To help, there is a simple framework that you can work with, known as the 'Think, Feel, Do framework'. Here is a summary of each aspect.

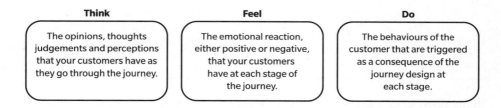

Putting the two frameworks together, the template below enables you to determine the desired state of your customer experience at each stage. Developing this holistic view is incredibly important for you to take ownership of every detail of the CX approach. For example, Netflix, the leading online video on-demand subscription service, says: "We own the Netflix customer experience from the moment they sign up, for the whole time they are with us, across TV, phone and laptop."[6]

To help with this exercise, it would be beneficial to actually get your customers to help you define each stage. When filling in the template try to use their own words or 'customer speak'. This should help remove any jargon or confusing terms that often creep into this type of exercise as you can easily revert back to thinking of the journey from your own 'company' perspective. To help, I have provided a few examples of how customers of Netflix could have considered each stage. I've left space in each box for you to fill it out for your own CX desired approach.

	Stage 1: Pre-acquisition	Stage 2: Acquisition	Stage 3: Engagement	Stage 4: Retention
Think	Ooh I really want to see that original show I saw advertised on that news website. Could be a great way to spend time with Mrs on the weekend as I know she would love it too.			You know it's actually great value for the whole family, maybe I'll continue it for a while longer.
Feel		Ahha free trial for 7 days, not bad so I get to watch the show for free and it's so easy to sign-up. I'm really looking forward to this.		
Do			Browse around to see what else is on here. I'll start at the recommended section.	

Remember, since you are trying to develop a customer experience that evokes an emotional response from the customer, you need to capture the 'desired' emotional outcome at each stage as well. This is done by looking at the template above and then creating an 'emotional experience map' of this desired state. The essence of this map is to illustrate how you would like your customers to feel when engaging with each part of the journey. Take a look at the figure below, on the X axis you have the stages of the customer journey and on the Y axis you have 'emotional sentiment' that goes from being positive to negative.

Emotional experience map

To illustrate, let's take Netflix as an example and hypothetically consider its desired emotional experience map. Ideally, it would like customers to feel increasingly positive about their experience at each stage of their journey. It's worth acknowledging that, if someone is intending to leave, there may be a dip that causes dissatisfaction, but by taking the right actions this too does not have to turn into a negative experience. You can see that we have also captured the type of emotion on the map that Netflix is trying to create.

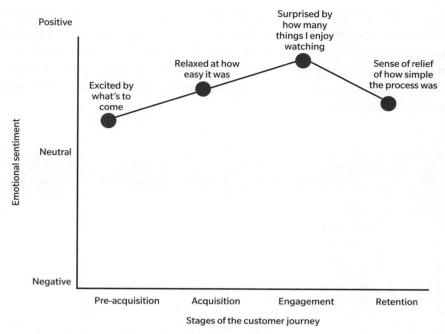

Hypothetical emotional experience map for Netflix

Using the blank template below, have a go at creating a similar style map for your proposition.

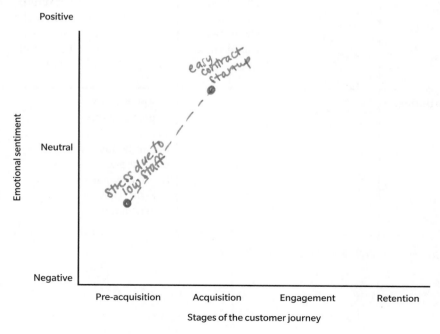

The final part of the process is to determine exactly how you are going to deliver the desired emotional appeal at each stage. To achieve this, we need to go back to our experience triangle and combine each element with the stage of the customer journey. Using the template below, I have once again provided some examples of how Netflix could consider this and left space for you to fill in with your own CX approach.

	Stage 1: Pre-acquisition	Stage 2: Acquisition	Stage 3: Engagement	Stage 4: Retention
Familiarity	Advertising shows in a relatable way across a variety of offline and online channels.			
Surprise		Easy to sign-up and free trial offer so they can effectively watch the show they wanted to for free.		Very easy to cancel, which makes it more likely they will return later on. No barriers, no fuss, no hassle.
Intuitive			The platform is so personalised that it recommends other shows based on what it deems they would watch.	

Experience triangle and the customer journey

Stage 2: Actual

You are now at a point where, with the help of your potential customers, you have developed an initial CX journey. Let's now assume that it's live and people have started to go through it. The next stage involves you evaluating whether your customer journey is having the desired effect in reality.

Interestingly, this is where you can really differentiate from the competition. Take for example, a study conducted by a CX consultancy firm Built for Mars, where it analysed the number of days it took to open an account by a number of banks in the UK. The results highlight the vast differences in actual CX in this space.

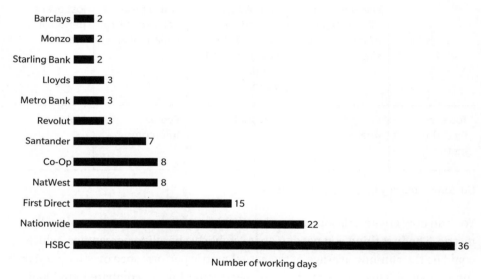

Number of working days

Source: https://builtformars.co.uk/banks/

In order to craft the ideal actual journey, you need to get customer feedback at each stage using a variety of metrics that help to indicate bottlenecks and issues. There are a multitude of metrics to choose from, but in keeping with advice from leading analytics expert and Google evangelist, Avinash Kaushik,[7] it's best to keep it simple. So for your purposes I recommend choosing the one metric that will allow you to generate the greatest insight at each stage. Below I have indicated my recommended metrics and some tools you can use to measure them.

	Stage 1: Pre-acquisition	Stage 2: Acquisition	Stage 3: Engagement	Stage 4: Retention
Metric	Drop-off rate/ bounce rate	Conversion rate	Customer satisfaction	Attrition rate
Description	The percentage of visitors to a particular website who drop off or navigate away from the site.	The number of visitors to a website that complete a desired goal (a conversion) out of the total number of visitors.	Extent to which a customer is happy with a product, service, or experience.	The number of customers lost over a period of time.
Tools to measure metric	Google Analytics	Hubspot	Feefo, Intercom	Hubspot

Customer journey measurement metrics

You can now create a dashboard and over time monitor performance of each metric. The first thing you need to do is establish a baseline percentage, which could be the running average of the actual metric performance over a period of three months. This is important as you need something to compare individual monthly performance to determine whether there are any bottlenecks or issues that appear in the journey. Over time, as you improve the experience, this running average will also improve and therefore you will constantly be looking at ways to make further improvements. Adopting this mentality is crucial as customer expectations themselves are forever evolving and it's therefore important to be ahead of the curve.

Here is a dashboard template that you can use to record your findings.

To help illustrate this step, I have added a number of hypothetical metrics at each stage.

Metric	Stage 1: Pre-acquisition		Stage 2: Acquisition		Stage 3: Engagement		Stage 4: Retention	
	Monthly actual	3-month running average benchmark	Monthly actual	3-month running average benchmark	Monthly actual	3-month running average benchmark	Monthly actual	3-month running average benchmark
Drop-off rate/ bounce rate								
Conversion rate								
Customer satisfaction								
Attrition rate								

	Stage 1: Pre-acquisition		Stage 2: Acquisition		Stage 3: Engagement		Stage 4: Retention	
	Monthly actual (June)	3-month running average benchmark	Monthly actual (June)	3-month running average benchmark	Monthly Actual (June)	3-month running average benchmark	Monthly actual (June)	3-month running average benchmark
Drop-off rate/ bounce rate	43%	15%						
Conversion rate			6%	17%				
Customer satisfaction					85%	90%		
Attrition rate							23%	25%

Based on the hypothetical situation, you can clearly see that the journey has a range of issues, particularly in the pre-acquisition and conversion stage in that month. It can be noted that there is a large number of drop-offs, which indicates that potential customers are not able to find what they are looking for easily and therefore leave the journey. In addition, you can see that the conversion rate is also pretty low compared to the running average benchmark, suggesting we have changed something that is not working. The other metrics suggest that you are around the on-target rate, which of course can be improved as well but it's less of an issue for the moment.

Take a moment to consider how you can collect the data for your dashboard template above and begin to uncover findings in the same way I did in the example above, by using Google Analytics or other analytics tools you have access to. Write some of your thoughts here.

Now, that you have determined some of the issues you are facing at a high level, you need to dig deeper to understand what is causing the issues in order to come up with appropriate solutions. To do this it's best to use real-time tools to get feedback in the moment from customers. This will be more valuable than feedback based on hindsight. You would have no doubt seen these tools in action from anywhere from your taxi service to restaurant delivery services. Here is an example from a leading meal delivery company. After placing an order on its app, customers can leave more details about the service, which it can then analyse.

How was your order?

Rate out of 5 stars

★ ★ ★ ★ ★

Great! What did you like about it?

⏲ Arrival time ☐

🍴 Food ☐

🛍 Packaging ☐

👤 Rider ☐

Write a review

Submit

App feedback from a leading food
delivery website

Another good tool to use for this is Drift (www.drift.com/), a conversational
marketing tool that allows you to have real-time chats with customers at each
stage of the journey. You can do this by setting up pre-set questions that appear
when a customer clicks on a certain section of the website, or you can have a
team member have a direct conversation. There are two things to determine.
The first are the key barriers and issues that customers are facing that have
caused the dip in the metrics. The second is understanding from customers how
they would want the situation resolved.

Let's move away from the Netflix example and consider a different context
for this next part and take the common barriers and solutions that may occur in
online food delivery. In addition to direct customer feedback, a very useful exercise to carry out is to understand what barriers and solutions your competitors
are facing by reviewing their frequently asked questions section on their website. It's likely that they are directly responding to customer feedback at different
points in the journey. This will enable you to also determine how they are over-
coming barriers, which is useful when developing your own solution.

Based on an analysis of a leading food brand's delivery service, we can
extrapolate the barriers faced (by the question posed) and the solution (by their
answer) in the top half of the template. I have left space in the template for you

to carry out this exercise by combining your own customer feedback with that of competitor insights, for your own CX journey.

	Stage 1: Pre-acquisition	Stage 2: Acquisition	Stage 3: Engagement	Stage 4: Retention
Key barriers/ issues Deliveroo	I want to know what types of restaurants are listed on the app	I really can't understand how the fees work on the app	I want to change my delivery address	I need to cancel my order
Key barriers/ issues				
Customer/ competitor insights to improve for Deliveroo	We personally curate a high-quality and diverse selection of restaurants in your area. This can range from a atop neighbourhood Italian trattoria to well-regarded national burger chain.	The closer you are to the restaurant, the lower your delivery fee. This helps us pay riders fairly. Some restaurants use their own delivery drivers. In that case, the restaurant sets its own delivery fee.	Sometimes things outside of a rider's control can cause a delay. Where we can, we will always try and proactively call you if we become aware that your order might not arrive within the estimated time of delivery, and our team will work to get your order to you as quickly as possible.	As long as the restaurant has not yet started preparing your order, you're able to cancel your order in Order Help. If the restaurant has already started preparing your order and you want to cancel, please get in touch with us, you can do this in Qrder Help as well.
Customer/ competitor insights to improve				

Barriers and solutions

Based on what you now know about the actual journey, we can do a comparison between your desired emotional journey and what you are actually seeing from our customers. Here is the emotional journey map template to use.

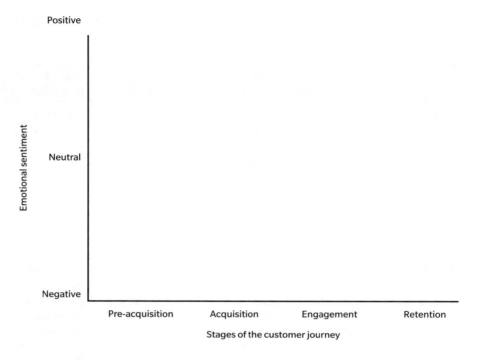

If you see a gap between your desired and actual emotional state of your customers don't panic. The good news is you are able to use the customer and competitor insights we have gained in the 'barriers and solutions' template to bridge the gap, which is what we will come onto next.

Stage 3: Realised

You are now at a stage where we have developed an initial journey, tested it and got feedback on where the issues are and how to make improvements. To achieve this, let's turn to the marketing mix to help you deliver on some of the changes required. What is important is not just to take the customer feedback at face value, as while their suggestions are valued they are unlikely to have the holistic view that you do. This is what Netflix experienced in its early years, where it lost 800,000 customers and 80% of its share price as it split its physical DVD and online streaming service, which was an extremely unpopular decision with customers.[8] However, had it not done this back then it would not have been the global sensation it is today, evidencing that sometimes it is about making hard decisions even if that causes a customer issue in the short term.

Ok, the first thing we do is determine the category where the problem is and what part of the marketing mix it relates to. For instance, we have determined that for the issues raised in the leading food brand's delivery service, the problems fall into the following categories. I have left blank boxes so you can fill this in for your actual proposition.

	Stage 1: Pre-acquisition	Stage 2: Acquisition	Stage 3: Engagement	Stage 4: Retention	Rationale
Promotion					Promoting the range of restaurants listed and having simpler navigation for a potential user to identify their preferred options.
Promotion					
Price					Simplifying the pricing structure on the platform.
Price					
Place					Making it easier to make changes such as an address or other elements such as different restaurant choices.
Place					
Product					Making it easier to do things like cancel the order directly on the app.
Product					

Marketing mix customer experience issue categories

Now, let's understand how you can use the different elements of the marketing mix to improve the experience. Once again bear the experience triangle in mind and fill in the template below. As a starter for ten, I have provided a range of examples of how companies, such as the leading food brand's delivery service, can improve their CX based on insights generated above.

	Familiarity	Surprise	Intuitive
Product	Service level enhancements: Create familiar spaces for customers such as different tiered areas or personalise the journey for them. Give certain loyal customers increased features and benefits to make them feel valued.	Surprise and delight: We introduced little additional gifts and surprises for your valued customers.	Improve navigation: Use comparison tables to clarity the different propositions on offer. In addition to this, we can use other tools such as pop-ups at different parts of the journey to make the navigation clearer. Tools such as Wisepops (https://wisepops.com/) work really well for this.
Product			
Place	Favourites: To help build familiarity you can add in customers' favourite restaurants or items that they continually would like to purchase.	Customised options: Given what you know about certain customers, offer them additional enhanced options about where to purchase their favourite items.	Simple navigation across channels: Make it very simple to navigate across channels, to locate different type of options and ensure the ones most demanded by customers are front and centre of the proposition.
Place			
Price	Free trial: Particularly for digital propositions, people are used to an initial free trial offer that allows then to see if it's right for them. Simple pricing structure: Have a very transparent, easy-to-understand pricing structure that allows the customer to easily understand what they get for the price they pay.	Incentives and discounts: Offering additional offers such as a certain number of free meals to new subscribers or discounts on restaurants in their local area gives them an incentive to become a member.	Referral programme: This is a powerful tool that rewards your existing subscribers for referring others. Usually the best 'member-get-member' programmes are when both the existing and new subscriber get a little something extra.

	Familiarity	Surprise	Intuitive
Price			
Promotion	Promotions work better when you get your customers to participate directly in the experience by developing and amplifying content. This plays into the word-of-mouth nature of marketing where, if you can get your customers to create shareable content, it has the potential at the most to go viral but at the least reach out to similar target audiences since your customers' posts will be seen by their network.	Refer your local restaurant competition: Here we asked our subscribers to take a selfie in a local vegan restaurant that was not currently listed in our directory and post it on social media, copying us in. If the restaurant later came on board, the subscriber would win a free meal on us in the same restaurant!	The final enhancement we made was to take a step back and look at the overall customer experience delivered. We wanted to ensure that at each touch point, the Vegan Life and Styles brand came through. This meant ensuring that everything in the platform, communications, customer services and even our partners had a consistent 'look and feel' and tone to it.
Promotion			

The evaluation and testing cycle

Once we developed this enhanced version of customer experience, it was time to put it to the test on customers and repeat the entire end-to-end testing process again that we had conducted at Stage 2. This should be a never-ending cycle of continual iteration, testing and feedback in order to constantly make it better.

Use the template below to map out once again the emotional journey of your customers that have gone through the improved customer journey.

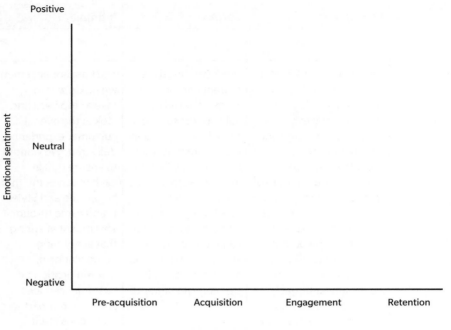

Emotional journey map: Realised

part 2

How to build your brand

chapter 4

Develop your brand

In Part 2 we will grapple with aspects of both brand development and expansion. Here we will look specifically at how we can build a brand that will really resonate with your target audience. Then in the subsequent chapters in this part, we will look at how we can scale and sustain a brand using a variety of tools and techniques.

When you look at some of the most iconic brands of today, such as Google, Amazon, Tesla, Instagram, Netflix, Spotify and Uber, to name but a few, it's worth reflecting on what they all have in common. They are all category disruptors and in a relative sense have not been around for that long. Amazon, the oldest, was founded as recently as 1994, and in less than 20 years has become the world's top brand.[1] This phenomenon is what marketing legend Seth Godin[2] accurately articulates by saying "established in 1908 used to be important. . . now it's a liability".

In many ways, the barriers to building a successful brand have certainly fallen over the last few years, as digital media has democratised access to audiences with the flick of a few buttons. However, at the same time we have seen customers become more discerning about what brands they engage with and trust.[3] Therefore, it is apparent that there exists a dichotomy for companies, where on the one hand there is an opportunity to create and bring new brands to the market while on the other it is increasingly challenging to sustain them over a long period of time.

360 view of the brand

To help you build your brand, I will use a new brand framework that I call the '360 view of the brand'. The benefit of this framework is its longevity, in that once we have gone through each stage it then acts as your ongoing brand archi- tecture or guidelines document. It can be used over time to articulate exactly what your brand does, stands for and how it expresses itself with multiple stake- holders, which is important for further expansion.

Here is a summary of the 360 brand framework.

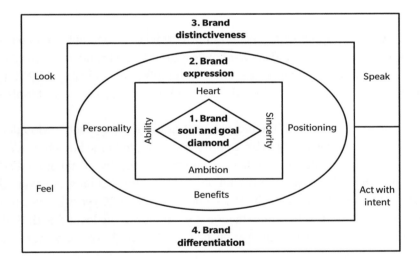

Brand soul and goal

At the heart of powerful brands lies the ability to form a strong connection with people as it promises to solve a significant problem. You may have come across the concept of a company purpose articulated through a mission or vision statement that is intended to highlight what the company aspires to achieve while in the pursuit of profit. However, herein lies a problem in that it is often very nebulous, broad and leaves both customers and employees with more questions than answers about the company direction. A good example is from a world-leading home furnishing company where their mission statement is along the lines of: To build a better everyday for everyone.[4]

Today, people are looking to connect with brands on both an inspirational and informational level to know how a brand provides value that aligns with their own values, but also to hold brands accountable to deliver on this. To achieve this dual dimension, here is a new model of what I call a 'Brand's Soul and Goal Diamond' that helps the brand you are creating articulate these dimensions.

It has four dimensions that look at a brand's intent (heart) and willingness (sincerity) that form the soul component. As well as a brand's capability (ability) and desire (ambition) to achieve the goal component. In the template, you will see a question attached to each aspect that you need to answer.

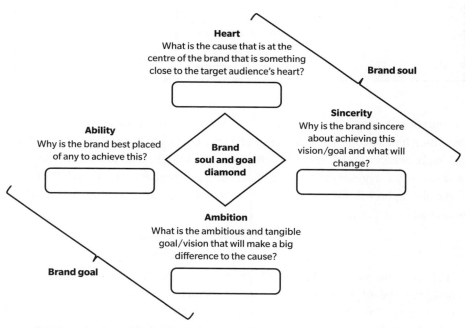

Heart
What is the cause that is at the centre of the brand that is something close to the target audience's heart?

Brand soul

Sincerity
Why is the brand sincere about achieving this vision/goal and what will change?

Ability
Why is the brand best placed of any to achieve this?

Brand soul and goal diamond

Ambition
What is the ambitious and tangible goal/vision that will make a big difference to the cause?

Brand goal

Brand's soul and goal diamond

To illustrate, here is an example using the renowned food chain.

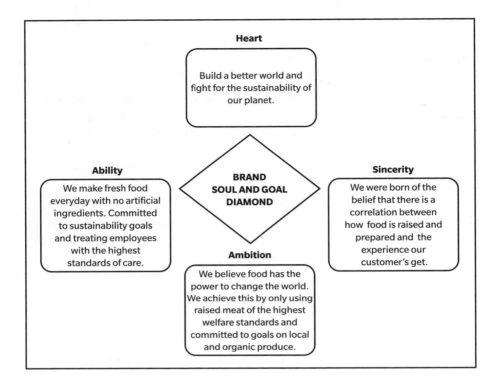

It's from this diamond that you are able to develop the brand story and narrative which helps people to understand and relate why the brand exists, what it's looking to achieve and why it will achieve it. In addition, this forms the basis on which you can generate positive PR to build goodwill for your brand. Based on the above, here is a summary of the possible brand story or narrative for the renowned food chain.

We believe that food has the power to change the world. We were born of the belief that there is a correlation between how food is raised and prepared and how it tastes. Therefore, we achieve some of the highest ethical standards in bringing our food from the farm to the table. We believe in freshness so prepare food each and every day with no artificial ingredients or microwaves, freezers or can openers. When you walk in to our restaurants you will see smiling faces as just like our food we believe in treating our employees right too.

Have a go at creating your own brand story or narrative, considering the example above.

Brand expression

The way your brand comes across and is perceived by your target audience is critical, which comes down to how the brand expresses itself. There are two dimensions for you to consider here.

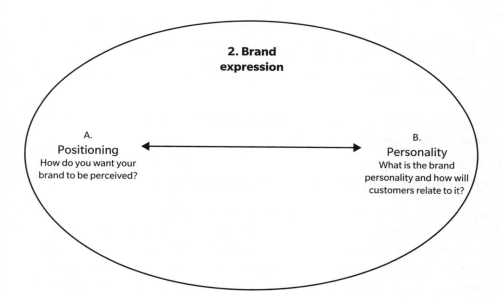

Positioning

Brand positioning is how you would want your brand to be perceived in the market relative to others. In fact, the most helpful way to consider this is to conduct a blind perception test, which is simply to think what would you want people to say about your brand if you were not in the room.

Try it yourself on a brand of your choice. Think of a brand that you engage with regularly (so you're likely to be in their target audience) and write in the box below how you would describe the brand in your own words. Is it funny, serious, expensive, aspirational, affordable, ambitious, caring, innovative? If the brand you had in your mind accurately reflects what it actually is (you will clearly need to research the actual answer), you can say that it has a strong brand position.

Crafting out a brand position is certainly a strategic activity and combines three key parts that lead to the development of an overarching brand position statement.

As we have already covered parts 1 and 2, let's focus on part 3 and then bring them all back into play.

Desired perception relative to competitors

In order to determine this desired perception, it's useful to use a tool called 'perceptual mapping' – remember we looked at it in Chapter 2, This is where you define the key industry characteristics and then plot your brand and competitors on the map to determine whether you have a unique positioning. It enables you to determine what your brand wants to be known for relative to the competition.

Before having a go yourself, let me illustrate using the restaurant industry Chipotle operates within. Let's say that on the one hand the industry can be divided into players that deliver healthy versus unhealthy food, and on the other those that deliver fast food versus a full sit-in dining experience. Now we can develop a perceptual map and then populate the various competitors we wish to have within the consideration set.

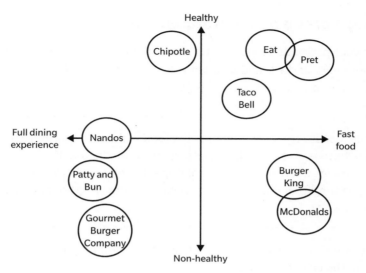

Perceptual map – Chipotle and key competitors

From this map it's clear that Chipotle occupies a unique position compared to others in its consideration set. The map helps us to determine the position that it has and understand what makes it unique compared to other competitors.

Have a go at creating a perceptual map for your brand, relative to competitors that you deem to be within its set. Start by considering the key industry characteristics that help you determine the dimensions of the map. Then decide who your competitors are and plot them on the map. Your goal should be to find a space or gap on the map where your brand can occupy a unique and differentiated position for all other competitors.

Defining a brand position statement

Based on your perceptual map, you need to articulate a brand position statement, a summary of the brand position you are adopting in the market. Here is an example based on what we know for Chipotle.

> Chipotle focusses on delivering healthy food with all natural ingredients to its customers and an in-dining experience that is categorised as 'casual dining'. Customers feel a sense of ease and comfort while eating at our restaurants and are happy to spend time enjoying the end-to-end experience.

Have a go at writing out your brand position statement for your brand here, referring to the example above.

Brand personality

The next element of your brand's expression is its personality. This is what people will experience, the 'feel' factor, when they engage with your brand at each and every touch-point. Increasingly, your brand personality must also form part of your company's internal culture, and with your employees, in order to create consistency both inside and outside.

A good example is how Direct Line, the UK's largest general insurer, was able to create an end-to-end culture as its brand embodied a 'fixer' mentality. It brought this to life through a marketing campaign based on the famous movie Pulp Fiction's character, Winston Wolf. The entire company focussed on 'becoming fixers' at every interaction, which was apparent to customers from the moment they took out a policy to making a claim.

To help you define your brand's personality let's use a technique I call 'personality moodboarding'. It has three simple steps to follow.

Step 1: Wireframe the personality framework

The first step is to wireframe the type of traits that you believe the brand encapsulates. This is where you create a skeleton wireframe using words to describe the different elements of the brand personality that you would like. Some examples are shown below.

WARM	LIGHT-HEARTED	HEALTHY
EXPERT	ETHICALLY CONSCIOUS	EFFICIENT

Here is a blank template for you to use.

Step 2: Gather inspiration

Now that you have determined the key traits that form the basis of your brand personality, you now need to get inspired by how we could bring this to life. To achieve this, you need to look for examples from a variety of places – from brands in adjacent verticals and even to celebrities that epitomise the trait.

Using the traits described, here are some examples.

M&S	Innocent	Graze
WARM	**LIGHT-HEARTED**	**HEALTHY**
Ellen DeGeneres	Jennifer Aniston	Jamie Oliver
Boots	Ben & Jerry's	IKEA
EXPERT	**ETHICALLY CONSCIOUS**	**EFFICIENT**
Google	Leonardo DiCaprio	Lewis Hamilton

Use the blank template above and add in your own inspiration for the brand traits listed.

Step 3: Develop brand personality characteristics

Clearly, it would be very difficult to adopt the personality of all the people and brands that you have seen at Stage 2, so you need to narrow this down.

Based on the personality mood board you can begin to generate a high level of understanding of how your brand personality will be articulated and brought to life. Fill out the template below based on the four areas.

Area	Description	Example	Your brand
Brand look	What is the visual identity of the brand?	Have a warm visual appeal that allows people to feel relaxed and earns trust due to expert signals and a strong colour scheme that highlights our ethical nature.	
Brand speak	What is the verbal identity of the brand?	Very conversational, we aim to keep things informal and simple. No jargon and slightly tongue-in-cheek to suggest we don't take ourselves too seriously.	
Brand action	What does the brand do that makes it different from competitors?	We are easy to navigate, demonstrate efficiency and do everything in the most environmentally friendly way.	
Brand feel	How does the brand make customers feel that makes it different from competitors?	We feel like we care, like we want to give you a hug, like we want you to join us, that everyone is welcome.	

Brand distinctiveness and differentiation

Remember, the purpose of a brand is to act as a shorthand cue to your customers so you remain front of mind when they have a need. So your brand has to really stand out above the crowd to get noticed and be so distinct that you are ingrained in your customer's memory structures that they only call on you when they have a need you can solve. Now importantly, in the brand development process you must treat these as different things. The first – how you stand apart from our competition – is what we call 'brand distinctiveness', while your ability to look and speak so uniquely that you get ingrained into your customer's subconscious is called 'brand differentiation'. The way you develop these different aspects is through the brand distinctiveness versus brand differentiation framework.

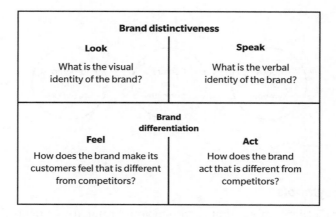

As you know, we have already begun developing the building blocks to these in our brand personality, so let's now dig deeper into each.

Brand distinctiveness

Mark Ritson, a renowned professor in marketing, said that he believed that 80% of the challenge for most brand managers should be codes, distinctiveness and salience.[5] This provides support that the way a brand looks and speaks is critically important when it comes to someone recalling it when needed.

Think about it. If I were to ask you which online company's logo had blue, red, yellow and green in it, you would probably instantly have the answer – Google (without having to Google it, ironically). If I asked what brand had the famous symbol, the 'Golden Arches', once again you would instantly know it and there is no way you would mistake it for any other fast food chain! This is because these brands actually sit in your subconscious memory structures and you can instantly recall them at any moment in time. We need to aspire to achieve a similar level of recall.

There are two key components that lead to brand distinctiveness – visual identity (its look) and verbal identity (the ways something is written or verbally expressed).

Visual identity

Logos and symbols

Your logo and other symbols that surround your brand are arguably the most important visual asset. A logo is used in a physical sense as an identifier. For instance, you can see 'Golden Arches' from many metres away due to its distinctiveness.

Logos and symbols also have a much greater underlying meaning that becomes part of the emotional bond a customer forms with them. For instance, the Amazon logo has an arrow that moves from the letter A to Z. This sends a strong message that it has all that we need and will deliver it quickly.

In today's digital context, arguably logos and symbols have grown in importance since digital real estate only gets smaller and therefore the only thing that is seen, say in a thumbnail, is a logo upon which people make purchasing decisions.

Developing a logo is a multi-faceted endeavour and you should consider the following five elements of logo characteristics.

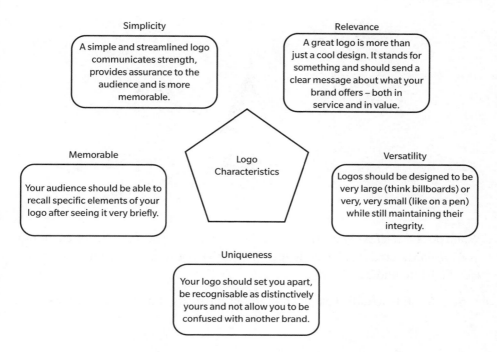

Colours and typography

You must pay close attention to both the colour scheme and typography as they reveal a lot about your brand. Colours, for instance, evoke a range of emotions and associations, although these are context-specific. For example, red signals passion, blue signals tranquillity, orange signals courage and so on.

It's also worth defining a primary, secondary and tertiary colour scheme with an indication of use. Here is an example (note the use of the colour code for accuracy).

Headlines:	Primary colour – 6D8700
Background to body text:	Secondary colour – 9DB300
Header and footers:	BAC600

Typography is also important and helps to bring out a brand's personality and intent. There are three typography families:

- **Serif:** They have nudges at the end and there is a significant weight distribution.

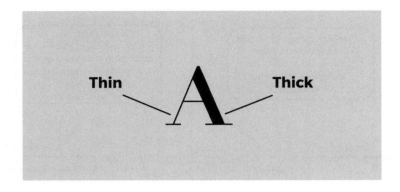

When does a Serif typeface work? Usually, if you are a luxury or historical brand and are considered reliable with an authoritative position. For example, Canon, Honda, HSBC and Burberry.

- Sans Serif: It actually just means without the serifs or nudges at the ends.

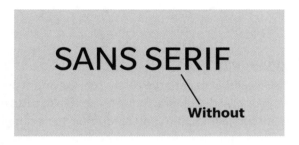

When do Sans Serif types work? Usually, a modern company, like a tech company, or one that runs an app, as the font shows a clean and new look to them. Good examples include Amazon, Facebook and Google.

- Script: This resembles handwriting.

When do Script types work? They are more playful and fun typefaces and can almost verge on calligraphy. For example, Coors Light, Coca Cola and Instagram.

In recent years we have certainly seen a movement towards the sans-serification of logos, especially in the fashion, tech and retail sectors. Brands such as Burger King, Pinterest, Spotify, Burberry and Saint Laurent have all taken the plunge to re-brand their logos in this way. Why? Well, firstly to fit into the logo characteristics we have considered above, given the need for example, to fit into digital assets seamlessly. Secondly, this font style is synonymous with 'tech' brands and therefore this forms an important signal to the market that they are transforming in this way.

It is also important to research other brands and ensure that you use fonts and typography that cannot be misconstrued or be seen to pass off as another brand. Here are some simple guidelines to follow in this regard.

Research key competitors' brands including their fonts and typography	Create a set of fonts and typography that is very distinct from competitors	Conduct research on customers to ensure that they feel your brand has a real uniqueness to it

Consider the type of colours and typography you would use for your brand, with your reasons why.

Photography and artwork

Finally, the type of photography and artwork we use is vital to draw a strong association with your brand. For instance, Disney uses illustrated 'cartoon' style artwork across its physical and digital assets, while Nike uses real-life sportspeople to highlight the enduring and persistent spirit of the brand.

So for your brand you need to define the type of photo and artwork to bring the brand to life. Consider the three directions below and fill out the bottom of the template.

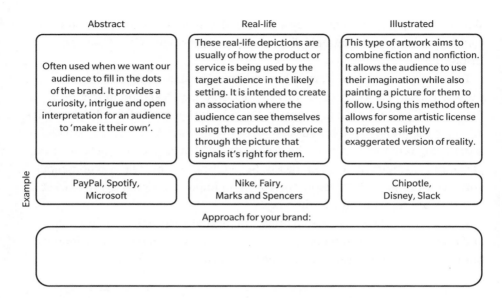

Abstract	Real-life	Illustrated
Often used when we want our audience to fill in the dots of the brand. It provides a curiosity, intrigue and open interpretation for an audience to 'make it their own'.	These real-life depictions are usually of how the product or service is being used by the target audience in the likely setting. It is intended to create an association where the audience can see themselves using the product and service through the picture that signals it's right for them.	This type of artwork aims to combine fiction and nonfiction. It allows the audience to use their imagination while also painting a picture for them to follow. Using this method often allows for some artistic license to present a slightly exaggerated version of reality.

Example

PayPal, Spotify, Microsoft	Nike, Fairy, Marks and Spencers	Chipotle, Disney, Slack

Approach for your brand:

Verbal identity

The way something is written or verbalised can leave a very lasting impact on the customer. Also, the tone and language used in copy has a strong influence on a customer's memory structures. For example, the way Innocent, the healthy drinks brand, was able to create funny, yet informative moments from the copy on its bottles was a key reason for customer loyalty and success. To determine how we can use these verbal cues and identity in your brand, we will cover three key areas.

Tone of voice and Language   Copy and Terminology   Music and Sound

Tone of voice and language

Think about how different people speak, from your parents, friends or even others who you may have overheard in a store. The way they speak, their accent and the type of words they use all help to create a mental picture of who they are. In the same way, your brand needs to achieve a similar thing, where it has a particular tone and language it uses in order to communicate across every touch-point.

It's important that the tone and language used reinforces your brand rather than creates confusion, just as you would be pretty confused (and a little concerned) if your doctor started to talk in slang during an appointment.

To help you achieve this, here is a framework called the 'Tone and language wheel' that shows the different styles you can adopt. There are four dimensions to consider where the wheel helpfully allows us to interrogate the polar ends of each dimension to determine what best fits your brand. A useful way to determine the right tone and language is to apply a common phrase across the dimensions to see what you believe best reflects the brand.

Here is an example of a tone and language wheel for a restaurant delivery service.

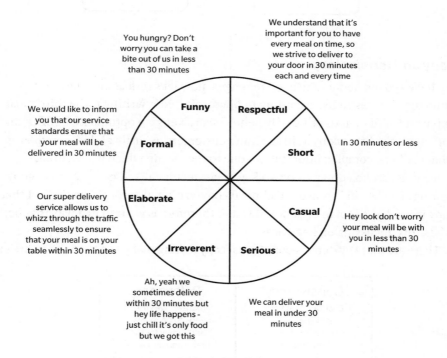

Have a go at doing it yourself using the tone and language wheel template. Pick a phrase that you think you would commonly use in your brand and fill out the various ways you think it could be written based on the descriptor.

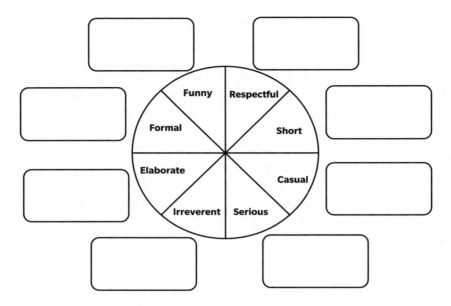

Copy and terminology

We have spoken about tone and language – now let's reflect on copy and terminology. Interestingly, according to Microsoft,[6] copywriting is the third most important skill in marketing only behind search engine optimisation (SEO) and data analysis. Great copywriting allows customers to easily glide through even what could be complex information, due to the way in which it is written.

It can be broken down into two key areas: technical and non-technical copywriting. The key difference is technical copywriting also considers the fact that copy is used as a tool to enhance SEO and therefore is written in a way that optimises this, focussing on keywords.

There are four key dimensions of great copywriting that you need to be aware of.

Consistency	Relevance
Ensuring that your style remains consistent at every touchpoint	Whatever we write it needs to be relevant and timely for the brand and audience
Grammar	Syntax
Poor spelling and punctuation is distracting and takes away from what the brand is saying	Create sentence structures appropriate for the audience and brand

Technical copywriting – keywords and terms

For your brand, you want to optimise 'searchability' and therefore need to consider keywords and terms within your copy. We will cover more on keywords searches in Chapter 8, but there are two simple techniques to use before developing copy in order to optimise this aspect. The first is to simply carry out your own search research where you type keywords into Google and see the results. This will give you an idea on the type of keywords to use with your copy. Second, you can turn to a tool such as Google Keyword Planner. Here is an example where I wanted to get other keywords to use related to vegan meals.

You can see the popularity of other keywords, as well as the level of competition for them, which helps you when deciding which of these terms to include in your

Q vegan meals		
Broaden your search: (+ vegetarian meals) (+ vegan cookbook) (+ diet meals)		
▼ Exclude adult ideas **ADD FILTER** 1,788 keyword ideas available		
Keyword (by relevance) ↓	Avg. monthly searches	Competition
☐ vegan food	10K – 100K	Medium
☐ vegan dinner recipes	1K – 10K	Low
☐ easy vegan recipes	10K – 100K	Low
☐ vegetarian food	1K – 10K	Medium
☐ plant based recipes	1K – 10K	Medium
☐ vegan dinner	1K – 10K	Low
☐ vegan pasta recipes	1K – 10K	Low

Source: https://ads.google.com/aw/keywordplanner/ideas/new?ocid=356548728&
euid=355931255&__u=3528410495&uscid=356548728&__c=6207910072&authuser=
0&sf=barebones&subid=uk-en-et-g-aw-a-tools-kwp_bb-awhp_xin1%21o2

copywriting. The sweet spot is a balance between attaining a high number of searches and yet a low volume of competition for them.

Music and sound

Music and sound form an increasingly important sensory component to a brand, just like songs remain in your head for a long period of time. In fact, sounds trigger recall to nostalgic moments that leave positive impressions on customers. Therefore, it forms a vital part of the brand impression and what makes a brand distinct. Mastercard, for instance, has recently created what it calls a 'sonic logo'[7] that will play each time someone makes a purchase to be reminded of the brand. This type of approach is becoming increasingly important as we turn to smart devices such as the Amazon Echo to consume content and information. Furthermore, Ipsos suggests that it is one of the most powerful ways to get your audience to remember your brand.[8]

To help develop a music or sound, you should begin by determining the kind of emotion you would like our audience to feel when they hear the sound, using the 'Music Mood Map'. This is where you identify the type of mood you want to trigger in your audience when they listen to the music you have created.

A good example of a company that put music at the heart of its brand is Just Eat in the UK. In order to attract a new urban, young audience it brought none other than the legendary rapper Snoop Dogg[9] to represent the brand. He created a bespoke song that was intended to be 'a memorable moment of light-hearted entertainment'.[10]

In the music mood map below, circle the word that best describes the mood you want to create. I have identified where Just Eat would sit on the map.

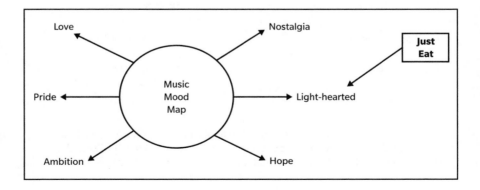

Brand differentiation

You are almost there in developing the 360 view of your brand and just need to develop the final element, brand differentiation. At the heart of any brand is the ability to add value to the consumer. In fact, one can argue that it forms the very cornerstone of marketing. It was Rory Sutherland, Vice Chairman of Ogilvy, who said, "Actions speak louder than words: make meaningful offers to help your customers." He talks of the importance of a brand that is able to 'walk the talk' and even goes above and beyond to help customers, which leads to them being highly differentiated.

However, simply taking action doesn't go far enough in the eyes of the consumer, rather it's actually the combination of 'intent' and 'action' that evokes a corresponding emotion in the customer where you can really differentiate your brand. Evidence shows that brands that are able to achieve this actually grow at more than twice the rate of others,[11] demonstrating the power of brand differentiation in this way.

There is a two-step process that we are going to go through in order to develop a clear brand differentiation approach for your brand that is centred in action, intent and customer emotion.

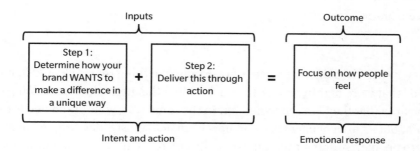

Step 1: Determine how your brand wants to make a difference

Let's turn to the recent Coronavirus pandemic as it was certainly a time when brands were able to differentiate themselves and truly stand out. However, according to an APCO Worldwide study only a handful of brands really stood out to consumers including Amazon and Walmart[12] due to their very clearly defined actions at the time. Furthermore, Laithwaite conducted an analysis and looked at how a variety of companies were taking action based on their values from banks (Standard Chartered) to FMCG companies (Unilever).

	Action		Value
Standard Chartered	Launched $50m fund to support victims of the pandemic.		Do the right thing
Coca Cola	Awarded $ 13.5m in grants to not-for-profit organizations responding to the coronavirus in North America and Canada.		We value workplace & Human rights
Pepsico	Distributing 50 million meals to at-risk populations.		Responsibility & Trust
Tata Group	Pledged $200m for affected communities, free education software and a COVID-19 patient tracker.		Responsibility
Nationwide	Shortened supplier payment time to 10 days for small businesses.		Act with honesty & Integrity
Lego	Pledged $50m to support victims and launched website enabling families worldwide to connect to play-based learning across social media.		Learning & Caring
Unilever	Donated free sanitizer, soap, bleach and food worth €100m.		Positive impact & Continuous improvement
BT	1.5% payrise for all 58,000 non-management staff to reflect efforts during the pandemic.		People first
Citi	Awarded an additional day of vacation to all 200,000 employees to reflect efforts during the crisis.		Act responsibly

Source: Laithwaite[13]

Through these two distinct pieces of research, one thing that is clear is that the brands that were highlighted as the ones adding the most value were doing so in the area that they are renowned for. In the same way, your brand needs to be clear about its area of expertise and how it can add most value, over competitors, to people. By doing this you can really create a win–win as not only does this action lead to higher brand equity but there is evidence to suggest that by being proactive in addressing the needs of your stakeholders your brand will be more resilient[14] and able to bounce back faster even during challenging times.[15]

So to do this, your brand needs to be able to answer the following two questions.

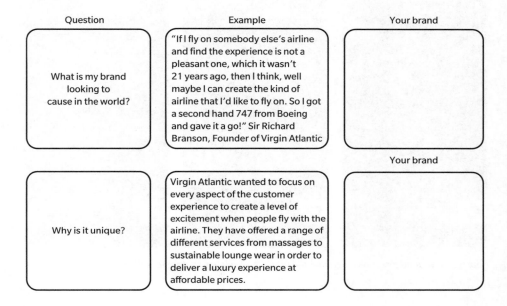

Question	Example	Your brand
What is my brand looking to cause in the world?	"If I fly on somebody else's airline and find the experience is not a pleasant one, which it wasn't 21 years ago, then I think, well maybe I can create the kind of airline that I'd like to fly on. So I got a second hand 747 from Boeing and gave it a go!" Sir Richard Branson, Founder of Virgin Atlantic	
Why is it unique?	Virgin Atlantic wanted to focus on every aspect of the customer experience to create a level of excitement when people fly with the airline. They have offered a range of different services from massages to sustainable lounge wear in order to deliver a luxury experience at affordable prices.	

Step 2: Deliver through actions

Once you have established what your brand is looking to cause in the world and why it is unique, you need to put a brand plan in place to deliver on this. At the heart of this approach is to ensure transparency and consistency, in what your brand 'says' and 'does' as increasingly we are seeing brands that are being tarnished with 'woke washing'. Alan Jope, the CEO of Unilever, says, "There are too many examples of brands undermining purposeful marketing by launching campaigns which aren't backing up what their brand says with what their brand does. Purpose-led brand communications is not just a matter of 'make them cry, make them buy'. It's about action in the world." Unilever for example, 'lives its brand' through its Sustainable Living Plan (available here: www.unilever.co.uk/ sustainable-living/the-unilever-sustainable-living-plan/) and has a very clear plan of action.

Source: www.unilever.co.uk/sustainable-living/the-unilever-sustainable-living-plan/

To develop a similar plan, use this template for your brand.

What is my brand looking to cause in the world?

Key brand objectives

When will you deliver these?

What are the key actions you will take?

How is it differentiated from the competition?

Emotional response: How people feel

By having the right intent and taking the right actions to deliver value to your audience, your brand will show that it genuinely cares and in turn forms a deep connection with its customers. It's worth considering how your brand, through its intent and actions, will make your customers feel. Or, said another way, what would be the optimal emotional outcome you would want your customers to feel when they engage with your brand?

This will allow you to monitor whether you are in fact achieving your desired response. To do this, we can use something I call the 'emotional wheel'. It allows you to plot the type of emotion you would like your customer to feel when they engage with the brand. You can also plot a number of your competitor brands as well to determine what emotion their brands evoke. Here is an example for a variety of different chocolate brands.

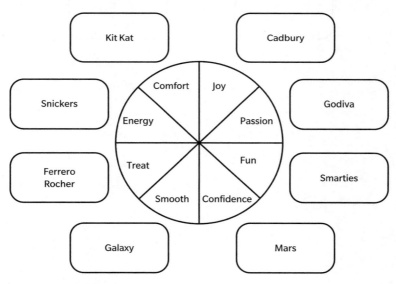

Emotional wheel

Use this blank template for your brand and plot some of your competitors.

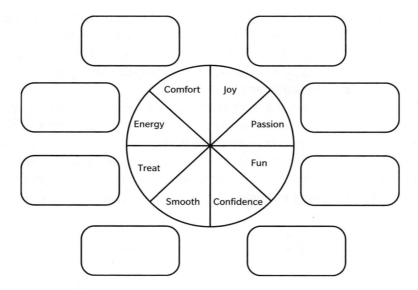

chapter 5

The secrets to scaling your brand

In the previous chapter, you discovered how to create a brand that is distinct, differentiated and above all connects with people on both a rational and emotional level. Now, you may be thinking that you have done all the hard 'ground' work to achieve brand success. Not so fast! Remember in the previous chapter, I mentioned that today the barriers to building a brand are lower than ever, yet sustaining it is harder than ever. Why is that?

Well, with so much competition it's very difficult for your brand to really stand out and gain traction, credibility and trust with your consumers. In reality, it's only a very small minority of brands that are able to break through to achieve any level of success. A good example of this is Tesla: in less than 20 years from it being founded, it has overtaken Toyota to become the world's most valuable car manufacturing brand.[1] This is certainly by no coincidence but rather careful design that enabled it to leverage its brand to achieve what it has in such a short space of time.

In this chapter, I'm going to reveal the secrets that brands like Tesla use when developing and growing its brand and take you through, step by step, the strategic choices that you need to make for your brand in order to be able to replicate this success. Here is the 'secrets of branding' model that consists of four layers.

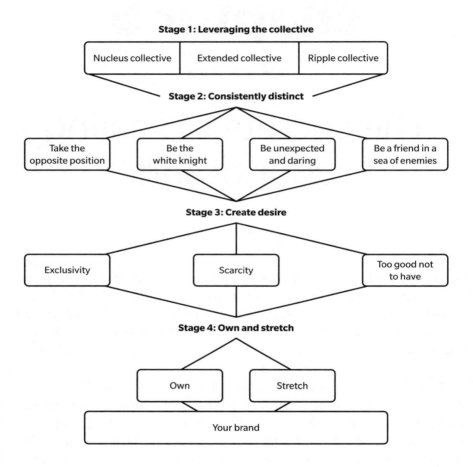

Stage 1: Leveraging the collective

At the heart of every brand is a collection of people who choose to come together to initially solve a problem, which then creates a ripple effect that encourages others to support the brand in a variety of ways, through their contributions, advocacy, custom and loyalty. At each stage, different groups of people play different roles in generating brand value, which I term 'people collectives', or 'collectives' for short. From well-known founding teams to renowned early-stage investors and influential customers, each play a role – and for you knowing how to harness them at different points is critical to give your brand the wings it needs.

Let me show how you can achieve this for your brand through what I call the 'collective brand model', where there are three stages to consider:

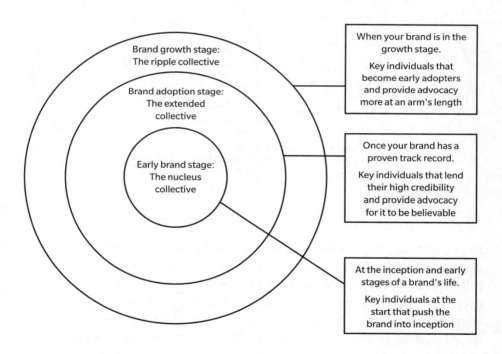

Early brand stage: The nucleus collective

At the inception of a brand, it's the founder that plays a crucial role in bringing a team of people together to solve a problem. It is actually this very team that is a brand's greatest asset in the early days as it's their credibility, ability and personal brands that you need to leverage. That is why it is so crucial to get the right team in place who can first convince others that your chosen cause is worth fighting for, and second, that together you are the right people for the job to lead the 'creation' of the solution due to a combination of skills, know-how, access and ability. These two dimensions are what I call the 'nucleus collective of the brand'.

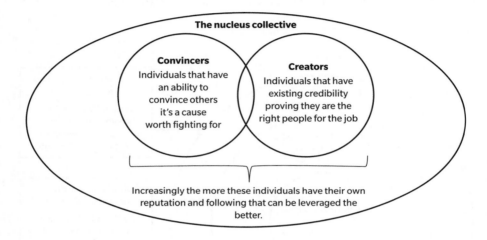

So as a first step, you need to analyse your brand's nucleus collective and develop it. Usually the founders take on the role of 'convincers' and typically have fairly charismatic, yet endearing personalities, combined with a deep appreciation for the sector. Good examples include Gary Vanerchuk of VaynerMedia to Steven Bartlett of Social Chain, who leverage their own personal brands to give a huge amount of credibility to the organisations they are associated with. At the same time, the team needs to be very credible with deep expertise in order to be able to deliver the ambitious task put forward.

Using the template, write down who in your team sits within the nucleus collective and compare them to the attributes on the right-hand side.

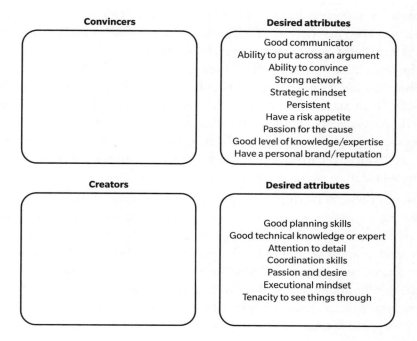

Convincers

Desired attributes

Good communicator
Ability to put across an argument
Ability to convince
Strong network
Strategic mindset
Persistent
Have a risk appetite
Passion for the cause
Good level of knowledge/expertise
Have a personal brand/reputation

Creators

Desired attributes

Good planning skills
Good technical knowledge or expert
Attention to detail
Coordination skills
Passion and desire
Executional mindset
Tenacity to see things through

If you identify gaps in this collective you must work hard to close them down. This could mean taking on some new people (not necessarily full time) to fill these gaps. One good way to achieve this is by inviting a number of very credible non-executive directors on to the board who can form part of your founding team.

The extended collective

Once you have your nucleus collective in place and your brand has seen some traction, you need to build on this, using the 'extended collective'. At this stage you are trying to build proof-points for the brand by leveraging the association with other highly influential individuals, who are not involved day to day. You can achieve this in a number of ways, depending on your brand strategy. I have listed a couple here for you to consider:

- **An angel or investor:** Often at this stage where a certain amount of traction has been achieved, a brand may look to bring on-board an early stage investor. There is a term used called 'smart money' here to suggest that this person should be someone who not only brings funding but can open doors, even just with their association. Check out a platform called Vintro (https://beta. myvintro.com/) to pitch to high-profile investors. A good example of this is Elon Musk himself who you may have assumed is the founder of Tesla. But it is not the case. It was founded by Ebenhard and Tarpenning in 2003 on the back of early successful tests of electric cars. They made the perfect backbone to the company given their engineering backgrounds and ability to deliver, but they missed one crucial ingredient, a statesman. Along came Elon Musk in 2004[2] as an angel investor who also became the chairman and together they formed the nucleus collective for Tesla.

- **Advisory board:** Putting together an advisory board is also a great way to become associated with some of the big names in your industry. They become a very valuable resource for strategic inputs, branding and also help through their advocacy of your brand with their influential peers. To develop an advisory board requires you to choose people with diverse skills and experience who believe in the cause and are willing to lend their name and time to help build the brand. A good example is the advisory board put together by the School of Marketing.

- **Brand ambassadors:** These are people who will actively champion your brand and help represent it on the ground. They are a group of very credible individuals who can spread the word about the brand and what it stands for. They should be someone your target audience admires or aspires to be like. For instance, Atom Bank had the famous rapper Will.I.Am as its brand ambassador, while the School of Marketing has 50 brand ambassadors known as the Founding 50.

Write down who and how your brand can leverage your extended collective.

The ripple collective

During the growth phase of your brand, it's important to focus on what I call the 'ripple collective'. These people are those who really buy into your brand, its values and what you deliver and are willing to not only become your early adopters and buy from you but also want to be a part of your community and vouch for your brand. These are arguably some of the most important individuals to your brand as they provide in-market proof-points of how you deliver to your promise. You must nurture these relationships at all costs and make them feel extremely valued so they feel like they want to help by adding to the brand story and go on the journey with you.

Here are some ways you can achieve this.

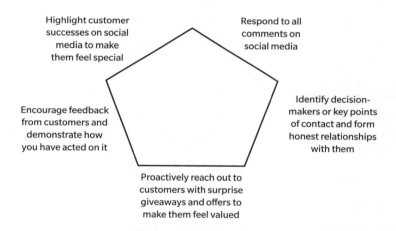

Highlight customer successes on social media to make them feel special

Respond to all comments on social media

Identify decision-makers or key points of contact and form honest relationships with them

Encourage feedback from customers and demonstrate how you have acted on it

Proactively reach out to customers with surprise giveaways and offers to make them feel valued

Stage 2: Be consistently distinct

It may sound like an oxymoron for your brand to be consistent and yet distinct, but this is exactly what you need to achieve. It actually is a two-stage process of first ensuring that your brand is being brave and bold as in the words of Mastercard's Chief Marketing Officer, Raja Rajamannar: "Sailing the sea of sameness"[3] just won't cut it. Once you have achieved this position, your brand needs to double-down on it, consistently reinforcing ownership of it over time.

A good example of this principle comes from another of Elon Musk's ventures, SpaceX, founded in 2003. It has an audacious and arguably the most extreme version of distinctiveness for a commercial entity to "revolutionise space technology". In the early days this position would have possibly been laughable compared to say its NASA counterpart. Yet, despite numerous setbacks, the single message to 'push the boundaries of human exploration' never wavered, which over time began to generate traction and credibility. Today, SpaceX as a brand is probably as well if not more well known than NASA for space travel, let alone actually helped NASA to resurrect US spaceflight.[4]

So let's explore how your brand is going to achieve these seemingly dichotomous goals. I will introduce you to four different techniques to consider, but you will only need to adopt one.

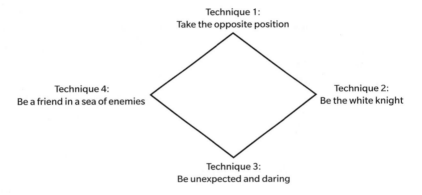

Technique 1: Take the opposite position

In order for your brand to stand out, when all others zig your brand should zag. This is a powerful technique where you show all other brands in the category as all being the same in one area and then your brand takes the opposite position. It's clever branding as although you are merely highlighting one key area of difference, it gives the impression that you are completely different from all others in the category.

A good example of this in the fizzy drinks category is Ugly drinks (https://uglydrinks.co.uk/). It was able to carve out a distinct position summed up in its tagline, "no sugarcoating. . . just sparkling water" making the not-so-subtle suggestion that all other brands in the space have a high sugar content in their drinks. Remember, it just focuses on one key aspect that makes it stand out from other brands and then doubles-down on that consistently reinforcing the message across all brand assets.

For your brand consider the one attribute where you can take the opposite position from everyone else.

Technique 2: Be the white knight

You are able to create a distinctive space for yourself by highlighting key industry and societal problems and then centring your brand on solving them in ways that no one else is doing. Importantly, the issue needs to be big and wide enough for people to care and want to actively participate in to have the largest impact. A good example of this is Marks and Spencer that highlighted the issues of planetary sustainability and focussed on the store's contribution to the problem. It then created Plan A, its sustainability initiative that became central to its entire brand strategy. More can be found here: https://corporate.marksandspencer. com/sustainability

Turning to your brand, what significant issues exist that you can play a key role in solving that are not currently being looked at by the competition? Fill in your thoughts here.

Technique 3: Be unexpected and daring

For your brand to achieve the unexpected, Benjamin Braun, CMO of Samsung Europe, says, "You have to dare."[5] Being bold and willing to take risks comes as part of the course when you have a brand that is centred around doing the unexpected.

It's this very mentality that led Burger King to achieve the Cannes Lions Creative Brand of the Year Award.[6] This is an award designed to recognise the creative risks that individual brands take to distinguish their product in different regions around the world. Burger King's brand has become a symbol for creative risk-taking, launching campaigns such as the Moldy Burger to highlight the lack of preservatives in its flagship item. It's the constant drive to deliver something creative, original and that has a shock factor at the heart of the brand.[7]

Consider what you can do with your brand that can deliver this kind of stand-out factor.

Technique 4: Be a friend in a sea of enemies

This final technique is used to highlight how for a long time the customer has been wronged in some way and they didn't realise it was happening. However, now a trusted friend is letting them know that there is a better way for them to save money, time or have less hassle. It positions the brand to be the trusted advisor, implying that they will look after the customer better than what everyone else has done or can do and therefore provides reassurance.

This has been a common technique used in a range of financial services brands where the need for trust is high. A good example is Transferwise that goes to great lengths to draw comparison between its fee structure and that of other institutions. At each point in its journey and communications it consistently highlights how much its customer saved by using its services. Consider how you could use these techniques in your brand.

Now that you have evaluated the different brand strategies in this area, circle which one best suits your brand.

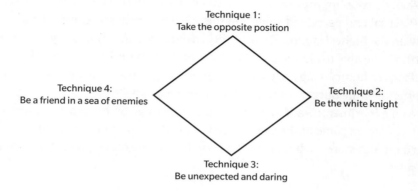

Technique 1:
Take the opposite position

Technique 4:
Be a friend in a sea of enemies

Technique 2:
Be the white knight

Technique 3:
Be unexpected and daring

Stage 3: Create desire

Brands that are able to generate significant traction and credibility are those that can actually evoke a sense of desire amongst their target audience. It's linked to the physiological feeling that they 'must have' the brand as it fulfils both a need and a want. There are three key techniques that brands use, represented by what I call the 'desired effect triangle'.

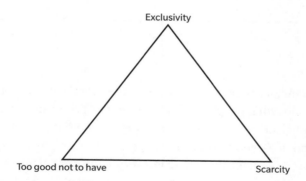

Exclusivity

Too good not to have

Scarcity

Exclusivity

A brand that creates desire through exclusivity plays on the principle that we all have an innate need for self-worth. The brand, therefore, acts as a mirror image of what someone either believes they are or wants to become. Associated with feelings of luxury this characteristic is also closely linked to superior quality with an expected price premium to match, which is where the saying "You pay for what you get" comes from.

When developing your brand in this way, there are two key elements to consider: actual and perceived value. On the one hand, you may want your brand to attain the highest standards of quality in every aspect, from design to service in order to be able to charge a higher price. In fact, many brands from designer handbags to luxury soaps rely on their ability to give their customers a luxurious experience while purchasing a product or service.

Do an experiment: walk into a premium store or go on its website, analyse and write down some of the aspects that made the experience more exclusive than a regular store – what forms the actual value the brand gives the customer. Consider.

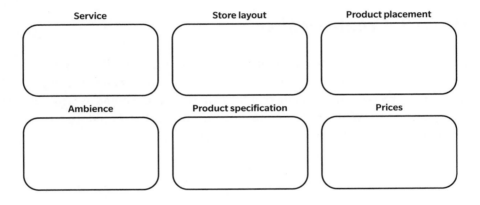

On the other hand, it's important to consider the perceived value of the brand as well. This is not what people see but how people feel when they think of your brand. Consider owning a home in a very prestigious part of town, such as Mayfair in London. Beyond the property specification and benefits of the surrounding area, the actual value, there is a very significant element for perceived brand value of living there for what it actually represents and reflects about an individual. In the same way, if opting for an exclusive brand approach you need to also reflect on the perceived value of the brand. To do this, consider and write down answers to these three questions.

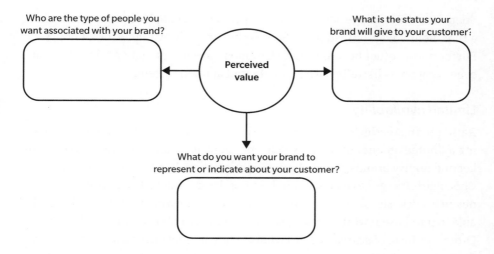

Who are the type of people you want associated with your brand?

What is the status your brand will give to your customer?

Perceived value

What do you want your brand to represent or indicate about your customer?

Scarcity

A brand that is based on scarcity to create desire focuses on the principle that we want what we can't have. There is often a close association between the role of scarcity and exclusivity, where by the very nature of being exclusive you become less available to everyone. However, it's important to note that scarcity also has a much wider applicability for you to consider as well. There are three core aspects that brands that focus on this aspect consider.

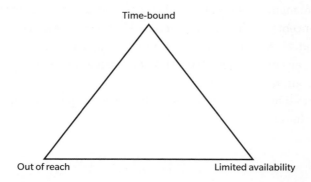

Time-bound

Out of reach

Limited availability

Time-bound

You would have no doubt heard of the term FOMO (the fear of missing out), where you only have a certain amount of time to purchase or experience something. This is the entire premise behind market-leading brands such as

Snapchat, the leading social media platform where people share moments in a time-bound way, or Instagram Stories that are only available for 24 hours. Furthermore, other brands such as Groupon have offers that only last a day and even companies like eBay use a time-bound auction system.

Limited availability

Rather than creating scarcity through time, limited availability focuses on having a limited amount of stock, which 'once gone is gone'. It applies to mass market and luxury brands, from a limited-edition chocolate such as Terry's White Chocolate Orange[8] to a new limited-edition Rolex watch. The reason for the desire is because customers want to feel special, knowing that they will only be able to purchase it while stocks last and thereafter nobody will be able to get it. Often this form of scarcity drives what is known as loss aversion, which drives desire to avoid a loss of not having something rather than for the gain it presents.

Out of reach

This aspect of scarcity is very interesting in that it plays into two different psychological states. The first is that it sits at a price premium and therefore only a certain segment of the market can afford it, which is what most luxury brands deliver, from cars to handbags. By purchasing that brand, the customer is instantly signalling their status which makes them feel somewhat superior in some ways.

On the other hand, it also refers to the fact that something is not out of reach from a price point of view but rather either only open to a select few or there is a significant wait to get it. Consider a private members club where the actual fee may be affordable to many people but it's only those who get referred who can join.

The two concepts can be clearly combined in certain instances as well, which makes the product even more scarce. A good example of this is a Hermes Berkin handbag that can cost up to £170,000 and have a waitlist of months before you can even get your hands on one.[9]

Consider if and how scarcity can be an important aspect for your brand. Write your thoughts here.

Too good not to have

I hope by now you have figured that creating desire is not limited to the high-end or luxury segment of the market. In fact, a brand can create a significant amount of desire by offering something that is so unique and/or great value that consumers do not want to miss out. Think about the psychology behind a retail store sale, which creates desire because what is on offer represents value that is just too good not to have. When applied to brand strategy it becomes a very powerful tool to create demand based on extraordinary value.

Brands from Poundland to Primark have recognised and executed this brand concept that drives volumes of people into their stores each day. It's the brand positioning of 'quality at low prices', which is seemingly contradictory, that creates the appeal and leaves the consumer wondering why they would shop anywhere else, as this is the savvy person's choice. It plays into the notion that we all have a desire to be seen to be making 'smart' choices when it comes to the brands we associate ourselves with.

When considering this brand position, you need to think about how you can achieve a juxtaposition between two seemingly opposing thoughts pivoted around a price-point. Here are a number of examples from companies that achieve this. Circle the ones you think may be applicable to your brand.

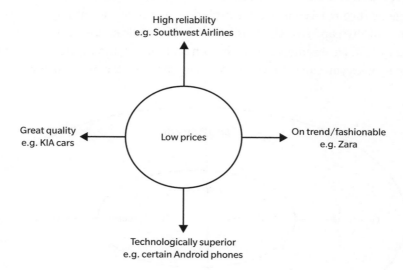

Finally, consider which technique would be most appropriate for your brand and circle it below. Write your rational in the triangle.

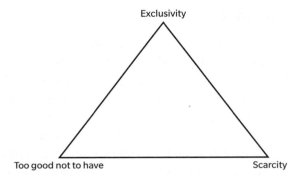

Stage 4: Own and stretch

The brands that do exceptionally well are all those that own a space or territory and become known for it. That is not to say that a brand is not able to extend its reach over time. In fact, great brands do just that, where they become known for a wider territory. For instance, take Amazon where in the beginning it started out as an online book retailer, compared to today where it is the largest e-commerce retailer in the world.

Similarly, Virgin began its life as a record label and today stretches into diversified areas from cosmetics to casinos. To get to where they are, these brands have gone through a considerable evolution over time and through a process of what I call 'own and stretch'. This is where they dedicate themselves to owning a territory and, once achieved, they stretch their brand into the next area. As your brand evolves you can achieve this by using the two-step model below.

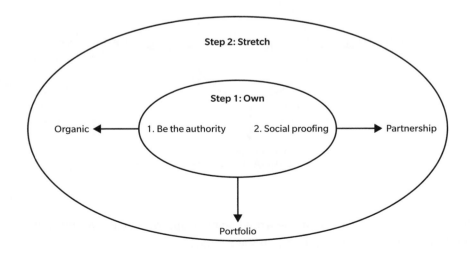

Step 1: Own

It is incredibly important that your brand is known for something. In fact, at the beginning the more it can be known for just one thing the better. For instance, TOMS shoes (www.toms.co.uk/) is a social enterprise known for its one-for-one business model (for every pair bought one is donated). And the Dollar Shave Club (https://uk.dollarshaveclub.com/) is renowned as the disruptive discount subscription shave company. It has managed to distil its entire reason for being into one simple, single message in an area where it saw a gap. You need to be able to do this for your brand.

To be able to own your space, there are two key techniques that go hand in hand that you will want to adopt in your brand: authority and social-proofing. Let me explain how you can use these to your advantage.

First, identify the one single message that you want to be known for and that you can deliver on. We have already touched on the fact that the more distinct, appealing and targeted at a specific customer pain point this single message can be, the better.

Reflect on this and write it here.

This single message must be front and centre of everything you do. It would also be advantageous to create a compelling brand story for people to relate to and see how it either fits into their lives or how they can be a part of the solution. For instance, Ben and Jerrys, the famous ice cream brand, focuses on why the founders started the company and takes a clear ethical stance.

Second, the more you can be seen on or get other 'authoritative' platforms to share your message the better. It's a form of social-proofing that if people hear about your brand from people they trust, they are instantaneously more likely to trust you. Interestingly, it works the same way with algorithms, where being associated with authoritative sources called 'backlinks' increases your online reputation and increases your search rankings (more about this later).

Many brands are able to gain publicity based on their mission and some initial traction. For instance, the School of Marketing regularly features in *Marketing Week* due to its social mission to help young people get employed in the industry. A final point here is that sometimes certain people's endorsement or recommendation of your brand can be even more powerful than a media outlet, due to the trust and number of followers they have.

Consider the types of media outlets or influencers you would want to talk about the brand and what would you want them to say.

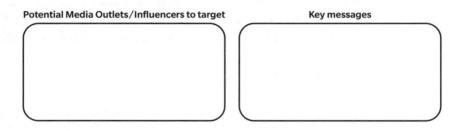

Potential Media Outlets/Influencers to target

Key messages

Third, have evidence to reinforce the brand through proof-points, ratings, reviews or customer testimonials that act as social proof for your brand. This could be how your brand is able to give an enhanced level of performance to demonstrate what others are missing out on. For example, Nutmeg, the online investment management company, does this by drawing comparison to its results versus a peer group, as shown in the example below.

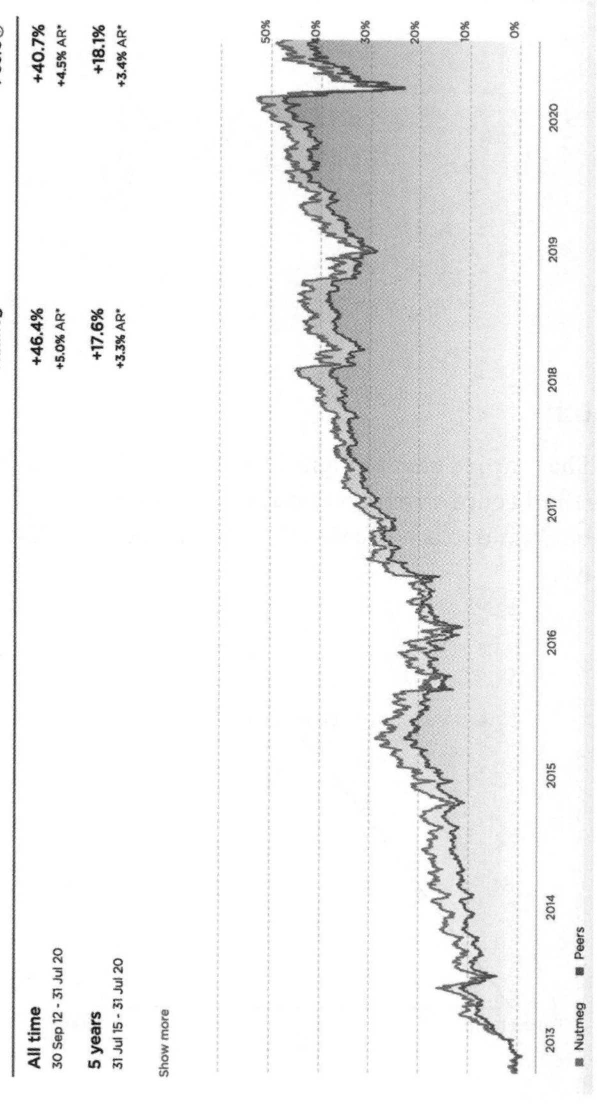

Nutmeg
Peers
All time
30 Sep 12 - 31 Jul 20
+46.4%
+5.0% AR*
+40.7%
+4.5% AR*
5 years
31 Jul 15 - 31 Jul 20
+17.6%
+3.3% AR*
+18.1%
+3.4% AR*
Show more
50%
40%
30%
20%
10%
0%
2013
2014
2015
2016
2017
2018
2019
2020
Nutmeg
Peers

Alternatively, Amazon has achieved a sustained degree of success over time and found its review and ranking system has been key to its social proof. It uses this function to demonstrate what others bought and how others rated the product.

Consider and write down how your brand can attain this type of social proof-points.

Step 2: Stretch

Once your brand has earned enough significant brand equity in a certain space it begins to have the 'licence' to expand into other areas or verticals. There are three ways for your brand to achieve this that you should consider, which are not mutually exclusive.

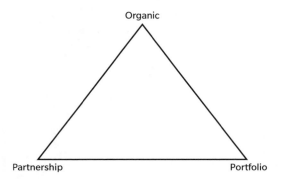

Organic

This is where your brand is able to lend the equity built in one area and apply it to another. Typically, this form of brand stretch takes incremental steps that enable it to build on some part of its existing advantage as it stretches into a new territory. Organic brand stretch should always follow one of the following approaches.

- **Related industries:** Your brand could stretch into a parallel industry, such as the Colgate brand stretching from toothpaste and into a range of oral hygiene products.
- **New customers, existing brand offering:** Your brand could stretch into new and expanded markets, such as American Express moving from a high-end brand to now catering to a high middle to upper market place through a tiered offering.
- **Same customers, new brand offering:** You offer the same customers a new brand category or offer. For example, the Dollar Shave Club targets its customers with a full range of grooming products.

Circle which option above could be applicable to your brand and write your rationale here.

Portfolio

The other way you can expand your brand is by actually creating a collection of brands within a portfolio, known as the 'House of brands'. This is where you create a series of different brands that come together under an overarching mother brand and each delivers something different to the market. It provides a good level of diversification and also provides protection in case one brand faces reputational issues. Certain companies use this to diversify within a certain category, such as Unilever where all its brands sit within fast-moving consumer goods. Or others diversify completely such as TATA or Reliance that are in cross-categories from cars to telco.

When thinking about a brand portfolio, there are a number of tools you can use to assess an existing portfolio such as the Boston Consulting Matrix or the GE-McKinsey nine box matrix, templates for which are widely available via Google. However, when considering how to add to your brand portfolio, you need to consider these four questions.

How does the brand add to the organisation's strategic and commercial objectives?

Does it operate in a space that is complimentary to our existing portfolio?

Does it extend our reach or enable us to deepen existing customer relationships?

Is it or does it have an ability to have a leading position in an area of interest?

Partnerships

The final way to stretch your brand is through partnerships and collaborations. This enables your brand to leverage another and vice versa. A very useful tool to understand the type of synergies you could generate by partnering with others is the brand asset validator, found here: www.bavgroup.com/ It's also worth noting that partnerships can also be with individuals that can help to further brand perception. A good example of this is BrewDog, the Scottish beer company, that on the back of a humorous tweet from comedian Ricky Gervais about the brand went on to form a partnership with him to help stray dogs.[10]

There are effectively two types of brand partnerships that you can consider:

- **Like-for-like brand partnering:** This is where a company partners with a direct competitor in order to realise enhanced scale and synergies. A term often used to describe some partnerships of this nature is 'frenemy'. This is where they could partner in certain areas for mutual benefit while also maintaining strategic distance in other areas where they remain competitors.

A good example is the strategic brand partnering of Slack and Amazon as they compete with a key rival product Microsoft Teams. It's a real win–win as Amazon gets access to leading communication tools while Slack is able to gain access to the latest cloud technology through AWS, making them a partnership to be reckoned with.

- **Category or channel brand partnerships:** This is when a company partners to gain access to a specific channel or gain closer access to some part of the value chain.

Haagen-Daz, a clear leader in the premium ice-cream category, understands that in order to win the hearts, minds and mouths of its customers it needs to be there at important and significant moments in their lives. To ramp up its in-home distribution it partnered with Secret Cinema to bring a new concept to customers called 'Secret Sofa'. It also teamed up with London-based gin company Sipsmith[11] and Jack Daniels[12] to provide the perfect alcoholic compliment to the ice cream.

Reflect on and write down if these partner models may be applicable to your brand.

Finally, when undertaking a partnership take the following steps.

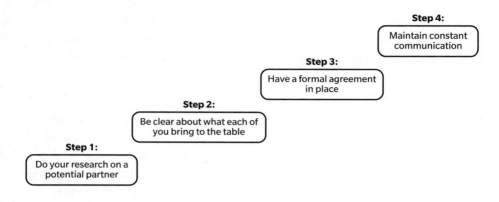

Step 4:
Maintain constant communication

Step 3:
Have a formal agreement in place

Step 2:
Be clear about what each of you bring to the table

Step 1:
Do your research on a potential partner

chapter 6

———

Build your brand's community through content marketing

In this chapter, I am going to talk you through the process your brand can go through to build a community and maximise its potential using content marketing. To help, I have created a model called the 'double loop community flywheel', an invaluable tool for you to apply. The model uses the term 'flywheel' to suggest that over time the flow through the model should become easier and self-fulfilling; but be warned–getting the flywheel started is often very hard, time-consuming and where most brands give up.

The most important relationship a brand can form is the one that it has with consumers. There is a simple formula to think about and that is 'whoever is closest to the end-consumer wins most', as they will have the best understanding of their customers' needs and be able to serve them directly in the quickest, most efficient way possible. This ability, for example, has been the key to leading fashion retailers Zara's success as it is able to pick up on trends almost instantly through its customers and then has new lines on the shelves within 10 to 15 days. It is also this rationale that has spawned the exponential growth of 'direct to consumer' or D2C brands as a way to foster a deeper, more meaningful relationship with customers, without any middlemen.

It therefore comes as no surprise that at the heart of many successful and disruptive brands is their ability to form direct relationships with consumers. Building this strong following or community is key as the psychological relationship between brands and consumers has fundamentally shifted. Previously, it may have been acceptable for brands to give consumers the hard sell, but today this is far from the case. Rather, consumers expect brands to earn their trust and they want to feel a part of the brand before making purchase decisions. Interestingly, there has been a significant shift in this regard where consumers are now more likely to trust a stranger's recommendation over a brand's claim. For instance, they are more likely to trust a review on Tripadvisor than a hotel's brochure, or follow a piece of advice from a mother they have never met on Mumsnet rather than a baby care brand or pay more attention to an Amazon rating rather than what the manufacturer says about the product. This has prolific impacts on the way we need to market to consumers and it starts with building a strong community.

Brands are able to engage in this two-way constant dialogue using digital channels, primarily social media, to build their trusted following where their community becomes their advocates, ambassadors and, over time, customers. It also acts as the modern-day form of word-of-mouth marketing for your brand, allowing you to gain access to new audiences cost-effectively through this social advocacy.

Here is the double-loop flywheel.

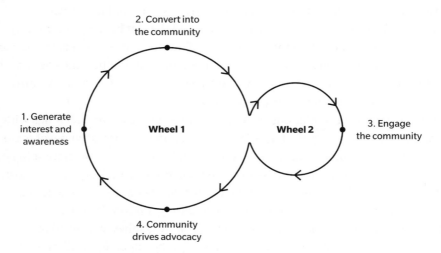

It uses a mechanism where you take people through a content process to make them part of your community and get them to a point where they become advocates and help promote you to their networks. In the model there are four stages, divided into two wheels for you to follow.

Step 1: Generate interest and awareness

At the beginning you need to create a content and engagement strategy where you look to engage a broad audience across social media. The sole intention of this is to get your audience to follow or subscribe to your page or profile because they are interested, entertained or intrigued by your brand and the type of content you are putting out there.

Step 2: Convert into the community

The next step is to generate permission from your audience to engage in a deeper relationship where you understand who they are as they are willing to share their data in exchange for the value you bring in sharing other types of content. This allows you to take the conversation from social media channels into more of your 'owned' channels.

Step 3: Engage the community

This is where you move into the second wheel where you nurture the relationship and make them feel part of the community across a multitude of channels.

Step 4: Community drives advocacy

At this stage, your community begins to do the talking for you, becoming your advocates and ambassadors to bring in new followers to engage with your brand and encourage them to follow your content. At this point the flywheel begins again.

Let's now take a closer look at each stage and see how you can develop this flywheel for your brand to foster and grow your community.

Step 1: Generate interest and awareness

Scroll through your social media feed and you will see a string of content that is produced by a variety of individuals and companies. Their aim is to drive awareness and engagement of their brand by getting people to like, share and comment on the content. In a similar way, you want to create a content and engagement approach that peaks your audience's interest where they want to engage and learn more about your brand, with the eventual aim of them forming part of your community. To achieve this, here are some simple steps to follow.

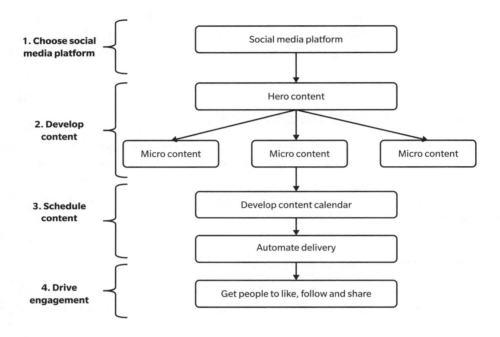

The first thing you need to do is carefully select the social media platform where you are going to cultivate your community. I recommend researching this carefully, considering the type of audience, demographics and other characteristics that you would like to attract to your brand. It is also worth looking at which platforms give you more organic reach with your audience. For example, at the time of writing both LinkedIn and TikTok generate some of the best organic reach of any major social media platform. Once you gain significant traction on one platform there is really no going back as you will have to start again from scratch.

The second thing is to design the type of content that you want to engage your audience with. Here is a list of the different types of content formats that you can use to achieve this. As you can see, there are so many options for you to choose from and it's best that you use a variety so people do not get 'content fatigued' when they see your profile on their feeds. This is where they subconsciously get used to the type of content and format you are using and therefore begin to scroll past it without evening noticing.

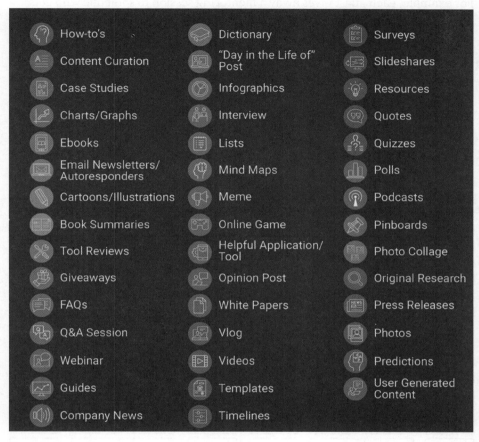

Content formats

When creating content, a good method to use for this process is to create a range of 'hero content' which is long form and acts as the headline for your audience. A good example of this is the School of Marketing's weekly virtual show called 'The Places We'll Go Show' where each week a new high-profile guest is interviewed. Increasingly, this type of content is generated in real-time and conversational in nature given emerging platforms such as Clubhouse. From this piece of hero content each week they create a series of micro pieces of content in multiple formats that go out throughout the week to keep engagement levels high. Also, considering ways to link the two together can be very useful. For example, each guest gives away a mentoring session to someone who gets announced as a micro piece of content in the following week.

Once you have determined the type of content, you should use a content calendar to determine the order of the content and use an automated tool like Hootsuite (https://hootsuite.com/) to schedule it in. The key is to not overdo the amount of content as there is a Law of Diminishing Returns which happens when you over-saturate your market and leads to less effectiveness. Here is a template that you can use.

Time	Monday	Tuesday	Wednesday	Thursday	Friday	Saturday	Sunday
09:00							
10:00							
11:00							
12:00							
13:00							
14:00							
15:00							
16:00							
17:00							
18:00							
19:00							
20:00							
21:00							
22:00							
23:00							
00:00							
01:00							
02:00							
03:00							
04:00							
05:00							
06:00							
07:00							
08:00							

Content calendar

Finally, and perhaps what most people forget, is that you need to constantly drive engagement by engaging in a two-way conversation with those who engage with the content. Here are a number of techniques to consider:

- Respond to every message or comment.
- Thank anyone who shares your content.
- Copy or tag relevant people into content you think they will enjoy.
- Use hashtags in your content so it becomes searchable.
- Form content collaborations with other brands so you can both benefit in the increased reach.

Step 2: Convert into the community

In this next step, your brand needs to gain permission from those who have engaged with you to take the conversation off social media and onto a range of other channels. This is very important for two reasons. The first is that other channels allow you to have a much more in-depth, richer relationship with consumers rather than one-off engagements with them. Second, there is a real risk with social media platforms that they either disappear or change their algorithm and you no longer have access to your audience. We have seen both these things happen recently with the ban of TikTok in certain countries and Facebook adapting its algorithm to reduce organic reach.

In order to achieve this deeper relationship, people must be willing to share their information and open to receiving communications from your brand directly. There is a clear value exchange here where if your brand gives them significant value they will be willing to give you their details and permission. This hook in marketing terms is what is known as a 'lead magnet'.

The more specific the lead magnet the more successful it is going to be. For instance, the School of Marketing has two different types of lead magnets. The first is the offer of free white papers or how-to guides which can be downloaded after the user provides basic information such as their name and email address. The second type of lead magnet relates to its content show, where if a user wants to sign up to watch the show live they must provide their details and agree to be kept informed about upcoming shows. Here is an example.

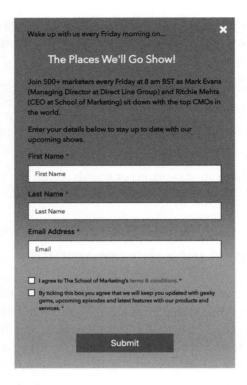

These two methods allow people to begin to form a deeper connection with the brand and see them as experts in their field. Interestingly, through this process these individuals are also more likely to like, comment and share what the brand puts out on social media as they feel more a part of it. The key is to be very clear about the value exchange and honest and up-front with people of what exactly they will get when they sign up.

Once you have converted these individuals and they have provided you with more information, you begin to move into the second wheel where you must continually engage them. Let's move on to see how you can do this.

Step 3: Engage the community

At this stage, you need to cultivate your community and continually provide value to them using a variety of methods and channels. Importantly, given they have entrusted you with their details, they expect that you understand them, so the more personalised you can make the interactions the better.

Importantly, these interactions should be aimed at adding value to the customer rather than trying to sell to them. You are trying to cultivate the relationship and without doubt by this point these people would have understood your wider commercial offering and will likely consider your brand when they have a need.

When developing your approach here, you need to consider three different dimensions of engagement. The first is the channels your community can reach you on such as your website or app. Being available to your community will give them confidence that they can open a dialogue with your brand at any point. The second is always on communications – these are a set of communications that are standardised and go out at set intervals to all customers. They can be personalised for different groups that we will talk about later on. The third is trigger-based engagements that are personalised based on the information you hold about individual members in your community, such as birthdays or other special occasions. This makes them feel that you really value them and solidifies the relationship further.

Fill in the template below with the channels and type of interactions you will have in these three areas for your brand–I have given you some examples to think about on the right-hand side. Once you have done this use the above content calendar template to schedule in your content.

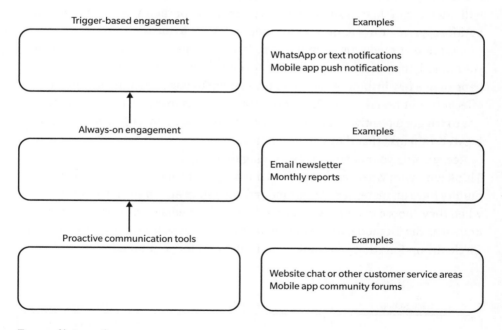

Types of interactions

Another very important aspect is for the community to get to know each other, and this inadvertently forms a deeper bond with your brand for facilitating the networks that others are creating. A good example of this is The Marketing Meet-up (https://themarketingmeetup.com/) that aims to bring people together both physically and virtually, thereby creating strong communities. Consider how you can foster ways to bring your community together using mechanisms such as roundtable discussions, mentoring sessions, networking events, conferences or even just facilitating one-to-one meetings.

Step 4: Community drives advocacy

As a natural by-product of engaging your community, they will begin to become advocates as they will feel part of your brand and want to be associated with it. Interestingly and importantly, as discussed in the previous chapter, your followers will be proud to promote your brand not necessarily completely altruistically but rather for the perceived association. It is very important that you nurture and encourage their advocacy so they feel even more valued when they promote you.

In fact, creating the moments where they can get involved in promoting your brand is key. For instance, the School of Marketing (https://schoolofmarketing.co/) will often tag in their most loyal followers and ask for their view or create competitions, prize draws or quizzes for their followers to answer.

It is often wrongly considered that followers, turned advocates, will promote your brand unprompted regardless of how much they value you. It is true it may happen in a few instances but not really enough to have a significant and lasting effect on your brand value. Rather your brand needs to create these opportunities to trigger a positive reaction, such as by offering them a reward for completing a certain task that they can post about.

Recognising your advocates and giving them higher social importance is key. Think win–win: what can your brand do to make the individual in the community have an increased status amongst the group and in turn help the brand when they choose to amplify it across their social media feed? Here is a model known as the 3R model to consider ways to drive advocacy from your followers. Circle the options that you think would work best for your brand.

Recognition	Reward	Referral
Talk about them on social media Give them a higher status Make them feel extra special	Offer prizes or incentives Access to money-can't-buy opportunities Discounts on premium aspects of your proposition	Access to other high-profile individuals Refer them to people/brands for other discounts Connect them to other members

part 3

—

How to scale your marketing

chapter 7

———

Creativity, storytelling and choosing the right media

In this chapter, we are first going to explore how you can embed creativity into your marketing activities and then take a closer look at how you can introduce one of the powerful creative tools, storytelling, to create a much greater impact.

I want you to do me a favour. I want you to close your eyes and think about an advert that really resonated with you. I'm sure with little thought you would probably be able to come up with 'the one'. Now, if I ask you to come up with your top three adverts you would probably have to think a little harder but I'm sure you would eventually do it. Now, if I asked you for your favourite top ten, you may really struggle and eventually give up. What this says is that throughout our lifetimes, despite the fact that we come into contact with thousands every day, most go completely unnoticed and even fewer are remembered.

The truth is that most adverts pass you by because they do not speak to you – they do not make you feel any emotion or tell you a story that you will remember. For those top three adverts that you can remember they all had one thing in common – they all were creative. They all told you something that meant something to you, that taught you something, that made you feel a certain way and because of this they stayed in your mind, potentially for years. This is the long tail effect of creative advertising where they get absorbed into the subconscious and remembered for a long time compared to average adverts that are easily forgotten.

It's this very role of creativity that is at the heart of marketing, and according to a Neilson study is the leading driver of marketing effectiveness, accounting for just under 50% of the reason why an advert becomes effective.[1] It should therefore come as no surprise that analysis conducted by Peter Field and Les Binet have shown that campaigns that win the most creative awards also most impact business outcomes.[2] A range of other studies also show strong links between creativity and financial performance[3] and increases in market share.[4] A good example is the Weetabix/Heinz PR breakfast Twitter campaign that went viral leading to an instant 15% rise in sales for Weetabix.

One can conceive that the case for creativity in marketing is rather simple and it goes something like this:

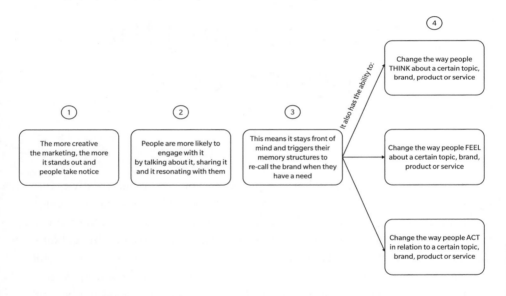

However, despite the resounding evidence for the case of creativity, it appears that it is currently in crisis mode. Over time we have seen the pendulum swing in favour of more short-term 'direct sales' campaigns as executives look for a quick return on investment.[5] This has led to a considerable decline in marketing effectiveness and brand differentiation that according to Binet and Field's 'The Long and Short of It' impacts the long-term revenue potential of a brand (we will learn more about this in Chapter 16).[6] Therefore, the current state of the market creates a huge opportunity for you to win based on creativity which can have a transformative effect on your marketing.

The truth is, for you to be a remarkable marketer and do remarkable marketing, you need to put creativity at the very centre of your approach. However, importantly this is not limited to just communications. In fact, the most creative executions are achieved by using all the marketing levers or mix (product, price, place and promotion) as well as executed through a creatively designed and targeted media plan in order to deliver value to the customer.

A great example of this is Burger King's 'Whopper detour campaign'. It got customers to go within 600 metres of its arch rival McDonalds in order to get a whopper for one cent via its app. It was a risky move that could have driven customers right into the arms of its key competitor. However, it certainly paid off as the campaign went viral, increasing its share of voice and delivered it an additional 1.5 million app downloads.[7]

Inputs to achieve a creative marketing campaign

Creativity can be a rather nebulous concept as it means so many different things to different people. It is synonymous with terms such as being novel, non-obvious, stand out, innovation and so on. However, perhaps of more use to you is to understand the various inputs that come together to make up a creative solution in marketing that cuts across the entire marketing mix:

There are five key interlinked inputs that make up creativity in marketing that you need to include in your activities:

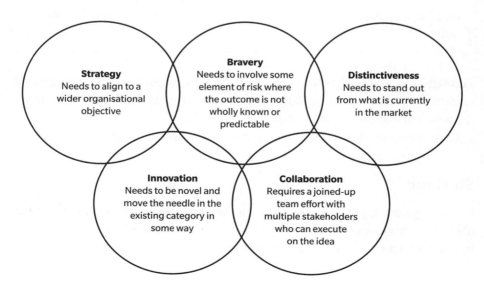

Strategy
Needs to align to a wider organisational objective

Bravery
Needs to involve some element of risk where the outcome is not wholly known or predictable

Distinctiveness
Needs to stand out from what is currently in the market

Innovation
Needs to be novel and move the needle in the existing category in some way

Collaboration
Requires a joined-up team effort with multiple stakeholders who can execute on the idea

Let me highlight each area through a case study.

Greggs, the UK's largest high street bakery, developed an exceptionally creative marketing campaign on the back of identifying a significant trend in the number of people turning vegan (literally quadrupling[8] between 2016 and 2019). It wanted to attract these new customers to its stores as well as incrementally increase sales to existing customers.

At the time, it was famous for a range of product lines but perhaps no more so than its classic, best-selling sausage roll. It decided to innovate on this and created a vegan alternative called the 'new sausage roll' (a rather brave name for a vegan product). By adapting its flagship sausage roll, it knew it would get existing customers to try it alongside the original option, while it would create a great deal of stand-out and intrigue for new customers to 'see what all the fuss is about' as well.

To draw a closer bridge between these offerings it even created an equivalent price-point to match. It launched with a distinctive marketing campaign, where it mimicked iPhone packaging and sent samples to key influencers, including Piers Morgan, that created a buzz on social media. Interestingly, at the same time it was not only distributed through the company's more than 2,000 convenient stores locations, but it also formed a collaboration to home-deliver its products with the app Deliveroo, which expanded its market further.

This creative campaign enabled it to creatively build on its existing brand, distribution, product line and pricing approach to add value to customers and beat the competition. The icing on the cake was it saw an 11% jump in revenue and its market value increased by around £700 million.[9]

Through this example, you can see how Greggs leveraged the entire spectrum of marketing levers it had at its disposal to create real value for its customers and the business in a very creative way.

Here are some take-aways to incorporate into your own activities.

Strategy

Like Greggs, it's important to link your marketing campaign to a wider strategic objective. This is critical as no matter how creative your marketing activity is, if it does not drive a strategic objective for your business it will all be for nothing. To achieve this, you need to develop a clear strategic creative brief that articulates your objectives on which your creative communications can be aligned with. Here is a template you can use.

Strategic creative marketing brief

1. Objective	4. Simple (and single) message
The objective must clearly state the over-arching business goals that the organisation would like from the campaign. Given the nature of creative campaigns it's important that a brief where a creative solution is required bears the hallmarks of a long-term ambition. Given the nature of creative campaigns, it's important that a brief reflects a long-term ambition.	The best briefs don't ask for too much, but rather can narrow it down to a single 'consumer message' that a communication should convey.
2. Target audience and trends	5. Creative components/expression
A clear description of the audience and any relevant trends that you see in the market. We have already talked about how to develop a customer persona earlier in Chapter 1, so it may be useful to do a similar exercise here.	This is where you can include any initial thoughts on a creative direction as well as the brand tone and guidelines, expression and other elements that are important.
3. Strategy	6. Consumer response: Think, feel and do
Creativity needs direction and therefore a clear strategy must be articulated. This must be defined as what the organisation is looking to achieve in the short and long term. It will enable the creative output to have some direction.	Here is where you articulate what you would want the end-customer to do differently on the back of the campaign, using the think, feel and do framework.

Bravery

Inherently, marketing is about taking educated risks. You need to be able to anticipate, through insight and foresight, where the market is likely to be and then be able to take a leap, recognising the unknowns. It requires bravery to stand out from the crowd – it requires you to stand up for something that is very different, unconventional and even controversial, just like Greggs did. In fact, the Effie awards show that the single biggest differentiator of effective marketing is this characteristic.[10] So the clear message is go forth and be brave.

Distinctiveness

You need to provide a unique and distinct offer that is embedded within and leverages existing brand styles, tones, designs and voice. This is the strategy adopted by Greggs using its brand and similar cues to its sausage roll range. This creates an instant familiarity coupled with curiosity in the minds of your customers. It also allows the customer to instantly mentally pigeon-hole where your product and brand fits in their lives, essential to increase overall brand recall and purchase over the long term. Evidence suggests that in achieving this, strong brands actually command on average a 13% higher price and achieve 31% higher operating profit over weak brands,[11] proving the value of leveraging this brand strength in marketing activities.

Innovation

There is no doubt that you need some level of innovation that actually extends the value of the offering. Typically, you may look to product innovation, but in reality the best campaigns are those that innovate across the marketing mix.

In Gregg's case, it recognised the declining nature of the high street and innovated across the distribution network through Deliveroo. Ironically, by doing so it was able to also buck the high-street trend and opened more physical stores.[12] It's a powerful lesson of the unpredictable nature of outcomes when trying new things, which reiterates the need for bravery during the process.

Write down how you can incorporate each of these elements into your marketing activities.

Now we have uncovered some of the key elements you need to incorporate into your marketing activities, let's consider the environment that enables this type of creativity to flourish so that you can replicate it in your organisation. It fundamentally comes down to three key factors that you must try and bring together in a cohesive way.

People and Partners

> Bringing the right people, with different skillsets, backgrounds and ideas together from across a larger ecosystem of partners is really key to fostering creativity

Culture

> They need to have the right organisational culture that allows people and teams to explore their creativity at the risk of failure and recognise when it goes right and don't criticise when it doesn't

Context

> Have a context that requires the team to be creative and challenge the status quo in order to get ahead

People and partners

Jim Collins in his book *Good to great* talks about the role of a (marketing) leader being like a bus driver. The bus is your company or department and you have a responsibility to steer it. He says, "So make sure you have the right people on the bus, the wrong people off the bus and right people in the right seats."[13]

It works in the same way in order to foster creativity. You need a wide variety of people with different skillsets, backgrounds and opinions, all working together to spark a new idea. Sir Clive Woodward said ideas can come from anywhere, "from the leader, from the grad, from the person in an entirely different department, from the person fresh out of school, from the person fed up with having their shirt pulled".[14] It's up to you to help your teams see the diverse perspective, empower them to be free to think of an alternative future and importantly be given the freedom to act on it.

Importantly, you must also get an outside perspective and mesh them with your own internal view in order for creativity to go to the next level. Fernando Machado says, "The vast majority of the ideas we develop are not ours. We surely collaborate, but our best ideas all came from having a solid relationship with our creative partners. You need creative partners who are also creatively ambitious."[15]

Write down the key people that you will bring together (internal and external) when coming up with new ideas.

Culture

Culture is very important when it comes to creativity as it forms the bedrock that enables your team to be brave, ambitious and audacious. If your organisation's culture is not accepting of risk-taking and puts the fear of failure into your staff, it is very unlikely anything very creative will emerge. In addition, if left to 'rule by committee', again it's likely the law of averages will play out and what you will find is a mediocre outcome.

On a more functional level, the organisations that exhibit the most creative solutions have cultures that encourage small teams, autonomous decision-making, encourage calculated risks, recognise and reward when it goes right and do not mind when it doesn't.

A good example of this is Spotify which organises itself into small autonomous units called 'squads'. They consist of teams of no more than eight people and they are accountable for a discrete aspect of the product, end to end. A number of squads collect to form a 'tribe' that are linked together by 'chapters'. They embrace news ideas and execution and go through an analysis of failures and successes every few weeks. They have an experimental-friendly culture with an emphasis on a test and learn approach. Spotify believes in "loosely coupled, tightly aligned squads . . . alignment enables autonomy – the greater the alignment, the more autonomy you can grant."[16]

What are the characteristics of the culture that you currently have in the organisation, that encourage or hinder creativity? How can you adapt to make the culture more conducive?

Cultural aspects that encourage creativity	Cultural aspects that hinder creativity

Context

The final aspect to consider is context – the environment that is created in order to let creativity shine. Stephen Johnson in his book *Where good ideas come from*[17] suggests that big workshops or creative sessions do not serve us well when it comes to idea generation. Rather you are likely to be far more creative and innovative over days, weeks or months as you are stimulated by a variety of people, contexts and networks. What is interesting is that he suggests the internet allows you to achieve greater connectivity which in reality could actually spar a whole new way of doing idea generation. So do use it to your advantage.

A key point around context is that you also need to get out of your own in order to be creative. For instance, Alex Stephany, one of the UK's leading social entrepreneurs, created Beam on the back of a conversation with a homeless person at his local railway station. He reflects and says, "Every day I would stop and have a chat and soon I learnt that he wanted to retrain but didn't feel like anyone wanted to help him". Using technology Beam was able to crowdfund the money required for this person to go to college. Alex simply stepped out of his own realm of reality for a few minutes each day, which gave him the insight to start a leading social enterprise.

Here are some tips and techniques you can use to create the right context to spark the creativity in your team.

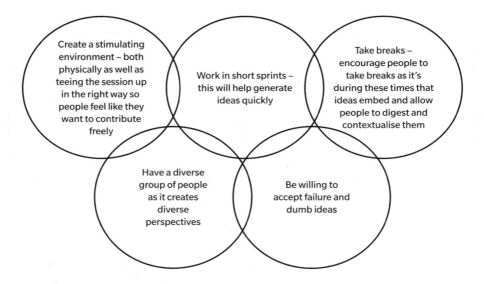

Create a stimulating environment – both physically as well as teeing the session up in the right way so people feel like they want to contribute freely

Work in short sprints – this will help generate ideas quickly

Take breaks – encourage people to take breaks as it's during these times that ideas embed and allow people to digest and contextualise them

Have a diverse group of people as it creates diverse perspectives

Be willing to accept failure and dumb ideas

Write down how you can adapt your own context in order to make it more conducive to generate new creative ideas.

Let's now move on to discover how you can use the art of creative storytelling to develop impactful marketing.

Creative storytelling

Although this technique dates back hundreds if not thousands of years, the role of storytelling in marketing has had a significant resurgence. Studies have shown that brands can increase the value of their product or service by as much as 20 times by integrating this technique into their marketing.[18] For instance, the Significant Object Study, where Rob Walker and Joshua Glenn bought 200 items off eBay for $250 and asked writers to create a story around each of them.

They then sold them back on eBay with the story attached for over $8,000. A good example is an egg whisk that they bought for $0.25 and sold it for $30. Goes to show that Seth Godin was right when he said, "Marketing is no longer about the stuff you make but the stories you tell."[19]

The question is how can you use this technique in your marketing activities?

The first thing to consider is some of the enablers you can use to bring your stories to life. Here are five to consider:

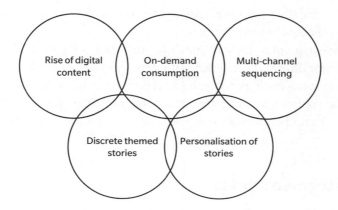

Rise of digital content

No longer are you constrained by the 30-second TV advert. You can now have a much richer narrative consisting of a storyline, characters, plot and climax. It's certainly not uncommon for adverts to last three minutes and resemble a mini-series rather than an advert. So consider how you can use digital content in this way.

A good example of this is Hewlett-Packard. Instead of doing a typical TV commercial, it hired Hollywood actor Christian Slater to star in a mini-web series called 'The Wolf'. The show is about the vulnerabilities of data hacking in a way that grips the audience with tension, drama and emotion – many of the ingredients used in blockbuster films.

On-demand consumption

When creating a story, you can have a number of episodes or instalments up online (say for example on your YouTube channel) at any given time. This allows people to immediately click on the next instalment of the content. It also creates longevity so you can benefit from the content you created for a long period of time.

Multi-channel sequencing

Another technique you can use is multi-channel sequencing, where different channels have different elements of the story and when combined creates the whole picture. Unlike, traditionally where channels were simply displaying the same thing, just in a different format, channels today have the ability to link different parts of the story together. This creates intrigue and makes your audience proactively seek out the next channel.

A good case in point is the way that Comparethemarket.com has been able to maintain its storyline of the meerkat family for well over a decade. The success of the campaign has been partially due to the way it unfolds the story across different media. For instance, it first launched the campaign on TV and then used digital channels and even created physical toys to keep people engaged in the experience.

Discrete themed stories

You also have the ability (due to longer ad lengths) to create themed discrete stories. Rather than having a continued story across a time period, you can opt to have a themed story contained within one communication, which becomes highly shareable.

A good example of this comes from Chipotle which has created a range of these discrete themed stories, the most successful being one called 'Back to the start'. This won it both industry awards and millions of views, shares and impressions.

Personalisation of stories

Finally, the more personalised you can make the story to the person watching it the better. There are three types of personalisation that you should consider. The first is user-defined personalisation where your customer has the ability to tailor the story, characters and ending etc. For instance, O2 created a campaign during the Rugby World Cup called 'Wear the Rose' that allowed people to choose their own avatar and virtually play the games. The second is behavioural personalisation where the creative approach adapts based on certain interactions by the customer. LinkedIn does this extremely well and tailors their messages based on prior interactions on their platform. Finally, there is tactical personalisation, otherwise known as 'in the moment' personalisation, which occurs as a one show and is usually attached to a wider 'surprise and delight' programme.

Consider how you would use these elements when creating your creative story.

Creating your own story for your marketing campaign

There are a number of steps you can take when developing your own story for a marketing campaign. Let's go through each.

Step 1: Cause/mission

Every great marketing story needs to have an underlying cause or mission, something that it is looking to achieve. You can take great inspiration from movies, TV shows and documentaries in relation to understanding the cause or the mission you need to attach to our stories. However, the key difference is that with a marketing story you need to marry up something that is extremely close to people's hearts with your brand narrative.

A good example of this is from the documentary 'Before the flood' starring Leonardo Di Caprio. It tells of the growing issue related to climate change. It's an eye-opening tale of the impact and potential consequences of this global challenge. The power of this story is in its relevance to what is currently happening around the world and what people care about.

Write down what could be your cause or mission for your story.

Step 2: Characters

Interestingly, leading marketing effectiveness consultancy, Ebiquity, demonstrates that a key element in creative marketing is what is known as 'fluent devices'.[20] According to System 1 group, this is defined as "a creative conceit (character) that is used as the primary vehicle for the drama of a long-running campaign".[21] Using characters in your marketing activities, according to Ebiquity, leads to higher market share, profit and increases the longevity of your marketing activities. It can therefore be said that the single most important aspect of your story is to develop it around a character that your audience can relate to and want to go on their journey.

There are a number of techniques to consider when developing characters:

- The hero character is almost someone who the audience can relate to in an almost 'it could be me' situation, although this is not always the case.

- The other characters should be those that they can almost visualise in that context or in their own lives and in many instances they can be exaggerated.

Let's take a look at some of the characters from Harry Potter to bring this to life.

Harry Potter characters

Harry Potter

Despite the attention lavished on him by the entire wizarding world, he remains more conscious of his failings than his successes, and doesn't let it all go to his head. He epitomises the slightly under-confident youngster, which is central to his likeability as he resembles so many young people out there.

Hermione Granger

Every hero needs his friends and Hermione (and Ron) are the perfect complement to Harry's character. She is at times an insufferable know-it-all, but she finishes them as an entirely sufferable, even loveable, know-it-all, someone who doesn't hide her smarts but also gives the people around her credit for intelligence as well. She is loyal and helps Harry solve many problems that he is exposed to.

Ron Weasley

He provides the light-hearted comedy factor to the duo. His relationship with Harry is not simply one of best friends, but a complex mix of love and envy. After all, while Harry envies Ron his large, loving family, Ron has to contend with his middle-child syndrome, and must contrast his own threadbare lifestyle with Harry's wealth. There's even a time when they seem to be rivals for Hermione's affection (at least in Ron's mind), and it's no wonder that there's tension there.

Albus Dumbledore

As wise as he is bearded, as eccentric as he is powerful and as fond of sherbet lemons as any man who ever lived, Dumbledore is a father figure and mentor to Harry – but one who isn't slow about sending him into mortal peril when the occasion calls for it. He has made a few errors of judgment in his time, making him more relatable.

Rubeus Hagrid

He's big, he's tough, and he has the soft heart of a 10 year-old girl. Hagrid is not, it's fair to say, the wisest, but he is perhaps the warmest. He makes no effort to hide how much he cares for his friends (and pets) and with that big sentimental streak always just under the surface.

Severus Snape

Snape is a puzzle-box of a character, layering secrets and riddles over a heart that remains hidden until the very end.

Write a description of all the characters you have in your story, using as many of the boxes as you like.

Your characters

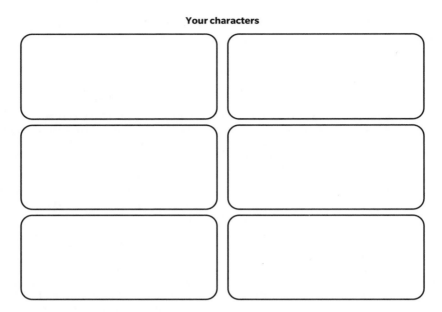

Step 3: Place and setting

The place and setting are very important components in the story and must be chosen very carefully. It helps the audience to visualise the story and embeds in it a particular place and period. Clearly, the location needs to align to the overall theme and narrative. It must also appeal to the senses of the audience and be as authentic as possible.

Consider the place and setting you would use for your story.

Step 4: Narrative or storyline

The next element you need to consider is the narrative or storyline. This is the flow of your story from the beginning to the end. What is very interesting about stories is that they tempt to exhibit a natural (almost universal-like) flow to them that you can use to your advantage. There is a five-step process that all stories typically go through that we can look at.[22]

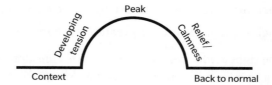

In this model 'context' sets the stage by introducing character and setting. Events within the story create tension and conflict that lead to the story's 'peak' by 'developing tension'. Once the peak has occurred, the story fully develops with a resolution ('relief/calmness') that leads to 'back to normal' (the characters return to normalcy releasing the audience's tension).

At each stage, the story has the ability to connect the other elements as we described above in order to achieve a high level of depth and bring the characters to life.

Based on the model have a go at writing a narrative for each of the five sections.

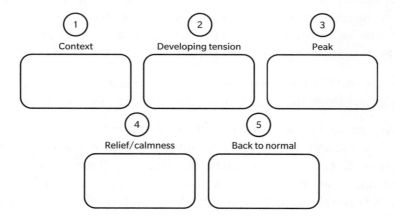

Media Planning

Designing the most creative communication would not have any effect or impact without being able to get it in front of your target customer. This is where media planning becomes important and is the process of determining the right channels (at the right time) to deliver your message.

When developing your media plan use a data-led approach to consider the following:

- Which channels are most frequently use by your target customer?
- Which channels compliment your creative idea?

- Which channels are being under-utilised by your competitors?
- Which channels will deliver you the greatest reach for the lowest cost?

To determine the right media mix for your creative, consider some of the different user dynamics across different channels, for example:

Viewability of video advertising: This is when an advert is actually viewed by audiences in a certain media channel, rather than to an empty room.

The evidence suggests that in over 25% of cases, people are not watching a TV ad although it is on their screens, while YouTube advertising has extremely high viewability. Meanwhile, many social ads are not viewable as they are scrolled past too quickly (less than 2 seconds in most cases).[23]

Dwell time: The amount of time an audience spends watching an advert and the highest likelihood of it being remembered.

TV still gets the highest dwell times, while digital media gets much less. Interestingly, despite many predictions that TV is dead, it still is the most cost-effective way to buy attention (as long as you have a big budget!). On the other hand, social media platforms such as Facebook give you low levels of dwell time. So the key message is when advertising on social media you really have to make your communication extra creative to grab people's attention![24]

Multichannel: Evidence suggests that when you combine channels it creates a much greater reach and effectiveness than when using a single channel.

How do you plan to hit your reach and penetration target?

There is a systematic way of achieving this that involves choosing your primary channel first and maximising reach and frequency of your target audience in that channel. Thereafter, once you have exhausted that channel, move on to the next and so on and so forth. Let's bring this to life through a rather iconic example:

Is advertising at the Super Bowl worth it?

The US Super Bowl is perhaps one of the most highly contested media spaces in the world, with a 30-second slot during the game costing $5.5 million in 2021. There is considerable amount of noise and controversy on whether this investment is indeed worth the money for advertisers, so let's take a look at the evidence:

Cost per impression and scale of reach

The first thing to consider are two concepts: cost per impression and scale of reach. Cost per impression is effectively how many eyeballs can you reach in the most cost-effective way. Typically, advertisers need to use a broad range of media in order to get to the same level of the 100 million impressions that can be achieved in one go at the Super Bowl. The second element is the type of reach you can achieve based on the types of customers that you want to attract. There is no doubt that the Super Bowl attracts a wide variety of watchers, many of whom will only occasionally watch TV and so advertising at this time can give advertisers the ability to reach new audiences effectively.

Viewability

Most people are inclined to use ad breaks as an opportunity to turn away from the TV; however, the Super Bowl is one time of the year where people actually stay tuned to watch the ads.

This time slot has become so renowned for its adverts that it has become a semi-competition during half-time to see which advertiser won during the Super Bowl. Therefore, the amount of dwell time a viewer spends watching the ads is far more than a normal period.

The knock-on effect of the TV advert; earned media

One of the big draws of the Super Bowl is the buzz it creates, people don't just watch it – they share, talk, engage and have an experience. It's like the ultimate occasion to spend with family and friends, both offline and online.

One of the major benefits for advertisers is how they can gain organic exposure across social media and therefore opening themselves up to new channels and ways to extend your reach and lifetime on air.

Building fame

According to the IPA studies, fame is one of the most important aspects when developing and building a brand. Merely being associated with being a 'Super Bowl Brand' gives you a huge amount of credibility and longevity in the minds of your target market. It's a classic way to generate brand equity and get into a select consideration set of your audience.

Based on the above, it's clear the Super Bowl gives advertisers the one-shot opportunity to reach a huge audience and not have to move to other channels to extend reach like they would normally. Therefore, it does become a very cost-effective and impactful way to achieve cost per impressions, scale of reach and high dwell time, making it a good option for advertisers who can afford it!

chapter 8

—

Use search marketing to scale your presence

We will now focus on search marketing, particularly how to develop a search engine optimisation approach for your website to rank the search terms that are desirable to your brand.

Four of the most powerful tools in the digital marketing armoury are search marketing, online paid and programmatic advertising, affiliate marketing and e-commerce. It can be said that these techniques have been at the heart of the democratisation of the entire marketing industry, enabling brands of all shapes and sizes to compete effectively with one another. Previously, brands required a very significant advertising budget to generate awareness, reach and distribution to get in front of their potential customers through mass marketing tools such as TV, press or outdoor media (although even now discount these channels at your peril!) and then fight for limited retail space. However, today even a start-up brand with a limited marketing budget has the ability to create highly targeted advertising through these techniques to reach its target audience and then instantly convert them into a sale. It's a real game-changer.

Perhaps, one of the most exciting aspects of these channels is their ability to either micro-target down to a local postcode or to springboard brands to go global literally overnight, using the power of their targeting and payment features. Through a few clicks of a button, companies can open up new market segments, truly proving that in today's interconnected world, borders matter less than bandwidth.

A major development in these areas is that what initially appeared as quite separate and distinct disciplines is certainly no longer the case. We are seeing a blurring of the lines between search, paid and programmatic, affiliate marketing and e-commerce techniques towards a more omni-channel approach. A good example of this is Google Smart Shopping that uses an auction system to serve rich media adverts on its platform and remarketing techniques to bring the customer back to Google to make a purchase. This is clearly not an isolated situation as the same could be said for Instagram Shopping or Amazon Ads as platforms look to create an integrated solution for their customers. This is for good reason as it's well evidenced that by using a range of channels together is more effective than using a single channel in isolation. In fact, good media planning involves the careful integration between the channels mentioned with a range of other more traditional channels in order to further enhance marketing's impact. Therefore, we must get these channels to integrate seamlessly together and with a range of other traditional channels using media planning techniques.

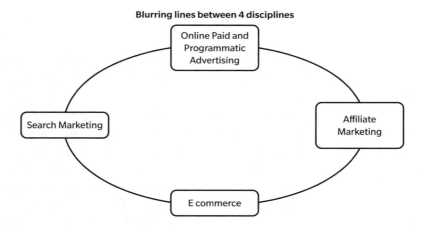

Blurring lines between 4 disciplines

Let's first get to grips with each of these areas. As you can see from the diagram, search marketing consists of search engine optimisation, online paid and programmatic advertising consists of paid search, paid social, paid display and affiliate marketing and e-commerce consists of marketplace or D2C.

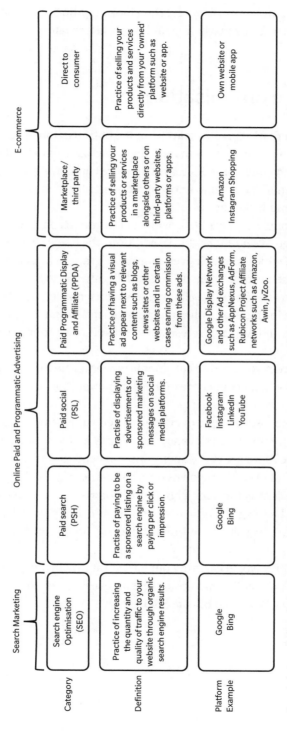

Category	Search Marketing	Online Paid and Programmatic Advertising			E-commerce	
	Search engine Optimisation (SEO)	Paid search (PSH)	Paid social (PSL)	Paid Programmatic Display and Affiliate (PPDA)	Marketplace/ third party	Direct to consumer
Definition	Practice of increasing the quantity and quality of traffic to your website through organic search engine results.	Practise of paying to be a sponsored listing on a search engine by paying per click or impression.	Practise of displaying advertisements or sponsored marketing messages on social media platforms.	Practice of having a visual ad appear next to relevant content such as blogs, news sites or other websites and in certain cases earning commission from these ads.	Practice of selling your products or services in a marketplace alongside others or on third-party websites, platforms or apps.	Practice of selling your products and services directly from your 'owned' platform such as website or app.
Platform Example	Google Bing	Google Bing	Facebook Instagram LinkedIn YouTube	Google Display Network and other Ad exchanges such as AppNexus, AdForm, Rubicon Project Affiliate networks such as Amazon, Awin, JvZoo.	Amazon Instagram Shopping	Own website or mobile app

Breakdown of search marketing, online paid and programmatic advertising channels and e-commerce

We will look at search marketing now and then look at online paid, programmatic advertising and affiliate marketing and e-commerce later.

Search engine optimisation

At the heart of search marketing lies search engine optimisation (SEO), which is the process of getting your website to rank highly across a variety of search engines for specific keywords (and increasingly voice commands). Here we are going to determine what you need to know and do in order to maximise the potential for your brand in this area.

It is interesting to note that over 80% of all click-throughs on Google happen from the first page of search results. In addition, voice search is becoming increasingly popular, which makes it even more important to rank in the top search results. This means that if you do not rank highly you are unlikely to generate significant traffic from this channel. It's worth noting that despite the dominance of Google in this area, other platforms such as Amazon (with the likes of Amazon Echo and Alexa) also use keyword and voice command search techniques.

The ultimate question you need to consider is how are you going to get to the top of these rankings when people type or voice command specific search terms or questions.

Google, for example, uses a range of criteria to determine a web page's ranking based on factors such as relevancy, popularity and authority. To optimise your website there are two dimensions you need to consider. The first is on-site or technical SEO which involves optimising the technical aspects of your website to make it easy for Googlebot (what Google uses to crawl your website) to pick up. The second is off-site or non-technical SEO which are things you can do around your website to uplift its authority and therefore make it more attractive.

Straight off the bat it's worth carrying out an SEO audit of your website using a tool such as SEMrush. It will enable you to get an overview of your presence on the internet, covering on-site and off-site SEO aspects.

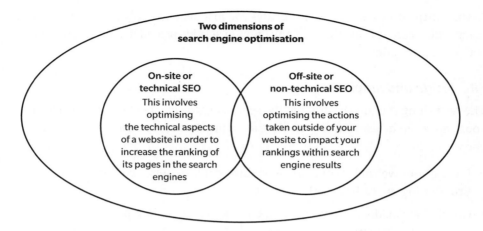

Two dimensions of
search engine optimisation

On-site or
technical SEO

This involves
optimising
the technical aspects
of a website in order to
increase the ranking of
its pages in the search
engines

Off-site or
non-technical SEO

This involves
optimising the actions
taken outside of your
website to impact your
rankings within search
engine results

On-site or technical SEO

With on-site SEO you are trying to make it as easy as possible for a search engine to understand what your website is about, how relevant it is for the person typing in a search term and the quality of the results you can provide. To do this you need to ensure that each technical aspect of your website conforms to certain standards that make it easy for search engines like Google to analyse.

There are seven key areas that you need to cover from a technical SEO perspective. There is a handy checklist at the bottom of this section for you to refer to as well. It is worth noting that different search engines are constantly updating their technical SEO requirements, so look out for their latest updates.

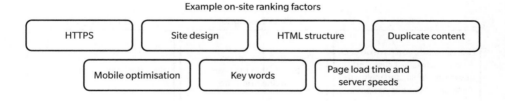

Example on-site ranking factors

HTTPS — Site design — HTML structure — Duplicate content

Mobile optimisation — Key words — Page load time and server speeds

HTTPS

You may well have noticed that many of the websites you visit have an https before the URL, of which the 's' stands for security. It suggests that the website has added levels of protection for the user including, encryption, data integrity and the need to authenticate the user. Given ongoing cyber security issues, this factor is increasing in importance and therefore something you must have.

Getting https status is easy to obtain and you just need to apply for an SSL certificate, which can be done through any domain service provider such as Go Daddy (https://uk.godaddy.com/).

Site design and map

The next thing is to make sure that the search engine can read or crawl through your entire site in a seamless way. Here are a number of very useful checks for you to conduct:

- Ensure your website is compatible on different browsers – you could use Browserling: www.browserling.com/.
- Check that you do not have any broken links as that will impact on a search engine's ability to find all your content. You can use Dead link checker for this: www.deadlinkchecker.com.

To make it easier for a search engine to go through all of your webpages, ensure that you have an up-to-date site map. Think of it as an easy-to-read table of contents for search engines so they know exactly what each of your pages contains and therefore find relevant information easier. This has a positive knock-on effect on your website's SEO ranking. There are many ways to create a site map and the XML-sitemaps tool does it for you: www.xml-sitemaps.com/.

HTML structure

Although we are getting a little technical here, it's important that your source code reflects your website's content and relevance. Here are some of the main elements to consider.

Title tag

This is the title you have on each page so make it clear and understandable, and make sure you only have one per page!

Meta description

This is the description under the title that the search engine brings up.

H1 Heading tag

This is the heading on each page.

Image Alt Tags

This refers specifically to images and is important from an accessibility point of view.

Canonical tag

A way of telling search engines that a specific URL represents the master copy of a page and avoids issues such as identical or 'duplicate' content appearing on multiple URLs.

To help bring this to life have a look at the picture below to see where each of these elements fit in.

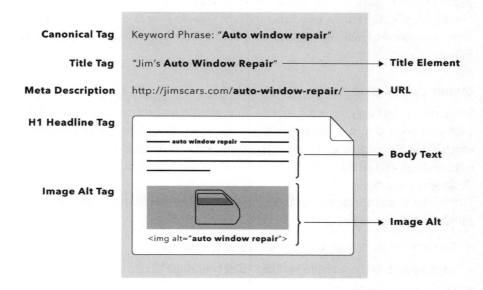

Page load time and server speeds

Another important element from a technical SEO perspective is how long your website takes to load. This is clearly important as search engines do not want users waiting around for ages to get access to the information. Worse still, if it takes too long it is reported that search engines could abandon the search altogether and exclude you from their results.

There is a very simple test that you should run to determine if your loading speed is up to scratch. Go to https://testmysite.withgoogle.com/ and type in your URL and all will be revealed.

Rich snippets

This is a very important concept from a conversion perspective. A snippet is a result Google shows to the user in the search results. Google shows the title in blue, the URL in green and a description of what the page is about. So you need to understand your website snippet using a snippet window: use https://yoast.com and then go to the snippet-preview section snippet-preview/.

Duplicate content

It is easy to have duplicate content that appears in multiple locations across the internet. This really confuses a search engine as it does not know which one to use in search results. There are two ways to deal with this issue. The first is to identify duplicate content using this tool the Google Search console. The second is to use canonical tags (mentioned above) to tell the search engine which URLs to use.

Mobile optimisation

With most of us carrying out searches, interactions and transactions on mobile each and every day, it is increasingly becoming an integral part of our digital experience. Recognising this, search engines such as Google, consider mobile optimisation as a ranking factor, importantly when returning results both on desktop and mobile.

In order to ensure that your website will comply to their standards, here are a number of things to check:

- **Content:** Is all my content compatible on a mobile view?
- **Page speed:** Is the website loading quickly enough?
- **Mobile responsive:** Is the website fully responsive?

To check your website's mobile design and responsiveness, you could use Responsive design checker: http://responsivedesignchecker.com/.

Keywords and BERTs

Previously, simply having the right keywords on your website was enough to get ranked highly on search engines. However, today the level of sophistication has certainly increased, using systems such as Google BERT, and now it's important to be both relevant and consider the search intent of the user.

To achieve this, put yourself in the user's shoes and think about how you can answer the questions that they may have. The more you can be specific to answer the question, the more favourable the search engine will be to you. To help, you can use a keyword planning tool, such as the one Google provides.

Finally, moving beyond user search intent you should also consider how you can engage the user once they have bought from you. So including FAQs, real-time support and ways for them to engage with you easily with any follow-up questions, could also enhance your SEO capability as well as build a greater level of trust with potential and existing customers.

Now you are aware of the key elements of on-site or technical SEO. It's time to put this into practice. Use this simple checklist to ensure you cover each aspect.

On-site SEO checklist	Tick box
Have you added an SSL certificate to your website?	
Have you created a site map?	
Is your website mobile-responsive?	
Does it perform well across all browser types?	
How fast is your website's loading speed?	
Are your title tags accurate and is there only one per page?	
Is your description under each title to the point and engaging?	
Are your headings concise and easy to understand?	
Do you have Alt tags for all your images?	
Have you included canonical tags where required?	
Do you have any duplicate content or URLs to remove?	
Have you considered a user's search intent when developing your content?	

Off-site or non-technical SEO

The second half of the SEO coin is off-site or non-technical SEO, which involves optimising all the other aspects around your website that have a material impact on your SEO rankings.

There are three key areas you need to consider and pay close attention to.

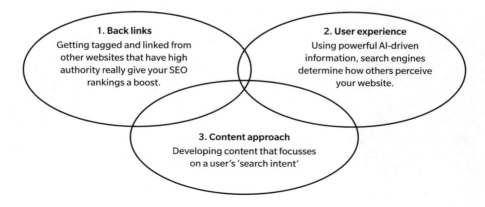

1. **Back links**
Getting tagged and linked from other websites that have high authority really give your SEO rankings a boost.

2. **User experience**
Using powerful AI-driven information, search engines determine how others perceive your website.

3. **Content approach**
Developing content that focusses on a user's 'search intent'

Backlink building

Considering the fact that the internet is also known as the 'web' to recognise its interconnectedness, one of the key ways that a search engine understands your content as being of good quality is by the type of other websites that are referring to it. The more credible the websites that link to yours, the most effective the backlink will be from an SEO perspective.

You can check your website's backlinks by using a backlink checker, such as the one provider by ahrefs: https://ahrefs.com and go to backlink checker. There are a number of key pieces of information to be aware of:

- **Domain ratings/link authority:** Shows the strength of the referring website.
- **Number of backlinks:** The total number of links that you have from other websites.
- **Referring pages:** These are all the pages that link to your website.

The key to a link-building campaign is to generate content that people love and then to really push that content as far and wide as possible. Once other credible sources pick up the content and link to it, it will generate much greater relevance with Google.

Here are a number of strategies to optimise your link-building efforts:

- Team up and collaborate with other credible publications.
- Do guest sections or posts on other websites that will link to yours.
- Develop a range of articles or white papers that then get referred to on other websites.
- Do things that get picked up by PR so you are covered by different media sources that link back to your website.
- Become a knowledge resource and known for leading insights that will attract others to your website and ensure you are referred to on their sites.

Write down which sources you would ideally like to get backlinks from.

User experience

Search engines such as Google have integrated artificial intelligence into their ranking systems, using technology known as Rank Brain. It looks at a range of information such as web stats to determine if people are able to easily navigate through the website. Here are three important web metrics to keep an eye on in this regard:

- **Click-through rate:** This is the percentage of people who click to visit your site from a search engine results page.
- **Bounce rate:** This is the percentage of people who leave almost immediately after landing on your website.
- **Dwell time:** The time people stay on your website.

You are able to determine all these metrics using Google Analytics: https://analytics.google.com.

Here are some suggestions to improve your website's overall user experience that will in turn impact your SEO ranking. Circle the ones that you believe are issues with your current website. We will take a closer look at these elements in Chapter 15.

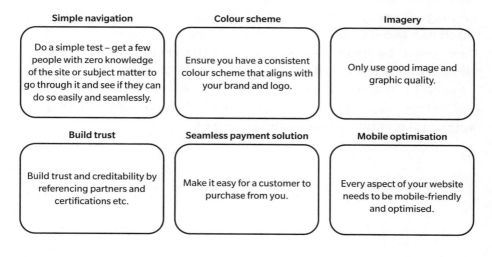

Simple navigation

Do a simple test – get a few people with zero knowledge of the site or subject matter to go through it and see if they can do so easily and seamlessly.

Colour scheme

Ensure you have a consistent colour scheme that aligns with your brand and logo.

Imagery

Only use good image and graphic quality.

Build trust

Build trust and creditability by referencing partners and certifications etc.

Seamless payment solution

Make it easy for a customer to purchase from you.

Mobile optimisation

Every aspect of your website needs to be mobile-friendly and optimised.

Content approach

We have covered the need to develop relevant content that focuses on a user's 'search intent' over just pure keyword matches. This is becoming more important as Google is placing more emphasis on intent and semantics when determining a match over anything else.

So how can you optimise your content for this? Here are a number of tips to consider. Feel free to write notes on the diagram.

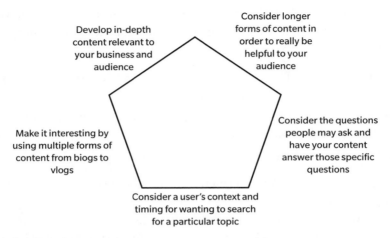

Develop in-depth content relevant to your business and audience

Consider longer forms of content in order to really be helpful to your audience

Make it interesting by using multiple forms of content from biogs to vlogs

Consider the questions people may ask and have your content answer those specific questions

Consider a user's context and timing for wanting to search for a particular topic

Improve your content

There are two key trends to bear in mind in this area. The first is that marketers are using influencers to help with content development that can be leveraged on and off your website. We will discuss this in further depth later in Chapter 12. The second is that search engines are placing a greater emphasis on video content, so it's worth investing in this format alongside rich text.

By now you should have got a good handle on the key aspects of developing your SEO approach. Let's now move on to uncover how to complement your organic SEO strategy with paid search techniques.

chapter 9

Online paid, programmatic advertising and affiliate marketing

Moving on from the previous chapter where you uncovered how to optimise your SEO approach, we will now look at the opportunity that online paid, programmatic advertising and affiliate marketing presents to your brand. Using these channels you are able to generate highly targeted and personalised ad campaigns that can have a direct impact on sales revenue.

As we have uncovered previously, there are three main types of online paid and programmatic advertising channels.

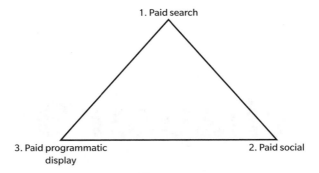

Paid search

Paid search allows you to advertise your offering on a search engine as a sponsored or paid-for advert and thereby gets you to the top or side of the search engine page. There are three key aspects to consider.

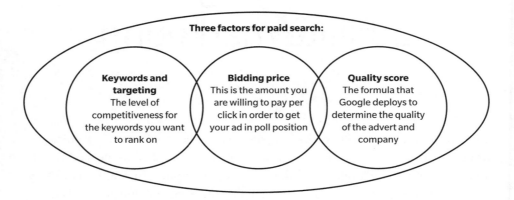

Keywords and targeting

The main driver of the effectiveness of your paid search campaign is the type of keywords that you want to rank for. For instance, some generic keywords are very popular which will mean that in order to have a chance of being listed for that keyword you will have to bid high and have a good quality score.

There are two broad strategies that you can adopt when deciding on the keywords that you would like to use, depending on the objective. Let me illustrate this through the vegan food example: say you are a vegan brand launching a new vegan banana bread. Use a keyword planner tool such as Google Keyword Planner, which is very useful.

Short-tail searches

On the one hand, if you want to generate brand awareness you may choose to opt for short-tail searches, which are more general and consist of one or two words. The benefit of this is that you are likely to be listed in more search results. However, you will have to bid higher in order to achieve this and the conversion rate will be low. In the table below, we can see that there is high competition for the term 'vegan snacks' and therefore will cost up to 96p per click. Using this tool, you can also see how other related terms perform and at what cost.

Keyword (by relevance) ↓	Avg. monthly searches	Competition	Ad impression share	Top of page bid (low range)	Top of page bid (high range)
vegan snacks	8,100	High	–	£0.31	£0.96
Keyword ideas					
vegan protein bars	2,900	High	–	£0.61	£1.36
vegan chips	880	Medium	–	£0.26	£0.82
vegan jerky	1,000	High	–	£0.22	£0.61
healthy vegan snacks	1,300	High	–	£0.46	£0.98
vegan crackers	590	High	–	£0.15	£0.77
vegan granola bars	320	Medium	–	£0.53	£1.40
best vegan snacks	390	High	–	£0.38	£0.95

Long-tail searches

On the other hand, you may want to generate a higher conversion rate at a lower cost but not reach as many people. You can opt for a long-tail search approach.

This is where you use a phrase that people search for in order for your advert to come up. For example, you can see if we use the phrase 'vegan banana bread healthy', the search volumes are much lower and in fact the cost per click will be negligible.

Keyword (by relevance) ↓	Avg. monthly searches	Competition	Ad impression share	Top of page bid (low range)	Top of page bid (high range)
vegan banana bread healthy	590	Low	–	–	–
Keyword ideas					
sugar free vegan banana bread	260	Low	–	–	–
vegan whole wheat banana bread	10	Low	–	–	–
healthy vegan banana bread recipe	20	Low	–	–	–
low calorie vegan banana bread	30	Low	–	–	–
vegan no sugar banana bread	210	Low	–	–	–
low fat vegan banana bread	20	Low	–	–	–
vegan banana bread recipe healthy	10	Low	–	–	–

Write down the type of keywords that you think are relevant considering your objective and short- vs long-tail approaches:

Targeting

In addition to deciding the parameters around keywords, you need to also determine who you are targeting. There are a range of factors that you can see from the diagram to consider from different geographies, languages and interests. You can use different groupings to adopt a test and learn approach with different audiences as well to find out which are most effective.

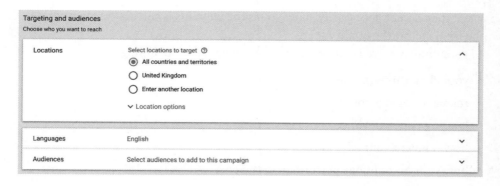

Write down your audience targeting preferences here.

Bidding price and quality score

The next factor is the bidding price – how much you are willing to bid for the cost per click. As you can see in the illustration below, Google will give you an indication of the number of click-throughs based on your daily spend.

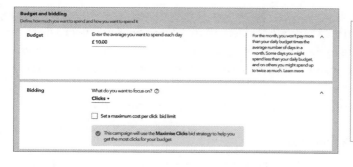

What they do not necessarily show you is the way this is calculated incorporates the final factor: the quality score.

Your quality score is made up of several elements,[1] including:

- your click-through rate (CTR)
- relevance of keywords
- landing page relevance
- how relevant your ad text is
- how your account has performed in the past.

Based on these factors the highest quality score is 10, while the starting quality score of a new campaign is 6. The most important variable of all is your click-through rate, as it indicates to Google that people are actually finding your advert useful. After all, success does breed success.

Let's take an example of how the bidding price and quality score come together. At the top of the table you can see the formula used to calculate which advertiser ranks higher than the next when competing for the same keywords.

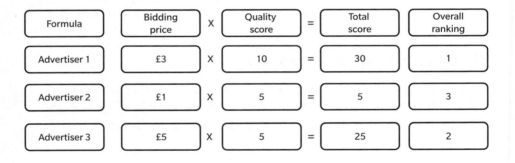

Formula	Bidding price	X	Quality score	=	Total score	Overall ranking
Advertiser 1	£3	X	10	=	30	1
Advertiser 2	£1	X	5	=	5	3
Advertiser 3	£5	X	5	=	25	2

We can see that Advertiser 1 actually bid less than Advertiser 3 and yet their advert ranks higher due to their quality score. This shows how important it is to improve this score as it makes running these types of adverts much cheaper for you.

There are a number of techniques that you can use to achieve this.

Target very specific keywords

Google allows you to determine just how restrictive you want your keywords to be, based on matches.

Phrase match	Exact match
This is where Google matches the phrase, although the search can include other things so long as the phrase is in there as well. N.B. Google recently merged 'Broad match' into this category.	The most restrictive match type, exact match tells Google to only match your ads to queries that are exactly the same, word for word, as your keyword.

To increase your click-through rates, you must try to narrow down your keywords as much as possible so that you are appearing only when someone really wants a service like yours.

Use negative keywords

This is useful when you do not want to show up in a search result when your keyword matches but the context does not. For instance, if you are the brand Direct Line, you do not want to turn up when people are searching for geometry concepts. Therefore, a negative keyword you would use is geometry or maths for example. You may find it difficult enough identifying keywords, let alone negative keywords, so it helps to use a negative keyword finder such as: www.wordstream.com/

Write down negative keywords that you would use.

Iterate your ad text

This is super important, as it is basically what engages and entices users to click on your advert. You need to keep experimenting with this. Here are some best practice tips when developing your ad text copy:

- Use the keyword in the headline and in the body copy.
- Describe the benefits of your service.

- Use site links in order to get additional real estate for no extra cost.
- Use long-tail keywords wherever possible as this enables a more targeted approach.
- Include a call to action.
- Include active verbs in your copy.
- Avoid repetition.
- Run an A/B test on different ads and see which generates a higher CTR.
- Iterate the ad text to optimise it.

Optimise your landing page

This is important on so many levels and we will go into more depth on this area in Chapter 15. For instance, a landing page determines your bounce rate as well as your conversion rate. Both of these are very important metrics. Here are some things you can do:

- Make sure your keywords are on your landing page.
- Use tools like Hotjar to see where people are getting stuck on your landing page, how far they get and what you can improve on.
- Make it simple and easy with an offer to match.

Paid social

Paid social is the ability to have sponsored advertising on a social media platform that can also be linked to other third-party links and feeds. The rise of paid social is certainly no surprise, given the volumes of people on social media – Facebook has over a billion people on its platform. From your point of view, this presents perhaps the best targeting option of any, allowing you to hone in on exactly the types of people you would like to see your advert in a way to suit any budget.

There are four key steps to consider when setting up a campaign using paid social.

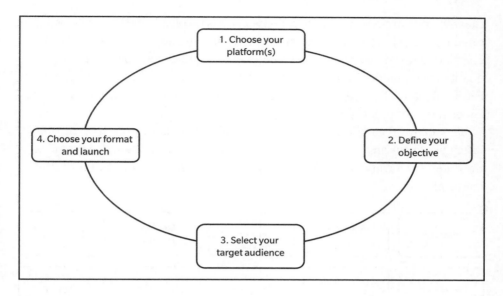

Step 1: Choose your platforms

This first step is important as all social media platforms serve different purposes and have very different types of people that use them. Therefore, you need to choose the platform that best represents your brand and your target audience. It's worth noting that choosing to advertise over a number of platforms can be advantageous for your brand for two reasons.

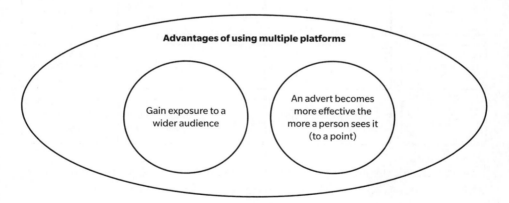

Clearly, there are resource and cost implications involved which need to be factored in. If you have limited resources it may be more advantageous to choose one platform and focus on really engaging those audiences. So in this case, quality over quantity. However, the good news is that certain platforms, such as Facebook, now allow you to post across both this platform and Instagram, so by choosing one you can very easily gain exposure on both.

It is worthwhile understanding the types of people that use each of the different platforms and base your decision on that. Here is an example of some of the criteria you could use when making this selection, using a sample of social media platforms.

Platform	Average age	Largest geographical markets	Median income	Purpose
Facebook	Middle to older demographics	US, India, Indonesia and Brazil	Middle income	Mainly social, keeping up to date with friends
Instagram	Younger to middle demographics	US, India, Indonesia and Brazil	Middle income	Mainly social but increasingly business
LinkedIn	Younger to middle demographics	US and India	Middle to higher income	Mainly business related
Snap Chat	Younger demographics	US, India and France	Lower to middle income	Fun engaging moments with friends
YouTube	Universal	International	All incomes	Entertainment, educational and informative
Tik Tok	Younger demographics	China, US	Lower to middle income	Entertaining and fun

Importantly, for the purpose of your brand you need to consider the context in which someone is going on these platforms when they might see your advert. For instance, if someone is on LinkedIn, they may be searching for a new job opportunity or client, while if on Facebook they may be having a little downtime and enjoying catching up on family news. It could be the same person doing this, but with an entirely different frame of mind on each platform, so bear this in mind when targeting them with any advert as it needs to be relevant for the context they are in.

Write down which social media channels will work best for your brand to advertise on.

Step 2: Define your objective

Due to this targeting capability, paid social advertising tends to be used for short-term offers that lead to a sale, whether that be directly on the social media channel using Instagram Shopping or directly to people to a separate website to close the sale. However, it can also be used as a way to generate awareness and build a community. You need to decide your objective – circle the journey in the diagram that is most relevant to you, remembering they are not mutually exclusive.

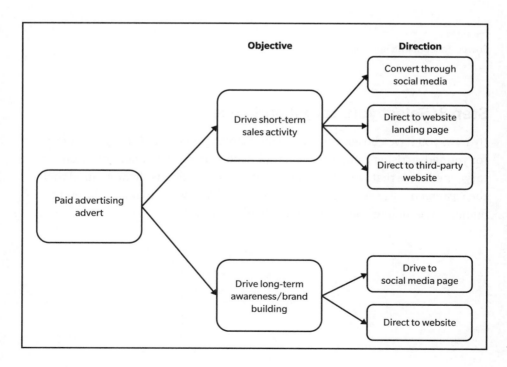

It is also worth going on to each social media advertising platform and analysing how they assess your advertising goals and objectives. For instance, here are the choices you will need to make if advertising on Facebook.

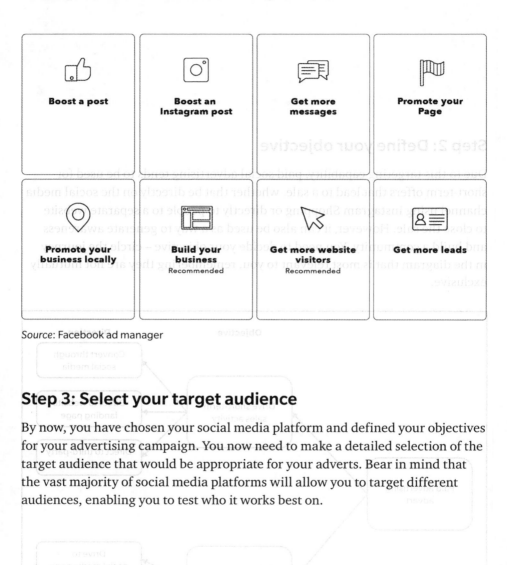

Source: Facebook ad manager

Step 3: Select your target audience

By now, you have chosen your social media platform and defined your objectives for your advertising campaign. You now need to make a detailed selection of the target audience that would be appropriate for your adverts. Bear in mind that the vast majority of social media platforms will allow you to target different audiences, enabling you to test who it works best on.

Here is Facebook's audience selection tool.

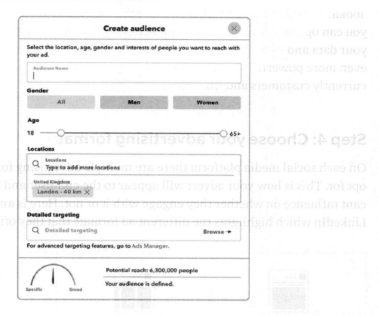

As you can see, you have fairly typical targeting options from demographics to geographical targeting. This is clearly important depending on the type of business you are and who you are servicing. In addition to this, they have much more detailed targeting options as well, as you can see from the figure below, as it allows you to focus on a range of variables on the left-hand side and drill even further as you can see with the example on the right-hand side.

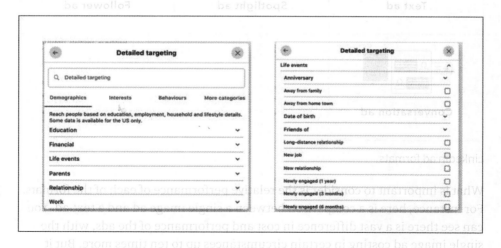

A relatively new feature from platforms such as Facebook is the ability to input 'lookalike audiences'. So rather than create your audience profile from scratch, you can opt for Facebook to determine a similar audience to yours by pulling your data and then matching it against their database. This could deliver an even more powerful targeted approach as it analyses the type of people who are currently customers and finds similar people.

Step 4: Choose your advertising format

On each social media platform there are multiple advertising formats you can opt for. This is how your advert will appear to the end-user and has a significant influence on whether they engage with it or not. Here is an example from LinkedIn which highlights the different ad formats that they offer.

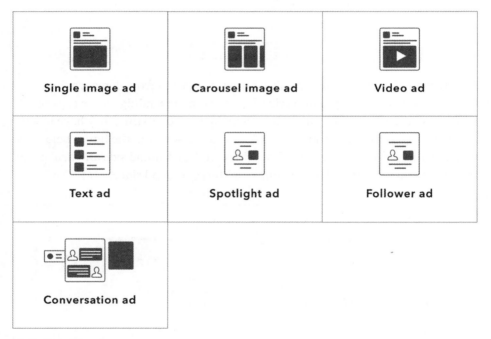

LinkedIn ad formats

What is important to consider is the relative performance of each of the formats. For instance, here is a comparison between a single image ad and a text ad. You can see there is a vast difference in cost and performance of the ads, with the single image ad costing in certain circumstances up to ten times more. But it could deliver vastly improved results.

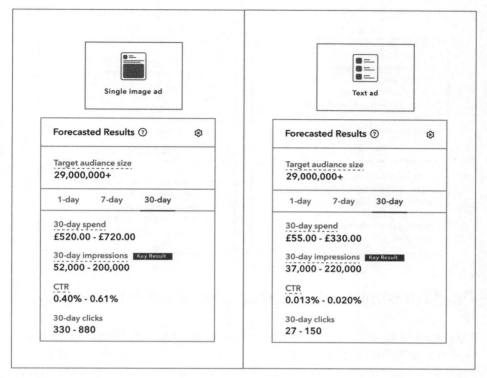

Forecasted results

In addition to performance, you also need to consider the format that best suits your advert type. For instance, for easy-to-understand offers the options above may seem feasible. However, if you need to explain something about your product or service you may need to opt for a video ad.

Facebook and other platforms have tools that enable you to automate the testing process so they service a variety of ad formats to similar customers so you can determine which is performing the best. It takes the hassle out of creating your own targeting selections and ad formats and delivers you results that you can rely on. To learn more, check out Facebook Automated Ads.

You are now ready to launch your advertising campaign. I would recommend adopting a test and learn approach and therefore start relatively small and test which ad formats served to which target audiences work the best. Once you have established that, you can then increase spending in the areas that you know are working.

Finally, here are a number of key tips to increase and improve your paid advertising performance.

Social stacking

Vary your targeting approach using different targeting factors, but use one ad copy and variant in order to maximise the social tools (Likes, comments and shares) of that one creative.

Get your potential customers into a Facebook Group

If you can get your potential customers into a social media group, you have the maximum opportunity to turn them into warm leads and engage them further down the line.

Offer great offers

With the level of competition only rising for these types of adverts, it is important to really make your offers stand out both from a visibility point of view and as an incentive.

Drive organic shares

Remember you do not pay anything when a user shares, likes or comments on your advert, so create content that they want to engage with.

Paid display and programmatic advertising

This channel in online paid advertising has many significant benefits that can take your advertising campaign to the next level. It sits at the heart of what is known as 'programmatic advertising', which is where a personalised advert will be delivered to someone based on three factors.

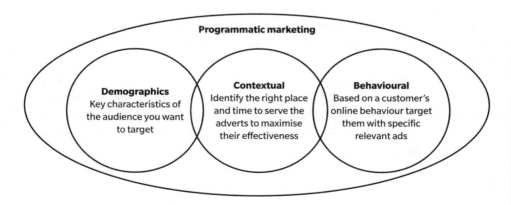

The power of paid display lies in its ability to serve ads across thousands of websites, through various ad exchanges and therefore not limited to a specific digital real estate in the same way paid social is. The good news is that it is relatively easy to set up these types of campaigns as there are sophisticated tools that automate the process for you, which we will come on to.

Before delving into the details it's worth understanding a little more about how programmatic advertising and ad exchange works. At the heart of this process is the ability to automatically buy and optimise digital adverts through ad exchanges rather than going direct to a publisher. To achieve this there is a real-time auction that takes places where an ad is bought at the same time as someone is loading a website. In the figure below, you can see that publisher or website owners (supply side) put out their ad space on to an exchange. On the other side, brands that have adverts do the same (demand side) and specify the conditions for their advert. For example, the type of websites to advertise on and under what circumstances, such as only if the user has been on their own website first.

| Publisher/Supplier | SSP (Supply-Side Platform) | Ad Exchange | DSP (Demand-Site Platform) | Brand/Advertiser |

Programmatic advertising and ad exchange process

As soon as a user lands on a publisher's site it triggers an auction based on all available adverts that meet the criteria. This happens in milliseconds between the time a person clicks on a URL and by the time the page is loaded. For example, if you are a dog food advertiser you can specify the types of websites to advertise on but also say only to advertise on those sites if the user has also been on your dog food checkout page but did not complete the transaction. This therefore acts as a retargeting message.

Based on this, you can see the major advantages that it brings to both publishers and advertisers.

Publishers	Advertisers
Reduces chances of not filling ad space	Ability to target based on strict criteria, therefore maximising effectiveness
Maximise revenue per space due to auction system	Gain unparalleled access to thousands of channels very efficiently
More effective space due to strict targeting leading to more valuable digital real asset	Maximise conversion rate

When deciding to use paid display you will need to determine if you use an ad network or exchange. Take a look at the figure that explains the differences.

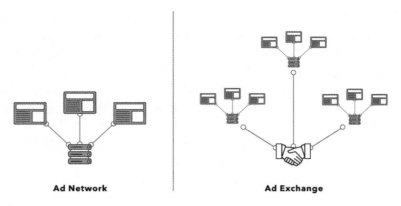

Ad Network   **Ad Exchange**

An ad network, such as Google's Display Network, is connected to a certain number of websites. Or alternatively consider using Taboola.com, which specialises in featuring your brand on trusted editorial sites. Publishers can also sign up to these platforms to offer advertising space which gets fed into the respective Display Ad Network. Publishers can sign up to Google AdSense (www.google.com/adsense/) where they can host their advertising space which gets fed into their Display Network. On the other hand, an ad exchange, such as OpenX (www.openx.com/) is like being on a trading floor that is made up of many ad networks from which you can buy ad space across a larger pool of platforms.

How does a paid display campaign work? Here is an example of how it could work in practice.

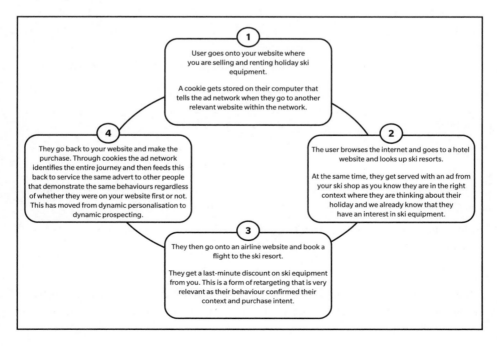

1
User goes onto your website where you are selling and renting holiday ski equipment.

A cookie gets stored on their computer that tells the ad network when they go to another relevant website within the network.

4
They go back to your website and make the purchase. Through cookies the ad network identifies the entire journey and then feeds this back to service the same advert to other people that demonstrate the same behaviours regardless of whether they were on your website first or not. This has moved from dynamic personalisation to dynamic prospecting.

2
The user browses the internet and goes to a hotel website and looks up ski resorts.

At the same time, they get served with an ad from your ski shop as you know they are in the right context where they are thinking about their holiday and we already know that they have an interest in ski equipment.

3
They then go onto an airline website and book a flight to the ski resort.

They get a last-minute discount on ski equipment from you. This is a form of retargeting that is very relevant as their behaviour confirmed their context and purchase intent.

Setting up a paid display campaign

Let's now uncover how you go about setting up a paid display campaign for your brand. There are a number of key steps to take full advantage of this type of channel.

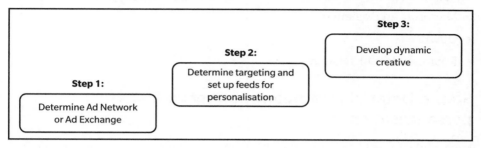

Step 1: Determine ad network or ad exchange

As an advertiser you need to decide whether you use an ad network or exchange to procure ad space. There are a number of key considerations to think about before deciding.

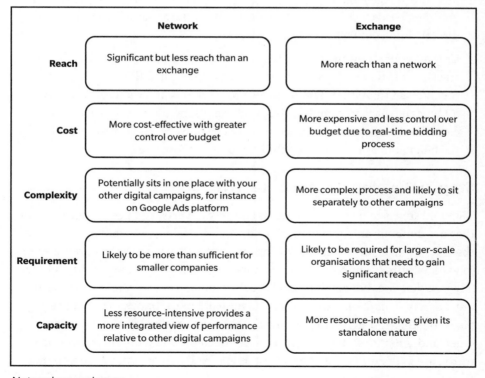

Network vs exchange

The most popular ad network is Google Display Network, but there are a range of exchange options to choose from. Here are some of the leading ad exchanges:

- AppNexus
- Microsoft Ad Exchange
- OpenX
- Rubicon Project Exchange.

Step 2: Determine targeting and set up feeds for personalisation

Each platform will have its own way for you to set up your targeting criteria. If you decided to opt for Google's Display Network, you are in a bit of luck since it uses the same targeting approach as paid search and therefore you have already gone up the learning curve. But there are a few additional things you need to do:

- **Install a conversion tracking code:** This is where the ad network or ad exchange knows when a sale has been completed. It is useful so it can optimise the journey and target people that have a higher propensity to convert. You can do this by installing the code given by the ad network or ad exchange directly into your website.
- **Upload your dynamic feed:** This is letting the ad network or ad exchange track people that go to your website and then continue their journey across the internet thereafter. It allows them to track this and then see if the customer came back to complete the purchase. Along the way, it personalises each the creative element based on the type of websites that are visited and the behaviours that the user exhibits while on those sites.

Step 3: Develop dynamic creative

The final step is to develop your actual display adverts. You need to ensure that they are dynamic and able to be viewed on both desktop and mobile. As part of the service, an ad network or exchange will provide you with the parameters to work within. It's important to remember, given the automated nature of the adverts, that you will need to supply each element from copy to imagery as separate assets. This is then used by the ad network or exchange to dynamically piece together the advert depending on where it gets displayed. Increasingly, video and other formats such as audio, connected TV and digital out-of-home media are being utilised using creative management platforms, such as Bannerflow (https://www.bannerflow.com/) that help to manage the process.

Here are a couple of example templates that Google use, to give you an idea of how your adverts then get displayed.

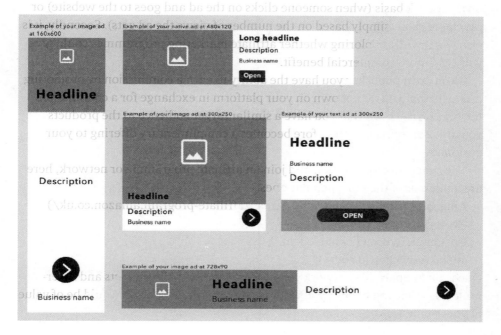

Affiliate Marketing

Finally, to this point we have largely talked about paid display and programmatic from the point of view of the advertiser. However, you may be or want to become a publisher where you give away ad space in exchange for revenue, given the amount of traction you may be receiving. There are a number of ways to achieve this by joining an ad exchange as a publisher, such as OpenX (www.openx.com/) or signing up to Google AdSense or Google Ad Exchange.

Write down any reflections on these steps and how it applies to your brand and advertising campaign.

As a publisher you really have two options on how you want to use your ad space. Firstly, programmatic marketing gives you the ability to generate revenue on a per click basis (when someone clicks on the ad and goes to the website) or per impression (simply based on the number of views the ad gets). Secondly, it is also worthwhile exploring whether affiliate marketing programmes could give you even more commercial benefit.

If you are a publisher you have the ability to earn a commission by promoting products that you do not own on your platform in exchange for a commission. It works on the basis that you have a similar target audience to the products you are promoting and therefore becomes a complimentary offering to your customer.

The first thing to do is find and join an affiliate programme or network, here are a number of the most popular ones:

Amazon Affiliate Programme (https://affiliate-program.amazon.co.uk/)

Awin (https://www.awin.com/)

Clickbank (www.clickbank.com/)

JvZoo (www.jvzoo.com/)

Once you are part of a network you need to browse their products and determine ones that you believe you would like to promote and that would be of value to your audience.

chapter 10

Develop an e-commerce strategy

We are now going to take a look at how to develop an e-commerce strategy for your brand. We will analyse the various e-commerce platforms and channels as well as the types of payment options available to you. As part of this we will also take a close look at the emergence of the 'direct to consumer' or D2C market-place and the opportunities that it presents to you.

For most businesses today, e-commerce is increasingly becoming the most important avenue for selling their goods and services. It presents companies with a huge opportunity to get in front of more customers, grow their presence and brand and deliver their products and services in a cost-effective way.

But what exactly is it? Well, as the name suggests, e-commerce is short for electronic commerce and is simply commercial transactions conducted over digital channels. So this means that whenever a customer uses a digital means to purchase a product or service, whether that be online or offline, they have engaged in the ever-growing world of e-commerce.

E-commerce has enabled businesses to transcend boundaries and has a grow-ing ecosystem of providers and solutions in order to create a more seamless and frictionless customer experience. The e-commerce ecosystem currently consists of four layers that you need to consider when developing your e-commerce approach. Importantly, these are not intended to be mutually exclusive, quite the contrary in fact as there is a drive towards omni-channel e-commerce where multiple payment options expand reach and maximum customer convenience when they purchase products and services. Let's briefly discuss each layer.

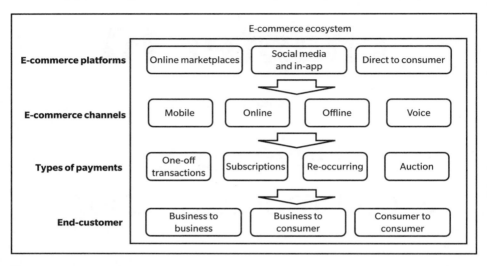

E-commerce ecosystem

E-commerce platforms

There are three underlying platforms that you can use to build your e-commerce infrastructure on. The first is a variety of online marketplaces such as Amazon, eBay, Flipkart or Ali Baba, to name but a few. These provide a ready-made, easy-to-set-up option with huge existing customer traffic. The second is social media and in-app shopping, where you use platforms like Facebook and Instagram 'shop' features to sell directly to people. Interestingly, we are seeing new technologies enhance the buyer experience, for example, Lens Studio by Snapchat enables users to try on new clothes or place a sofa in their living room, using digital augmented reality. It also covers third-party apps where we are seeing contextual targeting using Google Maps and Waze. For instance, you are driving down the motorway where an offer appears on your satnav of a drive-through that is 200 metres away. The third is 'direct to consumer' where you sell directly to people through your own platform where you plug in a payment solution or use an SAAS-based web tool such as Wix or Shopify which has in-built e-commerce capabilities.

Here is a summary of the various platform options. Circle which of them are most relevant to your brand.

Online marketplace	Social media and in-app shopping	Direct to consumer
Easy to set up and get started	Relatively straightforward to set up	Varying complexity depending on how you set up
Huge existing customer traffic	Seamless experience for customers from feed to checkout	Own the end-to-end customer experience
High fees for sales impacting margin, for example, Amazon charges between 20% to 30%	Ability to market products well and where an audience amplifies the ad	Keep all the margin
High level of competition on the platform	Contextual, timely and personalised based on behaviours of audience	Need to do your own marketing to get people to the website
	Fees per transaction	
	Need to do your own marketing	

E-commerce channels

There are four channels that can be used. The first of which has seen the largest increase over the last few years: mobile payments. This is where people opt to purchase products and services through their mobile phone via their browser, app or when making offline purchases through Apple Pay, for example. A major benefit for e-commerce providers is the ability to also gather geo-location information at the same time, providing greater context as to when and why certain purchases are made. The second benefit is online e-commerce which is the ability to make purchases online, from your supermarket shopping to signing up to a Disney Plus subscription. The third channel is offline payments, and you may not have traditionally considered it to sit in the realm of e-commerce, but increasingly it does. This is because many retailers are moving to 'smart point of sale' technologies that use mobile devices and tablets to carry out transactions. This is advantageous as it integrates directly with their online channels so they get to see the full picture of the customer journey and sales cycle.

Finally, a new emerging channel is voice due to the increase in voice activation and command technologies from Apple's Siri to Amazon's Alexa. It's important to note that these channels are becoming more integrated, which increases the need to have capability across them.

Here is a summary of the various platform channels. Circle which of them are most relevant to your brand.

Mobile	Online	Offline	Voice
Convenient and easy to use for customers	Most widely adopted e-commerce channel	Integrates with the backend system to generate an end to end view of customers	Automatically adds items to the shopping cart based on voice commands
Seamless verification using face or thumb print	Ability to make more complex selections and pay with ease through checkout functionality	Uses mobile phones or tablets as point-of-sale machine	Integrates with other payment channels Easy and convenient way for customers to make a purchase
Purchase through browser, app or 'tap and pay'	Ability to save previous purchase for ease		
	Handles a variety of payment options from cards to bank transfers		

Types of payments

There are four types of payments you can use. The first is the simple one-off payment in exchange for a particular item or service. It could range from buying a pair of Nike trainers to a toothbrush. The second is a subscription payment where a customer is charged the same amount at set intervals. These payments range from a Netflix to a digital newspaper subscription. The third is a recurring payment that is of a different amount at each interval, such as a gas bill or an insurance premium. Finally, the fourth payment type is an auction or variable payment where the price depends on supply and demand. For instance, where an item is sold through an eBay auction. An interesting development in this space is the growth of software that links payments to other back-office functions such as stock control to accounting (Xero: www.xero.com) and taxes (Avalara: www.avalara.com).

Here is a summary of the various types of payments. Circle which of them are most relevant to your brand.

One-off	Subscription	Recurring	Auction
Simple to execute using any e-commerce platform	Regular interval payment at same price	Regular interval payment at different price	Based on highest bidder is willing to pay leading to higher level of uncertainty for company
Least valuable from a long-term perspective	Creates long-term value, especially if attrition rates are low	Creates long-term value, especially if attrition rates are low	Provides novelty and engagement
Need to continually drive incremental purchases	Customer pays regardless of usage	Price based on what is consumed	Could be loss-making or very profitable

You should also consider your broader pricing strategy as it can have a dramatic effect on the take-up of your products or services. One model that has come to the fore in a digital context, is that of freeium pricing used by a range of organisations from Spotify to Adobe. This 'try before you buy' approach or enabling limited features and functionality on a non-paid for basis, allows customers to really consider the value of the product or service and allows for a smoother glidepath to the purchase than the typical instance buy.

End-customer

There are three main types of end-customers to consider. The first is perhaps the most common where a business sells directly to an end-consumer. This could be a simple purchase of groceries to a car (yes, you can buy a car online now). The next is business-to-business where one business pays another through e-commerce channels, such as card payments, bank transfers or setting up regular recurring payments (direct debits or standing orders). Finally, an emerging area is that of customer-to-customer payments where increasingly people are paying others for things that range from small transactions such as splitting a bill to large items.

Here is a summary of the various types of customers. Circle which of them are most relevant to your brand.

Business to consumer	Business to business	Consumer to consumer
Consumers make payments in the way that is convenient for them in their channel of choice	Uses a variety of payment solutions to cater for small and large amounts	Simple and easy solution for consumers to make payments to their friends, relatives and colleagues

How do you decide which options to select for your e-commerce strategy?

Given the number of options you have available, it can certainly be a challenge to determine the best e-commerce tools and techniques to consider. To help here is an evaluation tool that you can apply, called the 'E-commerce evaluation hexagon'.

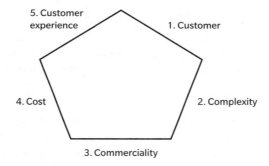

There are five criteria to use to determine your e-commerce approach. Begin with the customer and consider whether you serve a B2B, B2C or C2C audience. The second criterion is to determine what makes most sense in relation to payment type. You need to consider your business model and balance the ability to generate short-term revenue with what will maximise your business potential in the long term. The third is to consider the level of complexity of the solution depending on the capabilities of your team. Certain e-commerce solutions require no technical expertise, such as a listing on Amazon, while others require a high level such as integrating a payment gateway with your own website or app. This leads us to the fourth criterion, cost, which you must consider for the various solutions involved. Typically, off-the-shelf solutions come with certain monthly and transaction fees, while more integrated solutions are likely to have higher up-front costs. The final criteria is to determine the overall customer experience you want to achieve to make it as easy and seamless as possible for customers to engage and purchase from you.

Here is a visual template for you to use on how each of the criteria fit when making decisions across the e-commerce ecosystem. Start at the bottom and work your way up, circling the areas that are most appropriate for you. Remember you can choose more than one option in each layer.

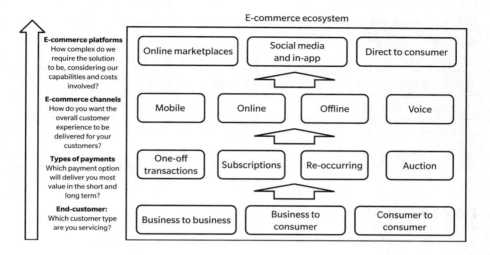

Write your reflections once you have completed the template above on the type of e-commerce approach to take.

From this point on, I will focus on each of the three e-commerce platform options as this is where the majority of innovation happens that would be useful for you to consider.

Online marketplaces

The world of online marketplaces is certainly heating up as more and more customers use them to buy their products and services. In the space there exists both global players, like Amazon and eBay, and regional players such as Flipkart in India and Ali Baba in China. When deciding where to list your items it's worth determining target audience differences and whether you are looking to sell in a single market or 'go global'.

There continues to be a lot of innovation taking place in this space both on the demand side (what the customer sees) and the supply side (how orders are fulfilled). Here are a number of developments that can materially impact your approach in this area.

Demand side	Supply side
Marketplace rankings	International fulfilment services
Video and livestream	Local one-hour delivery
Voice commerce	

Demand side

In a similar way to SEO, all online marketplaces have an algorithm that helps them rank which items go to the top of the list. There are three main factors to consider.

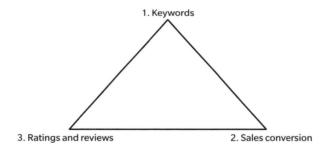

Keywords

It is important to integrate high-volume and relevant keywords as part of your listing. You need to do your research using tools such as Merchant Words (www.merchantwords.com/) or KeyworX (https://keyworx.org/). Be sure you only use keywords that are relevant to your product. In the same way we discussed with SEO, you may also want to consider keywords that have a lower volume of searches so you rank higher. Good copy is also essential to really stand out, so do invest time in building engaging long-form, descriptive copy integrating the keywords you discovered.

Sales conversion

There is no getting away from it – the higher your sales volumes, the higher you will rank. Here are some tips to improve your sales:

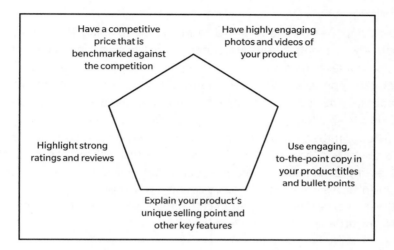

Ratings and reviews

The number and quality of ratings is also an important component to consider. In fact, without a minimum number of ratings you will not appear highly in any marketplace ranking. Here are a number of things you can do to increase them.

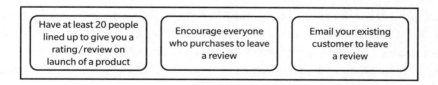

Video and livestream

Given the level of competition on online marketplaces, it's essential to stand out. One way that is growing in popularity (and favoured by ranking systems) is the use of video on product pages. It gives you an opportunity to talk about your brand story behind the product. You can upload a video, for example, to the product detail page on Amazon.

An interesting development you can also use is livestreaming to have an open dialogue with your customers in real time, just as you would in a physical store.

Many of the online marketplaces including Amazon allow certain customers to do this. To learn more go to Amazon Livestream.

A good example of this is how farmers in rural China used this technology during the coronavirus pandemic.

Recognising the significant need of farmers to keep going, JD.com and Alibaba-owned Taobao quickly launched rural livestreaming initiatives. The companies helped farmers and merchants set up online stores with expedited approvals and showed them how to design the content of their broadcasts. They made their apps more intuitive and used their logistics networks to ship the products directly from farm to home.

So from a rather traditional farm-to-market way of doing business they were now able to go straight to the customer, which has increased benefits such as improved margins for farmers and shorter lead times for customers. All in all, it's likely that from a crisis comes an opportunity like no other for these rural farmers to communicate directly with their end-customers and form strong relationships with them.

Voice commerce

Despite being relatively new, voice commerce has gained tremendous traction given the number of people who now own a voice assistant in their homes. It creates a big opportunity for your brands to differentiate themselves further; however, to achieve this you will need to rank very highly or have a very recognisable and memorable brand. Let me explain.

Say you are selling a new form of organic tomato ketchup. If someone 'asks Alexa' for organic ketchup your brand will be in the mix with a range of others and be left in the hands of the algorithm to decide which one it offers. However, if you create a brand that is so well known and your customers ask for 'Your brand organic tomato ketchup' you are in poll position every time. So the reality is that building your brand is going to be key to win in voice commerce.

You can also optimise your items on voice commerce to move up the rankings. Here are some tips to achieve this.

| Highly rated and ranked products with the marketplace badge of approval (such as Amazon's choice badge) will be advantageous | Optimising those keywords to consider what a customer may say when asking for a product is key – put yourself in their shoes and think what voice description they would use for your product | This channel is very conducive to repeat purchases and therefore get your customers to purchase once and the marketplace will remember their preference for the next time |

Write down your thoughts on how you could implement some of the best practise above:

Supply side

International fulfilment services

One of the major benefits of e-commerce is the ability to 'go global'. However, it's not that simple especially when you consider logistical issues such as shipping and taxes. The reality is it takes a long time to ship across borders, especially when customers expect their product in a matter of days. Furthermore, local tax and custom requirements can be a significant hurdle that you need to overcome. So the question is how do you ensure your products can serve international marketers and be with your customers in hours, while adhering to all local market regulations and tax requirements?

Well, two innovations in this space have come to the rescue. The first is that most online marketplaces will offer what is known as fulfilment services.

These fulfilment services are a game-changer as you are now not even required to hold your own inventory or have the hassle of packing and sending the product to your customers. Not to mention, you can sell around the world and have your customers receive their product very quickly, using services such as Fulfilment by Amazon (check out the URL for more details: https://services. amazon.co.uk/services/fulfilment-by-amazon).

To help solve the issue of local taxes and regulations, you can use services such as Avalara (www.avalara.com) that automatically calculate all local tax requirements no matter which country you are selling into. This again removes the complexity in selling internationally and allows you to focus on growing your business.

Local one-hour delivery

In a related service, the local one-hour delivery transforms the way people shop for convenience products. It works off a simple warehouse and fulfilment system where products are stored in convenient locations across different cities. Customers order products that are available in the nearest warehouses and it gets dropped off to them within an hour.

If you operate in the convenience product space you can opt for your products to be stored at these local centres and be part of this type of delivery service, such as Amazon Now.

Write down any thoughts on how your brand and products could take advantage of these innovations.

Social media and in-app

As we discussed in previous chapters, a key advertising channel is social media, particularly given the ability to build a community and target very specific individuals that value your products and services. Given the overarching premise that you need to make the end-to-end experience as seamless as possible, what better way to achieve this than to advertise on social media and then let your customers purchase the product in the same platform.

There are three ways to achieve this.

Business pages	Shoppable posts	Live stream
Your effective hub on the social media platform to showcase your brand, stories, news, updates and product range	Posts that you can add shopping tags on so your followers can make instant purchases while remaining on the social media platform	Host live sessions with your audience on social media to answer questions, overcome objections and lead them to buy off your page

The strategies you need to adopt for each of these are quite different so let's talk through each.

Business pages

This page is effectively your hub on a particular social media platform. Its purpose is to showcase all the latest updates for your company. It's a place to help build your community as they are likely to use this page as their port of call if interested in what you have to offer. It is also the account from which all your posts will originate from, so the more engaging the better.

Although it is not strictly a direct sales channel, your business page acts like your shop window, but rather than just giving potential customers information about your products it gives them a much richer view into your brand and why they should become part of your community as a follower and customer. There are a number of things you need to have on your business page.

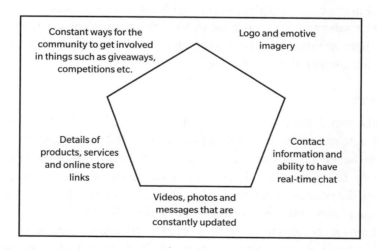

There are also a number of advantages of having a business page on platforms like Facebook, Instagram and LinkedIn. They give you enhanced levels of analytics and insights on user engagement, which are key when generating revenue on these platforms.

Shoppable posts

The second development is the ability to create shoppable posts on platforms such as Instagram and Facebook. This allows you to create compelling content and label various items that can be purchased directly with a few clicks. This integration between advert and e-commerce presents a fantastic opportunity for you to shorten the purchase journey for your customers and thereby increase conversions.

Since your posts go out to your existing followers and their followers if amplified, you already have a significant base of warm leads who are interested in the type of product you sell. So as they become inspired by your posts, they can at the same time become a part of your journey through their purchase. This is very powerful in-context marketing.

To be able to use this feature on platforms such as Instagram, you need to have the following:

A business account | The latest version of the app | Compliance with their physical goods policy

There is a major caveat to this feature. Your followers do not want to feel directly sold to with sales messages. So if you overuse this feature you run the risk of turning them off rather than on. It's therefore best to use it sparingly and as part of a broader content marketing strategy.

Livestream

In a similar way to livestream on online marketplace platforms, you can achieve a similar outcome using social media platforms. In fact, livestreaming could be even more beneficial for your business using social media given your existing community. Using livestream is a very effective way to get people to engage with you, check out your latest offerings through product demonstrations and you can even overcome any objections they may have in real time.

There are two options to use to get started with livestreaming across social media. The first is you can use the in-platform 'live' functionality that most social media platforms have. The second option is to use a third-party tool such as Zoom (https://zoom.us/) or YouTube Live to stream across all of your social media channels at the same time and thereby increasing your reach and effectiveness.

In-app e-commerce

Being able to catch someone when they are in the right frame of mind to make a purchase is key. The vast majority of the time people glance over products and services that may not be relevant for them simply because they are not in the mood to buy. Therefore, the ultimate marketer's dilemma is not just to target people who have a need but doing so when they may be receptive to listen and take action as well. This is where in-app e-commerce becomes relevant – where you combine the following elements to create a very conducive environment to make a sale.

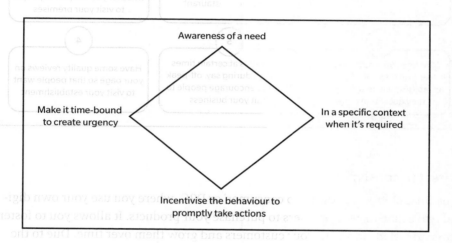

Your customers use a range of apps almost on a daily basis from listening to music on Spotify to turning on Google Maps or Waze to find their way to a restaurant. Increasingly, it's this type of app that you can tap into to promote your products and services that are relevant at the moment for customers using geo-location functionality. For instance, if your customer is in the gym listening to a podcast while working out. Using geo-location a company could know their location and how long they have been there and then present them with a time-bound offer of a discount of a refreshing energy drink that they can purchase in the gym's café. They could present the discount code in the app using push notifications.

This example uses all the elements of the diamond to create a highly relevant, compelling offer for the customer. As importantly it fits in seamlessly into their lives in a very non-intrusive way and therefore delivers an exceptional customer experience.

A good way for you to get started is to tap into the Google network that owns both Google Maps and Waze. Here are the steps you need to take to 'get on the map', so to speak.

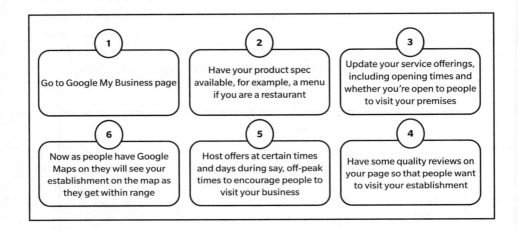

Direct to consumer

The final platform is 'direct to consumer' or D2C, where you use your own digital real estate to get customers to purchase your products. It allows you to foster direct relationships with your customers and grow them over time. Due to the advent of digital technology many brands, both established and disruptors, are opting to engage customers in this way. It allows them faster access to market, control over the route to market, ability to deliver and be responsive to customers and maximise their margins as it cuts out the middleman.

Companies from Pepsico[1] to disruptive health brand Ugly drinks are all adopting some form of D2C strategy, so it's important to consider this e-commerce approach. Let me first show you how the mechanics of a D2C strategy works before jumping into how you can take advantage of it. Here is a diagram of the four stages of the D2C cycle.

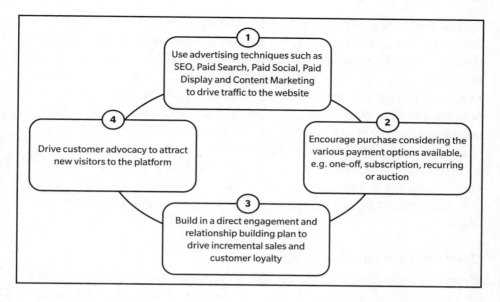

There are three different types of D2C platforms to consider.

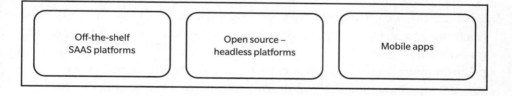

Off-the-shelf – SAAS platforms

These types of solutions are the easiest to set up and get started with. They involve using a third-party platform that enables you to choose your template and populate it with very limited technical knowledge. Platforms such as Wix (www.wix.com) and Shopify (www.shopify.com) are market leaders in this area where they literally have hundreds of 'off-the-shelf' templates to choose from.

The good news is that all your standard integrations from e-commerce capability to social media plug-ins can be easily done on these platforms. So if you are just starting out, with an unproven track record and limited resources, this type of solution could be ideal. These companies have certainly done the hard work for you and you can use the full range of integrated e-commerce solutions they have. For example, Shopify has a product known as POS or point of sale that you can use in any store, event or other app where physical payments are required. For example, Kylie Jenner used this approach when she opened her pop-up stores.[2] The major advantage is you get a single back-end platform with clear insights between online and offline sales.

The disadvantage is that although the up-front costs are low, you will be charged ongoing fees that can rack up. In addition, you will be tied to their infrastructure, which can be limiting as you won't have total control over the design.

Open source or headless integrations

These types of integrations allow you to use your own digital infrastructure and effectively plug into it to deliver you e-commerce capability. If you think about any of the big retailers or supermarkets, they would use this approach due to the complex needs associated with their products.

Amongst the most popular e-commerce integrations are Stripe and PayPal, leaders in this area. They not only allow card payments but a host of others from bank transfers to traditional invoicing (important for business-to-business transactions).

Furthermore, they allow you to collect a variety of payment options from one-off to monthly subscriptions. Unlike SAAS-based tools, this option offers you a lot more customisation based on your website and business model. For example, you could create customer areas and have saved orders and previous history, making it easy for people to hit repeat purchase. In addition, depending on the package you choose you only get charged per transaction, which could save you considerable costs over the long term.

However, they are often more complex to integrate and require a high degree of technical expertise to set up and achieve all the things you may want to do.

Mobile apps

Mobile commerce is becoming increasingly important and therefore you need to build your solution with this in mind. There are effectively three ways to ensure you have mobile commerce enabled that form part of your solution.

Mobile-optimised website including checkout functionality	Use an off-the-shelf app builder e.g. Good Barber or Appypie	Build a progressive or native app and integrate a payment gateway via the app store or payment provider

There are larger considerations of which options you use, of which e-commerce functionality is a key component. The main consideration in this respect is to make sure it's a seamless experience from customers adding to their carts, checking out, paying for their products and storing their shopping history.

Mobile commerce is also important as it lets you 'join up' the customer journey more seamlessly and reduces bottlenecks when paying at a variety of establishments. A good example of this is the recent experience Starbucks had in China.

Starbucks, a company that understandably was badly hit in the pandemic since "social distancing" has been enforced, has carved out its plans in China in a post-Covid world. There are a number of prominent actions it has taken that give us some indication of how things might unfold elsewhere in the world.

At the time of writing, 98% of Chinese Starbucks outlets have re-opened, but with a slight twist. Over the last decade or so Starbucks recognised the importance of digital in its overall journey and that is now paying dividends as it enters a new phase in its evolution.

Kevin Johnson, its CEO, says: "Traditionally we've seen 80% of our business be stay-in and enjoy their drinks in the cafés. As Covid hit, we hit a peak of nearly 80% of transactions being digital orders. Those digital orders were all set up with the contactless experience through walking in the stores and picking up your orders in Mobile Order & Pay and then the rest of it was delivery. . . What we're seeing is that there is a higher percentage of to-go orders taking place in China and we expect that trend to continue. If there is a silver lining, I think it is forming a new habit in China, where you are seeing more people take to-go orders and get used to doing that."

It appears that this will be a regular scene for some time to come as Starbucks adheres to the health protocols within the nation.

What can be learnt from the Starbucks China experience? Well, it's likely the role of the physical location or store will evolve balancing 'stay-in' and 'take-out'. However, perhaps the most insightful intel is the way the customer will use technology to augment the overall experience. Digital will permeate through the journey from pre-order through to (in many cases) delivery. This is a step-change for many of these types of businesses that have relied heavily on the face-to-face element to deliver the service.

Finally, mobile apps in the context of consumer-to-consumer commerce are very important as we are increasingly seeing people making payments to each other. There are a range of apps and mobile solutions available for this from Barclays Pingit (www.pingit.com) in the UK, to M-Pesa in Kenya (www.safaricom.co.ke/personal/m-pesa).

chapter 11

The art of social selling

We will next explore both the practical steps you need to take as well as the consumer psychology to consider when carrying out social selling activities using a three-stage process.

Stage 1:
Building your social reputation

Stage 2:
Approaching prospects on social

Stage 3:
Moving towards the sale

In previous chapters we discussed the changing nature of consumer psychology when it comes to the sales process. Today, it will probably come as no surprise that the majority of the buying decision-making process is done without ever making contact with a human. Therefore, brands need to respond to this by finding, engaging and educating new prospects using digital channels such as social media, a process known as social selling.

Stage 1: Building your social reputation

Before engaging in any form of social selling you need to build up your own reputation and profile across the social media platforms that you will be using. It may sound obvious but for a prospect to take you seriously they need to think you are credible, knowledgeable, experienced and someone they could learn from and not just be sold to. Also, there needs to be an element of familiarity which comes from having common connections, interests or associations. This can be achieved through regular posting of content that positions yourself as a thought leader and that fosters engagement with others across social media, which your prospects are bound to see and even engage with.

Here is a model to consider to build your social reputation.

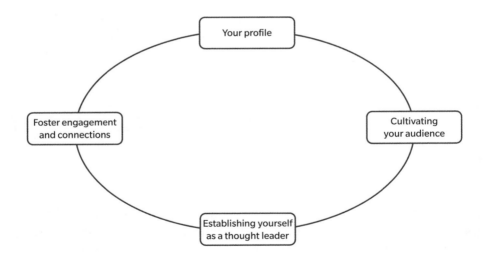

Your profile

This is like your personal landing page and is the single most important element and opportunity for you to build credibility. A good tip when developing this page is to see it through the lens of your target customer and think about what they would want to learn about you and your business. They will be looking for clues about your expertise, professionalism and things they have in common with you.

Here are a number of basic things to consider:

- clear and professional profile picture
- easy-to-understand job title
- summary of your skills, expertise and how you can add value to them
- contact information
- examples and testimonials of your previous work
- up-to-date summary of previous education and work experience
- list of all clubs, universities, organisations and associations you are a part of.

In addition, here are some enhanced-level tips to consider.

Include a distinct tagline that makes you stand out. For example, a distinguished copywriter, John Esprian (https://www.linkedin.com/in/johnespirian) said key to his success was his tagline, "relentlessly helpful technical copywriter". He said the term "relentlessly" is almost always played back to him when dealing with new prospects

On the featured section of most social media platforms such as LinkedIn, Facebook and Instagram, ensure your achievements, talks or content that show you as a thought leader in your industry are kept up to date

Maintain and encourage endorsements and testimonials from high-profile people who are likely to be known by your prospects

On platforms like LinkedIn a simple tip to get people to look at your profile is to view theirs so you come up on their 'viewed profile' list, which makes them more likely to check yours out!

Cultivate your audience

A key way to build your reputation is to be seen to know other experts or high-profile people in the industry and one way to achieve this is to build up your connections and followers. Use this model – what I call the 'circle of influence' – and consider some of the people you should be connected with.

Follow others who are influential who you do not have a direct connection with

Through association ask your connections to **connect** you to who they know who is of interest

Connect with who you know, e.g. work colleagues, university alumni, people you met through your network

Circle of influence

Most people don't realise that the more connections you have and influential people you follow, the more access to information, insight and opportunities you can leverage to make yourself more credible and known. In addition, it opens up your ability to have an open dialogue with these people, thus fostering deeper relationships and also enhancing your own social credibility through the association.

Here are a number of key ways to build your audience.

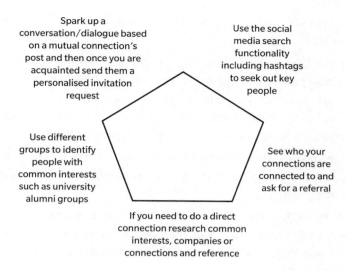

Spark up a conversation/dialogue based on a mutual connection's post and then once you are acquainted send them a personalised invitation request

Use the social media search functionality including hashtags to seek out key people

Use different groups to identify people with common interests such as university alumni groups

See who your connections are connected to and ask for a referral

If you need to do a direct connection research common interests, companies or connections and reference

Establish yourself as a thought leader

Building your social reputation requires you to position yourself as a thought leader. To achieve this requires you to be proactive across social media and continually post content that is engaging and informative. Over time, you will begin to be recognised for your area of expertise and people will proactively come to you when they have a need. When this happens a very different dynamic is created between you and prospects, as more psychological power lies in your court, rather than the other way around.

You can use many of the content-generation techniques we talked about in Chapter 6 to develop and schedule content. It's worth considering how you can use both 'created' and 'curated' content, the first being content you create and own; the second being third-party content that you share.

However, to simply share content is not enough. To get the most value out of it you need to optimise your approach in order to maximise your reach. Every social media platform uses an algorithm that determines the amount of reach your posts gets and to whom, so there are a few things to consider in this regard:

- When you post, the algorithm will send it to a small base of people to assess appeal, engagement and interactions. Usually, the first hour is the most important to determine the trajectory of the post, and therefore you are really looking for maximum engagement at this time.
  - How can you help this? Understand what the best time is to post your content, who to copy into the post to drive engagement and continually engage

with people who like, comment and share your content, especially within the first hour.

- Once the post has received engagement in the first instance, it then gets filtered to a larger audience across your connections. It's likely at this stage your posts will get maximum exposure, as your connections will engage with it that will lead to their connections seeing it as well. How you respond to this amplification is crucial in order to expand your own circle of influence:

  - How can you help this? Respond to every comment and in particular if you see someone outside your connections commenting make sure you cultivate that dialogue.

  - You can bring in others into the conversation by tagging them in if you believe it's relevant to them. Consider people who have high influence that you know on some level as everyone in the stream will then know you are associated with them.

- Over the next few days the post will continue to organically grow and reach people outside your connections. Continue to push this reach through engagement. Here are a number of ways to achieve this:

  - Comment on every interaction and ask open questions so others can respond back.

  - Cultivate the relationship with new connections and when appropriate send them a personalised invitation request. Now they become part of your network and therefore your posts will more easily be amplified to their network in the future.

The key to growing your social reputation in this way is to have patience, persistence and dedication. Often people give up way too soon as they see little return after a few weeks. You need to break through as building any reputation takes a very long time. For example, Grant Cardone, who has one of the biggest reputations in the sales industry, said he made 12,000 videos to get to where he is.[1]

Foster engagement and connections

In the previous section we discussed the role of you proactively putting out content regularly in order to become a thought leader. This may seem like the more sexy side of social reputation-building, but make no mistake there is another side of the coin that is important, which is active engagement on your connections' social activity.

By being a strong supporter of your connections' content, you are building good will, trust and actively demonstrating you want to help with something they care about. Also, regardless of how seasoned a content creator your connections are, everyone is nervous about how their posts will perform, so you being an advocate of them will not go unnoticed.

Interestingly, there is also a biological reason for doing this. Simon Sinek, the world-famous author and speaker, suggests that when someone engages in social media posts and receives a response it releases a chemical called dopamine, which makes them happy. So over time, your prospects will begin to associate you with an increase in their happiness levels.[2]

In a similar way to your own content, you also have a way to extend your network by responding to other connections' posts by creating an open dialogue and also encouraging your connections to join the conversation. Don't forget that once you have engaged with anyone outside your network you send them a personalised invitation request.

Here are a number of additional tips to consider.

Look out for key influencers' or decision-makers' posts and ensure you respond to them quickly	Try and identify posts from these people that do not have many likes/comments as your response will stand out
Share useful insights from your connections that will add value to your audience and also make them feel important – it's a real win–win	Write a personalised note when sending connection invites, making reference to what you have in common and your reason for connecting

Stage 2: Approaching prospects on social media

Today, social media platforms give you the ability to directly approach your connections and even certain people outside your connections using the direct message (DM) feature. It goes without saying that in order to increase the chances of a positive response, it's best to have cultivated a good social reputation using the guidance in the previous stage. Too often, people try to use this DM feature too early in the process as they are looking for instant results. Resist this temptation and remember this fundamental rule: 'Customers don't buy when you have a need, they buy when they have a need.' This means that by constantly filling their inboxes with direct sales messages you are only doing your own social reputation more damage.

To illustrate, these are a number of real examples of messages that people have sent on LinkedIn:

Example 1: Hello, it is my absolute pleasure to have you as a friend. Hope you are well?

Example: 2: Hello, let me ask you this. Is your project constantly missing deadlines? Are your production costs just way too high? Do you want to have increasingly high margins? We would like to offer you a FREE customised design by allocating eight man-hours of highly skilled people to help.

Five days later after no response: Just to let you know we are an infographic design company. We want to give you eight skilled man-hours to work on any of your projects. Let us know when you want us to start.

Example 3: Hi, wondered if I could ask you something? I am currently seeking out companies that have IT issues that are just too big for their teams to handle. If you know any such companies, it would be great if you could recommend me.

All the messages really do fail to understand how they will be perceived at the other end and therefore are very likely to not even get a response, let alone a sale. They adopted a fairly typical 'spray and pray' tactic and it's likely that hundreds of people received the same message. The net effect is that it is going to elicit a low response, create negative brand perceptions, trigger an unintended action. The list goes on, but in short it will have exactly the opposite effect than what was intended.

On closer inspection, here are some of the reasons where they went wrong:

- **Over-familiarity too soon:** In the first example, they wanted to come across as friendly; however, just by using the word 'friend', when it's apparent that they have never even met, creates an instant barrier.

- **Being too generic:** In the second example, they have used terms like 'missing deadlines' or 'want to increase margins' which are so generic that the receiver will doubt their integrity and wonder how many people this message was sent to.

- **Lacks a link between what they define as a problem and how the company will solve it:** A common marketing technique is to identify a problem and then have a solution for it. However, by pitching a generic problem and then a solution that does not obviously solve the problem leaves many questions in the mind of the receiver.

- **Asking the end-user to take action that is of little benefit to them:** It would only seem natural that if someone asks you for a referral you should have worked with them before. Otherwise it just seems fake.

All the examples represent a lack of creativity or personalisation.

Now you have recognised the pitfalls and what to avoid, here is a three-step model to consider when making an approach on social media.

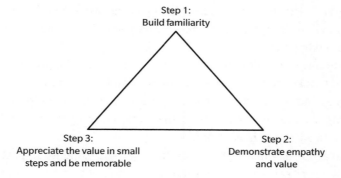

Step 1: Build familiarity

We have talked about the need to build familiarity in the previous stage, and it most certainly is the starting point when making an approach to a prospect. There is a very easy three-step guide to this:

1 **Being seen on:** Being seen on a range of relevant media channels can be very useful, which you can then amplify through your own social media tools. A good example of this is when guru Jay Shetty was seen on popular TV shows like Ellen in the US. It was also uploaded to YouTube and then he used it across all his social media channels.

2 **Being seen with:** Another great way to generate familiarity is to be seen with other influential people that creates an association but also you get access to their network by tagging them in posts. These types of partnerships are very popular and a good example is the Gary Vee show where he interviews a range of prominent and distinguished guests such as Joe Rogen.

3 **Being seen to:** The final piece of this is being seen to be an expert and sharing your points of view on certain things. A good way to achieve this is to use offline techniques to drive your online presence further. For instance, speaking at industry conferences and networking thereafter with relevant people is a great way to spark up connections that can be followed up on social media afterwards.

Step 2: Demonstrate empathy and value

When you are comfortable that you have built a considerable social reputation, you can take the next step and DM people in your network. Remember that it's likely others will be doing the same. So how do you stand out and get them to want to respond to you?

You need to have a considerable amount of empathy and approach it in a personal way that makes them feel that you understand their circumstances, issues and challenges and therefore are the best person to be able to help solve them for them. This will create an element of an emotional connection which will help draw them in to what you have to say.

In order to achieve empathy, however, takes patience and it's important to remember that it's likely to come on their terms and not your own. It may also mean that when you message them you do not mention anything to do with your product or service – rather go in with an open mind on how you can help them.

At the same time, you need to prove your value to them which acts as a rational proof-point. This can be achieved by providing access to information or other ways they can get a taster for what you can bring.

Here is a simple framework to use when considering how best to develop empathy and demonstrate your value:

- **Who:** Do not go for a blanket, generic targeting approach, as you saw in the examples above. Rather, quality is better than quantity so take your time to really research the people you would like to contact. Get to understand their situation through what they are posting or other forms such as articles, interviews and videos. Also, try to connect with them on an emotional level so you understand what they are passionate about and incorporate it into the message.

- **When:** Remember the golden rule: try to establish the right moment in time when they have a need rather than the other way around. You can do this through things like press releases or they may post on social media with a specific requirement. Timing is everything.

- **What:** Having an appropriate solution to meet the prospect's needs is one thing, but convincing them that it will work is certainly another. Therefore, giving them an opportunity to 'try before they buy' will certainly be helpful and it's likely that most people continue their relationship with this approach. There are a variety of ways to achieve this from freemium offerings where you give access to certain parts of the solution for free to trial it, or free access for a certain period where they can check out all features. You need to decide which is appropriate for your audience.

- **How:** The more personalised you can make your approach and message, the better. So really craft the message with this in mind. Remember that one really well-crafted message is worth ten generic ones (at least).

Often, due to the number of messages that important people receive, it's likely that even if you make a genuine and well-personalised approach it will be ignored as we have become accustomed to filtering out messages from people we don't know. Therefore, a good way to get around this is to find someone you have in common and ask for an introduction. That way you are no longer a stranger and they are more likely to respond given the mutual connection.

Step 3: Appreciate the value in small steps and be memorable

You may have heard of the old English proverb, 'softly, softly, catchee monkey', to mean that you need to take slow steps to achieve your eventual goal. Often, on social media it becomes easy to be very generic and ask for something that overstretches where you are in the relationship with your prospect (for instance, asking for referrals for big IT projects as we saw in the example above). Recognising that trust is built over time is important and that if you go too fast people will not be very responsive, as largely they will be risk-averse.

Here are a number of examples of smaller steps that you could request that are likely to yield more fruitful results.

Ask for a 15 minute call so you can explain more	Get their email address so you can send them more information
Seek their guidance or advice on something	Ask a personal question about something that you are likely to have in common

Once you have established a relationship, you have an expanded licence to operate to ask for other things. In fact, it links to a behavioural science theory known as the Benjamin Franklin effect.[3] It quite conversely reveals that people like you more after they have done you a favour. Furthermore, they are more likely to provide even more help later down the line if they have done you a favour before.

Finally, with inboxes filling up with hundreds of messages each day it's just so easy for someone to read your message, and even if it's relevant they may be in the middle of something, so think they will get back to it but don't. So the best way to avoid this is two-fold.

First, have a constant presence in their minds. For instance, we discussed the need to create great content and constantly share that across social media. This will mean that people will continually be reminded of the services that you offer.

The second is to actually try and have a conversation with them outside the social media platform, for instance, via email or even WhatsApp. That way you have automatically differentiated yourself from everyone else and they are more likely to have you on 'speed-dial' should the need arise than anyone else.

Stage 3: Moving towards the sale

In the last section of the previous step, you took a lot of care to adopt a slow approach when engaging with your prospect – and that has now earned you some trust. The next step is to convert them to a customer. Interestingly, and as mentioned above, at this stage you want to take the conversation off social media and on to another form of communication. Why? Well, consider the fact that your prospects receive many multiple messages each day on their social channels. The more you engage with them there, the more opportunity there is for you to blend into the crowd. By moving things off social media you have already gained 'preferred' status in the mind of your prospect.

There are three stages to consider to take the sale to fruition.

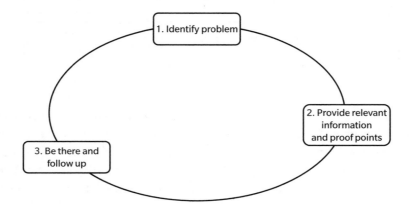

Identify problem

The first is taking time to understand the problem they are facing. You could do this through an exploratory call, coffee or video conference. It's still too early to propose your solution although there is no harm in sending them a presentation with further information about who you are and what your company does. I would highly recommend using trackable presentation software like Slidebean (https://slidebean.com/) so you can see who viewed the presentation and which slide they spent the most time on. It will give you invaluable insight into who the decision-makers are (who you can subsequently connect with on social media), as well as which product they found most attractive.

Also, at this stage ensure that everyone you come into contact with you connect with on social media. This will open you up to more decision-makers who will see your content, where you are positioned as an expert. Also, if the conversation goes no further at least you will remain front of mind for next time.

Provide relevant information and proof points

The second thing to do is provide relevant information and proof-points based on their needs. At this stage you are trying to use your social reputation to your advantage by directing them to a range of social proof points.

Case studies that are relevant to them that are posted on social media	Reports and presentations that you have on social media
Video customer testimonials that are on your social media pages	Recommended references to speak to with their social links

Clearly, anything confidential you can send them through more secure channels but in the document or presentation ensure you link back to your social channels, as set out above.

By using this technique you are signalling your transparency to your prospects, which is very important. Also, at this stage it is likely they will conduct a deeper level of research on you and your company. By directing them to pages that you control you are helping to own the narrative and portray yourself in the best possible light. They are also likely to see common connections and therefore likely to go to them for a reference which will work in your favour.

Be there and follow up

The third aspect is to have open lines of communications and constantly follow them up in relation to the immediate opportunity – and if it doesn't work out still keep in touch for the future.

There are plenty of ways to keep the lines of communication open both on and off social media. The key from a social media perspective is to send them a message from the platform so it's at the top of their inbox just letting them know you can be reached through this channel.

Finally, following up is incredibly important both in the short and long term. Using an automated tool such as Hootsuite (https://hootsuite.com/), you can schedule in when you should touch base with the prospect again at regular intervals. In the meantime, you are safe in the knowledge that they are connected with you and that they will continually see all the great insights you put out on social media, which will keep you in front of their minds.

chapter 12

—

Develop an influencer marketing strategy

In this chapter, you will learn about the various dynamics, challenges and opportunities that influencer marketing presents to your brand and how to navigate through it. We will cover how to create an influencer marketing strategy that is right for your brand and what to watch out for.

Influencer marketing is certainly one of the new kids on the block and is one of the fastest growing areas of marketing, set to be worth around $15 billion dollars by 2023.[1] It has been fuelled by the rise of new media channels, such as social media, virtual worlds and computer gaming, where key figures in these spaces are able to generate huge community followings and thereby become 'influential'.

At the heart of this discipline is the trust that audiences have in these influencers, that enable them to shape how people think, feel and behave about certain products, services and situations. So much so that top influencers such as David Attenborough achieved 1 million Instagram followers in four hours,[2] or Kylie Jenner who is reported to get paid around $1 million per post.[3] However, it's not just mainstream influencers that have seen incredible growth. Even more niche areas such as the world of esports, for instance, which is essentially virtual gaming where others watch people play, is estimated to generate over 500 million viewers by 2023.[4] Its top influencers such as Peter Dager is said to have earned over $3 million and amassed a following of over 200,000 followers.[5]

Importantly, influencers play an extremely important role in fuelling the always-on marketing trend that we are witnessing. Rather than opting for big bang campaigns a number of times a year, brands need to continually engage with their audiences sometimes even ten times a day using social content. The path to achieve this level of quality content through conventional routes is a non-starter, since it's just too expensive and time-consuming. However, if brands harness the development of micro-content using influencers, this helps to create a significant amount of content cost-effectively, which can be posted on a brand's page as well as an influencer's page. This opportunity presents your brand with the ability to constantly engage your audience with new, relevant and exciting content while also finding new audiences at the same time through your influencer's network.

Developing an influencer marketing strategy

There are five steps to consider in creating an influencer marketing strategy.

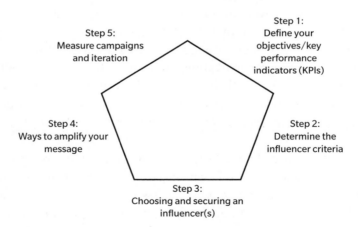

Ok, so let's get started with each.

Step 1: Define your objectives/key performance indicators

Before delving into trying to find the right influencers to work with, it is important to outline your objectives for doing so. This could range from trying to reach new audiences that an influencer has influence over, or perhaps you are looking for a brand ambassador to help champion your brand or cause in some way. It's important to recognise that an influencer can add significant value over and above reaching out to their followers.

You must also be very conscious that an influencer will be cautious over who they work with and what they promote, since it's the very fabric of trust that built up their reputation in the first place. Therefore, you must consider how you would also be a good strategic fit for them.

Here are a range of objectives to consider that specifically relate to on-boarding an influencer. Consider each and circle the ones that align most with your objectives for your brand.

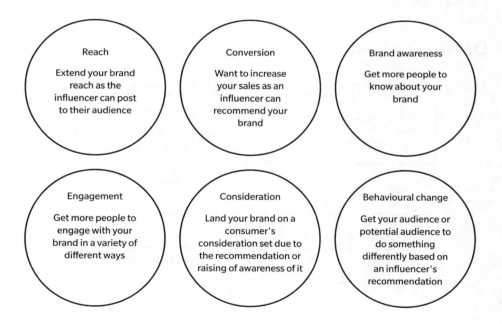

In addition, I would suggest considering why an influencer would want to work with your brand. Look at it from their point of view and consider how they can leverage some of the capabilities you have to grow and strengthen their relationship to their audience. Write your thoughts on this below.

Step 2: Determine the influencer criteria

Before deciding on which influencers you would like for your campaign it's worth developing some criteria to benchmark them against, consider the following:

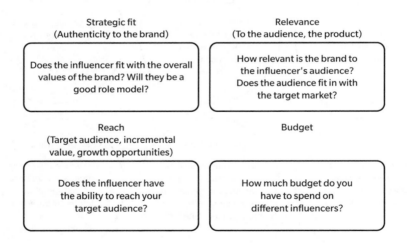

Strategic fit
(Authenticity to the brand)

Does the influencer fit with the overall values of the brand? Will they be a good role model?

Relevance
(To the audience, the product)

How relevant is the brand to the influencer's audience? Does the audience fit in with the target market?

Reach
(Target audience, incremental value, growth opportunities)

Does the influencer have the ability to reach your target audience?

Budget

How much budget do you have to spend on different influencers?

Use this template to decide the type of influencers you think may be appropriate.

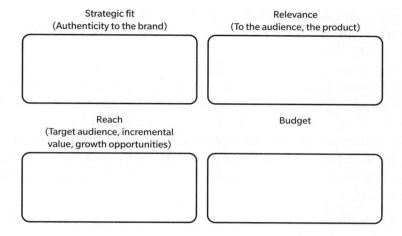

Now that you have determined your criteria you need to understand the different types of influencers you can choose. Influencers come in all shapes and sizes and the type of influencer depends very much on the niche they have created for themselves.

There are broadly three types of influencers.

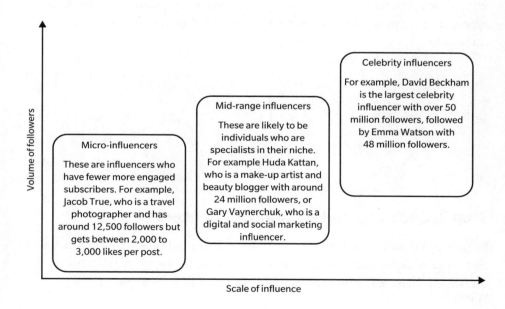

It's worth understanding there is typically a volume/value trade-off when considering different influencers – more engagement on the posts or volume, or greater reach per post.

On the one hand, choosing an influencer who has a huge following will ensure that you get significant reach. On the other hand, an influencer with fewer followers may well have a more intimate and trusted connection with their fans, as they can have a higher level of engagement with each one.

It is important to recognise the inverse relationship between volume and engagement, in that the more followers an influencer has, the less engagement is likely to occur per post on a percentage basis. Research from AdWeek[6] shows the following:

- Influencers who have an audience smaller than 1,000 typically have engagement rates of around 15%. That means a person with 1,000 engaged fans might earn 150 likes on each post.

- Influencers with 1,000 to 9,999 followers often have engagement rates of around 7.4%. That means a person with 2,000 might also get around 150 likes per post. Engagement rates fall to just 2.4% by the time a person has more than 100,000 fans, meaning they might only get 2,400 likes per post.

Write down your reflections and the type of influencers you deem to be most appropriate for your brand and campaign, considering the volume/value trade-off.

Step 3: Choosing and securing influencers

By now you should have a good sense of the criteria and types of influencers that may be suitable for your brand. However, you need to pin down a shortlist of individuals that meet your criteria. Here is an easy process to follow.

Finding suitable influencers	Approaching influencers	Negotiating with influencers

Finding suitable influencers

In order to find the right influencers, you should carry out your own form of research and investigation. You can also take on the services of an agency to help with the selection process, but in any event it's worth you also independently doing your homework.

There are a number of ways to identify key influencers and typically the mid-range and celebrity influencers are likely to be easier to identify. However, remember the value/volume trade-off and the fact that they need to fit with your brand. I would recommend doing the following.

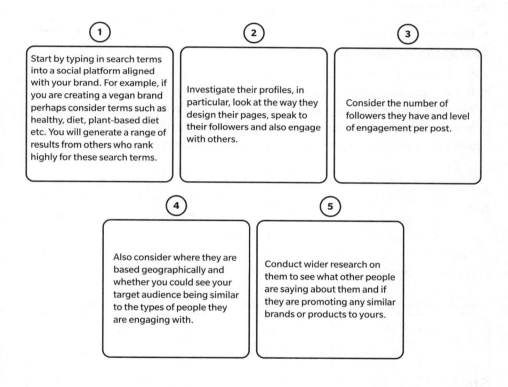

1 Start by typing in search terms into a social platform aligned with your brand. For example, if you are creating a vegan brand perhaps consider terms such as healthy, diet, plant-based diet etc. You will generate a range of results from others who rank highly for these search terms.

2 Investigate their profiles, in particular, look at the way they design their pages, speak to their followers and also engage with others.

3 Consider the number of followers they have and level of engagement per post.

4 Also consider where they are based geographically and whether you could see your target audience being similar to the types of people they are engaging with.

5 Conduct wider research on them to see what other people are saying about them and if they are promoting any similar brands or products to yours.

In addition, it is worth seeking out recommendations or commissioning an agency to work on the selection process on your behalf.

Another big issue that you will need to navigate is the rise of influencers buying followers using bots or zombie accounts to inflate their influence.

The question is how you can spot whether an influencer is using fake followers or genuine ones. Well, the answer is simple. Genuine followers will have genuine interactions with an influencer, while fake follower interactions will range from none at worst to superficial at best.

Here is a checklist you can use to assess if followers are genuine.

Engagement rate	Track engagement rather than number of followers for starters.
Engagement type	Determine where engagement is coming from, if it's frequently unrecognisable groups it could be bots or a pod.
Follower location	Usually influencers have followers in a specific region where they are based, if the majority of their followers are elsewhere it merits further investigation.
Follower growth	Use https://socialblade.com/ to see how an influencer has gained their following. Unusual spikes should cause suspicion.

Approaching influencers

There are several ways that you can approach an influencer, which tend to fall into two categories: direct and indirect.

The direct route is when you identify an influencer through social media, perhaps once you have seen their posts and have begun to follow them for a while. You can contact them directly and see if they would be interested in working with you.

Alternatively, there are several influencer agencies or platforms that you can work with, such as Tribe (www.tribegroup.co) which is the indirect option. This would give you much greater visibility of the market and you can pick an influencer that really meets your target market's needs.

There are also a number of ways you can work with an influencer which are important to consider.

Influencer as content creator	Influencer as creator and distributor	Influencer as distributor
This is where the influencer becomes a content creator for your brand and uses your platform (not their own) to distribute the content. This is an emerging trend where influencers are establishing 'micro content agencies' for clients.	This is where the influencer creates the content and distributes it to their audience as well	This is where the influencer acts as a distribution channel for content not created by them but leverages their audience

Increasingly, companies are opting to use influencers as micro content creators (as discussed in the introduction), and therefore rather than considering their audience size they are more interested in the quality of content that they produce. Remember influencers know their audience intricately and since they should align with your own audience, they can become a valuable source of insight into what works and what doesn't. Therefore, they can become an important strategic partner over the long term that you can leverage in a number of ways.

Write down your reflections on the types of services you would use from an influencer, including strategic guidance, reach and content.

Negotiating with influencers

It's worth noting that influencers are typically paid through any of the following.

Pay per post — Involves paying influencers for each post they create

Pay per result — Involves paying influencers for every click-through, conversion or social media impression they generate

Barter — Free products and/or experiences

The amounts involved vary tremendously depending on the type of influencer and range from $1 million per post for celebrity influencers to around $20 to $30 per post for micro-influencers.

As a rough guide, rates range from $75 per post for an influencer with fewer than 10,000 followers to more than $500 per post for influencers with more than 100,000 followers in the micro-influencer segment. A recent study from Rakuten Marketing[7] in the UK found that marketers would pay up to £75,000 for a single post mentioning their brand by someone with over a million followers.

So you can see there is very wide variation in the pricing model, making it a rather unpredictable environment for marketers. However, quite often influencers are willing to offer their services in exchange for other intangibles such as exposure and association with brands that can help them achieve their goals. Therefore, as part of the negotiation process I would consider what are the things that you can offer that may enhance a deal for an influencer that may not necessarily cost you more money.

Finally, and interestingly, as the model evolves certain platforms such as Tribe allow brands to have less risky ways of working with influencers. For example, you can get influencers to actually create examples of work and only get paid if you use them.

Let's now move on to look at how you can measure your influencer marketing activities.

Step 4: Ways to amplify your message

So you are at a stage where you have chosen the influencers you want to work with and you want to ensure that you are generating the maximum amount of reach for your brand.

Here are a number of techniques to consider:

- Be creative with your content (see my guidance on creativity and storytelling) – the more it stands out the more likely it will grab people's attention.
- Post regularly and consistently using the latest tools such as YouTube's Short and Instagram Reels.
- Hashtags – use around five as this helps people search for your posts.
- Shift the emphasis to your followers – ask them to create content for you.
- Create engagement through discussions and competitions.
- Link up with other influencers.
- Advertise on platforms such as Insta Advertising.
- Use geo-tagging.
- Use the right keywords, check on Google Trends, Google Keyword Traffic Estimator or Google Keyword Planner or use UberSuggest. Make sure you have targeted keywords in your video title (especially in the beginning of your title).
- Use the same tags as other popular videos so you can become a suggested video.

Step 5: Measure campaigns and iteration

One of the most contentious and debated areas is how to measure the return on investment of influencer marketing campaigns. Therefore, to circumvent this it's worth considering putting measurement techniques in place from the outset.

Let's consider four techniques that you can use to measure your influencer marketing activities.

Technique 1: Establish campaign reach via followers, post impressions, and referral traffic

To examine influencer reach, measure the following key performance indicators (KPIs).

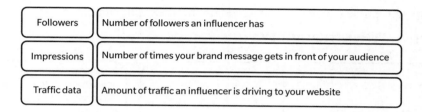

Followers	Number of followers an influencer has
Impressions	Number of times your brand message gets in front of your audience
Traffic data	Amount of traffic an influencer is driving to your website

Technique 2: Measure campaign engagement via clicks, likes, reactions, and shares

To measure the engagement an influencer brings to your brand, track these types of engagements.

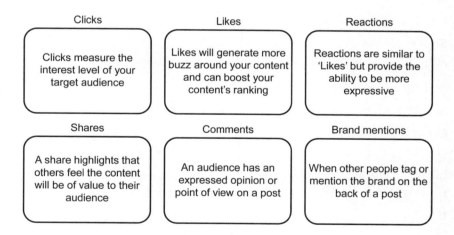

Clicks	Likes	Reactions
Clicks measure the interest level of your target audience	Likes will generate more buzz around your content and can boost your content's ranking	Reactions are similar to 'Likes' but provide the ability to be more expressive

Shares	Comments	Brand mentions
A share highlights that others feel the content will be of value to their audience	An audience has an expressed opinion or point of view on a post	When other people tag or mention the brand on the back of a post

Technique 3: Quantify social leads via Google Analytics' acquisition overview report

This is a technique to be able to determine the return on investment (ROI) of your influencer marketing campaign. You can do this using Google Analytics. In your GA dashboard go to Acquisition and then Overview to see your traffic channels. Next, in the list of traffic channels (Social, Organic Search), click Social. This will give you an understanding of whether your Instagram or Facebook strategy is working better. It's a strong indication that if your influencer is working in one platform then their content is working to drive traffic to your site.

Technique 4: Analyse the origin of sales via UTM parameters

There are three direct ways to measure sales conversion against your influencer campaign. Circle which one you would use to track your campaign.

Measure 1

Create affiliate links that influencers can use in their marketing efforts. So viewers click on the link and then make a purchase.

Measure 2

Promo codes are a good way to attribute sales. Similar to an affiliate link, customers simply input a unique promo code that can be traced back to an influencer.

Measure 3

Using Google Analytics Campaign URL Builder, you can add Urchin Tracking Module or UTM parameters to URLs to track your influencer campaign in Google Analytics. You then receive data about the site where the ad appears, the campaign name, keywords used, and more.

part 4

—

How to engage your customers

chapter 13

—

Develop a customer relationship management approach

We will now take a look at how you can use a variety of customer relationship management or CRM techniques to initially understand your customers and then put in place a range of proactive and reactive activities using tools such as email, instant messaging and even video messages, to remain front of mind, meet changing needs and maximise the value derived. To achieve this for your brand, you can utilise a framework that consists of what I call the four killer question model of CRM that we will go through.

Four killer question model

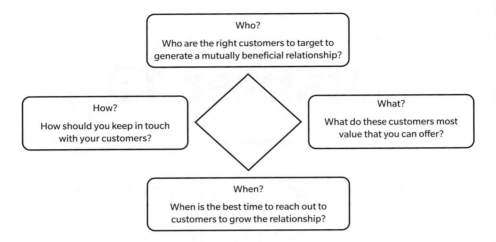

You would have no doubt heard the saying 'that it's cheaper to sell to an existing customer then to a new one'. This in many cases is certainly true but does not go far enough to explain the importance of nurturing strong mutually beneficial relationships with your customers. Often, companies rely on their ability to develop and grow these relationships over the long term in order to turn a profit.

Take for instance a typical example of purchasing an insurance policy. It is likely that beyond the product quality itself, the price to attract a new customer will consider the following:

- Endeavour to beat competitors in the market to attract new customers.
- Incorporate the cost to acquire the customer, for example, marketing spend.
- Consider the average anticipated cost to service the customer.
- Ability to up-sell the customer on to a higher package or buy more.
- Ability to retain the customer over a number of years to spread the acquisition costs.

Given the level of competition, it is highly likely that the overall costs to acquire and service a customer in the first year on a standard policy is either more or around the same as the premium charged. Therefore, the ability to get customers to buy more over time and stay for a number of years is not a 'nice to have' but an essential in order to run a business profitably. It works in exactly the same way across multiple industries from razor blades to utilities.

Regardless of the sector, CRM encompasses the techniques used to nurture the customer relationship over time to meet their changing needs. Traditionally, the way different industries achieved this was quite different. From fast-moving consumer goods that heavily focussed on repeat purchases to service industries such as telecommunications that focussed on stopping attrition or churn at renewal. However, increasingly all sectors are adopting more data-led approaches and beginning to form direct relationships with customers across each stage of the customer journey.

Let's get started on the four killer question model.

Who?

When developing your CRM approach the first thing you need to do is identify the right type of customers to focus on. At this stage, it is important to identify those customers that will deliver value to you and determine the optimal cost to service them while maintaining a high level of satisfaction.

Remember you do not have to generate equal profit from all customers nor give every customer the same treatment. Take for example an airline experience: in order to run a profitable airline you need a wide range of customers from economy to first-class passengers. They each arrive at their destination at the same time, yet the service experience, based on the value they give you, is completely different. It works the same way in all businesses, although perhaps it is not always that obvious.

To achieve this, you need to balance two viewpoints.

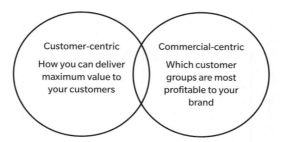

Customer-centric

How you can deliver maximum value to your customers

Commercial-centric

Which customer groups are most profitable to your brand

Importantly, within your existing customer base there will inevitably be customers who are more profitable to you than others and for a CRM approach to work effectively it's important to identify these differences in value. It will allow you to make much smarter decisions about how much you can afford to spend on acquiring, servicing and retaining certain customer groups over others.

To achieve this, you need to understand the different customer lifetime values (CLV) of your customers. This is the total amount of revenue and profit that you will earn from that customer over the lifetime of the relationship you have with them.

A great example of this is Amazon and its Prime membership option. Analysts estimate that the 'lifetime value' of a Prime membership customer is $2,283 compared to $916 for non-members.[1] Armed with this information, Amazon would make very different decisions about how they nurture its Prime customers versus non-Prime customers, not to mention where it would place its efforts to perhaps convert more customers to a Prime subscription.

In the same way, you need to develop a similar customer value analysis to determine different value segments so you can then put robust CRM strategies in place to increase their value in different ways. Let's see how you can do this.

There are a variety of factors that could feed into your CLV modelling that will be very context-dependent and beyond the scope of this book. Therefore for illustration purposes, I will use two common factors that are standard across multiple industries to present an estimation of CLV from a revenue perspective: frequency/number of product purchases and time as a retained customer. By combining these two factors we can break down all your customers into three segments: low, mid and high value. You will see in the low-value segment I have further broken it down into low/high potential as you have the ability to grow some of these customers while others have very little potential to do so.

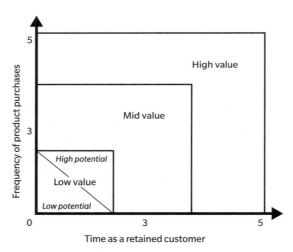

Customer lifetime value segmentation model

Here is the key.

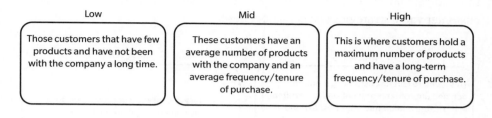

Low

Those customers that have few products and have not been with the company a long time.

Mid

These customers have an average number of products with the company and an average frequency/tenure of purchase.

High

This is where customers hold a maximum number of products and have a long-term frequency/tenure of purchase.

Now you have determined the groups there are a number of very tangible actions you can take.

The first is to determine how you intend on growing the value of each of these segments, for instance, turning your mid-value customers into high-value ones (in the same way Amazon would convert more non-Prime to Prime membership customers). This is illustrated below.

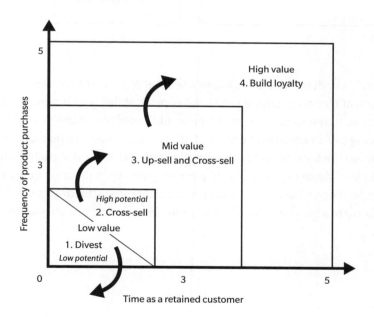

You will notice that there are a number of customer value strategies included that indicate how you can maximise the value of each segment. There are four customer value strategies you can adopt here.

Divest

This is where certain customer groups are deemed unprofitable and unlikely to be different in the future and therefore it's best to remove from the portfolio. If opting for a 'defensive' strategy this would be the first port of call in a bid to remove costs.

Cross-sell

Here is where you get customers to buy more relevant products from you from your portfolio.

Up-sell

Here is where you get customers to 'premiumise' their existing products with you.

Build loyalty

There comes a point where a customer segment is delivering all the value it can to the company and therefore the key strategy is to nurture them in order to keep them for as long as possible.

The second is to determine how you can profitably grow the relationship with each segment by understanding the level of profitability you require from each. For example, in the same way an airline would know how much they can spend on servicing say an economy versus a first-class passenger. To do this, you need to determine the level of revenue generated and cost to service each group. This will give you a sense of gross margin per group and then more strategic decisions can be taken to determine how much further investment you would like to make when growing the value of each group. Here is an example illustration.

Segment	Revenue per product per customer per year		Number of years	Average total lifetime Revenue per customer	Average total cost to service	Margin	CRM strategy
Low	$100 + NA + NA$	×	1	= 100	− 74	= 26	Determine how much margin to use on growing the relationship using the four customer value strategies outlined above
Medium	$65 + 45 + 55$	×	2	= 330	− 240	= 90	
High	$35 + 55 + 75 + 25 + 10$	×	3	= 600	− 400	= 200	

It's worth remembering a simple formula: the more products a customer has with you the more 'sticky' or loyal they become. Hence, why in the low and mid-value segments by increasing the frequency of product purchases, you are increasing the time the customer is likely to stay with you. In the high-level segment, a customer has largely saturated the number of products they are likely to buy from you and therefore the approach needs to be to do everything you can (within reason) to keep them for as long as possible.

Here is a blank template for you to use for your own brand.

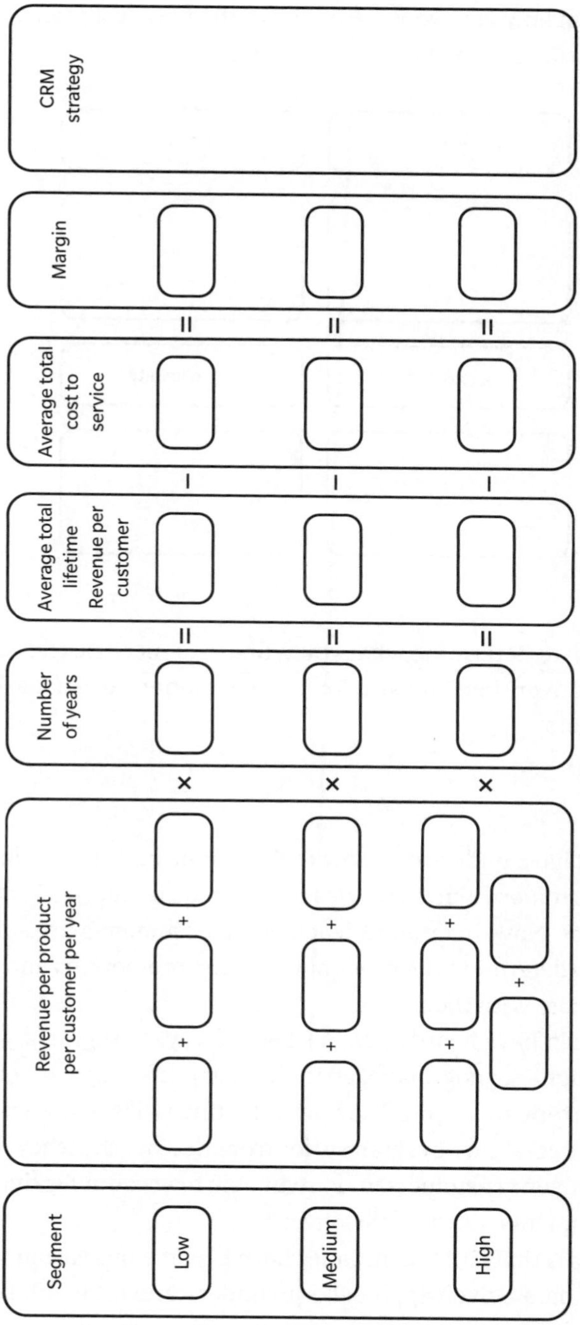
Segment
Low
Medium
High
Revenue per product per customer per year
Number of years
Average total lifetime Revenue per customer
Average total cost to service
Margin
CRM strategy

Now write down how you would use each of the four customer value strategies above to maximise the value of your customers.

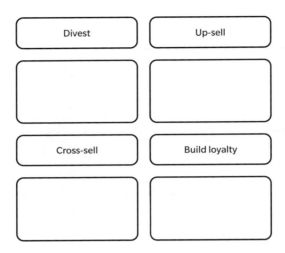

Divest	Up-sell

Cross-sell	Build loyalty

Let's now move on to determine what you will use to increase the value of each of these segments over time and also look at what more we can learn about these segments using data.

What?

To this point, you have understood how to determine customer value and consider different customer value strategies to use on different segments to grow these relationships. Now, in order to reach out to customers with something valuable you need to determine the types of products, promotions and offers that would most resonate with them.

You will no doubt have heard about a range of ways to segment your customers from demographics, geographic, attitudinal and life-stage, all of which are undeniably important and typically act as a starting point to understand your customer's preferences. However, all suffer from the fact that they make generalisations about your customers and are unable to account for dynamically changing environments in which they live.

The good news is that CRM techniques have become increasingly sophisticated. They use data-driven approaches to understand individual customer behaviours and then respond with appropriate offers and solutions that consider a customer's circumstances and context in real time. Over time, these get more personalised in nature. You can use tools such as Personyze (www.personyze.com/) to achieve this. It works like this.

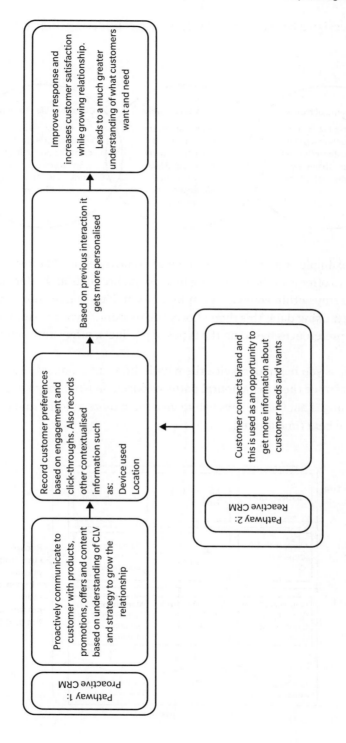

You need to design a behavioural CRM approach considering three key components.

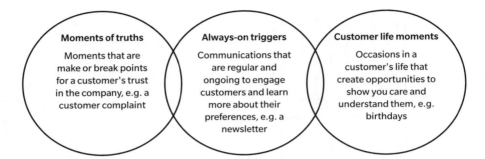

Below is an example of how all these elements come together. The key to identifying what to offer is in the beginning to keep the products and offers wide, ensuring you stay within your CLV margin limits and aligned to your customer value strategy. Using data, this then allows you to identify your customers' behavioural preferences based on the types of products, offers and content they choose.

Over time, as you begin to service them with different products, offers and content you can see their behavioural patterns based on what they are clicking on and choosing. That then allows you to give them more tailored and personalised offers the next time around.

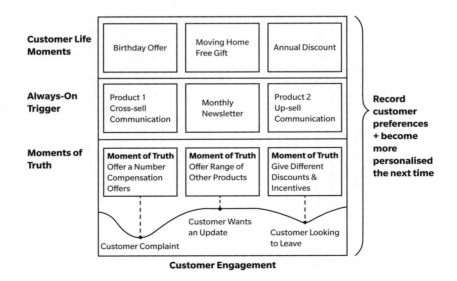

Here are some examples of where each of the components become relevant to build into your CRM plan.

Moments of truth
- Customer complaints
- Updates on their service
- Response when they get in touch
- At renewal

Always-on triggers
- Cross-sell communications
- Up-sell communications
- Monthly newsletters

Customer life moments
- Birthdays
- Anniversaries
- Life events, e.g. having children or moving home

Use this template to determine the types of behavioural triggers you will use in your CRM approach.

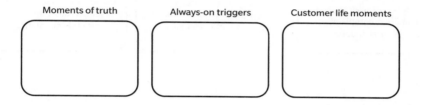

Moments of truth

Always-on triggers

Customer life moments

Here is a blank template that you can use to populate your products and offers that acts as the first point for you to learn more about your customer's preferences.

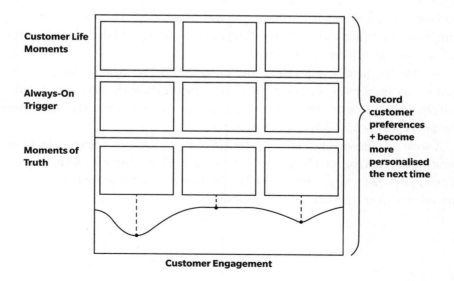

Customer Life Moments

Always-On Trigger

Moments of Truth

Record customer preferences + become more personalised the next time

Customer Engagement

Now let's move on to determine when the right time to contact your customers is.

When?

There is certainly an art of sending communications to your customers at the right moment in time. Many studies out there will each tell you slightly different things about when is the best time to reach out to your customers. To really get to the bottom of this, you need to divide your communications into three areas.

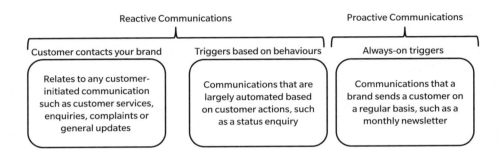

Let's take each one in turn.

Reactive communications: customer contacts your brand

In this instance, it is important to prioritise a customer's communication when it has originated from them. Customers today expect access to companies 24/7 and want very fast response times (even within minutes). This can pose challenges to your brand especially if selling internationally and therefore requires support across different time zones.

In these instances it is advantageous to use technology to aid in the process and seamless delivery of customer services, whether it be through automated telephony channels or your website. The more personalised you can make these instant types of communications the better.

A good and increasingly effective tool to use are chatbots, delivered by Drift (www.drift.com) or Intercom (www.intercom.com). It overcomes a customer's frustration where they may have had to fill in a form and wait for it to be attended to over a period of 24 to 48 hours.

It is a sophisticated version of live chat on your website, but rather than having people at the end of the line you use artificial intelligence or AI to work through the best answer for the client and deliver it to them in real time. It's pretty unique and does have an option to switch to a human at any point when it realises that the question is out of reach for the bot. However, since it uses machine learning, the next time someone asks the same question it will be prepared with the answer.

Reactive communications: triggers based on behaviours

These are usually communications that are automated and triggers based on certain customer interactions. The immediacy of these is very important as a customer has just completed a certain action that you deem important or relevant to deliver a follow-up communication, whether that be a service or marketing communication.

Proactive communications: always-on triggers

These types of communications are when your brand sends customers communications proactively, ranging from newsletters to cross-sell or up-sell communications. The optimal time to send these communications to your customers is based on several factors, including:

- type of communication – a service notice versus a cross-sell communication versus a monthly newsletter
- channel of communication – email versus a text message
- seasonal factors such as holidays
- even a customer's individual schedule
- stage of relationship with customer – are they coming to renewal?
- the context of the customer – what and where are the customer when they receive the communication?

When you combine all these factors, there can be no perfect time to send a customer a proactive communication. Rather you are looking for the optimal time to maximise open and click-through rates at an aggregate level.

To achieve this, you want to create a testing structure to determine what works best for your customers. Here is a template you can use for this.

Time	Monday Communication Open and Click Rate		Tuesday Communication Open and Click Rate		Wednesday Communication Open and Click Rate		Thursday Communication Open and Click Rate		Friday Communication Open and Click Rate	
09:00										
10:00										
11:00										
12:00										
13:00										
14:00										
15:00										
16:00										
17:00										
18:00										
19:00										
20:00										
21:00										
22:00										
23:00										
00:00										
01:00										
02:00										
03:00										
04:00										
05:00										
06:00										
07:00										
08:00										

How?

The final part of developing your CRM approach is to consider how you are going to communicate with your customers – through which channels. Today, there are so many channels you can reach your customers on from email to instant messaging that you need to decide which ones are most appropriate for your customer base. There are two key considerations here.

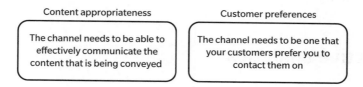

Content appropriateness

The channel needs to be able to effectively communicate the content that is being conveyed

Customer preferences

The channel needs to be one that your customers prefer you to contact them on

Content appropriateness

There are certain communications that are more conducive to specific channels than others. In addition, some channels create more immediacy than others which can be used depending on the urgency and confidential nature of the communication and necessary action.

Here is a table to help you assess this for your communications.

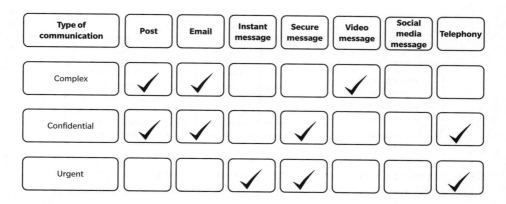

Type of communication	Post	Email	Instant message	Secure message	Video message	Social media message	Telephony
Complex	✓	✓			✓		
Confidential	✓	✓		✓			✓
Urgent			✓	✓			✓

Customer preferences

At the same time, you need to ensure that you are only communicating with customers in a way they want you to. Typically, at the beginning of a relationship your brand would ask customers for their channel preferences when getting them to sign up. Importantly, you must allow your customers to update these preferences at any time. This not only creates greater trust between your brand and the customer but also ensures that you are building the relationship in the right way.

It can sometimes be quite challenging to maintain a list of all your customers' contact preferences and therefore it is often easier to use automated CRM tools such as Salesforce (www.salesforce.com) or Active Campaigns (www.active-campaign.com/).

Predictive analytics

To this point, you have used CRM to not only give your customers an enhanced experience while also increasing the value for your brand. During the course of this process you have also begun to collect some incredibly powerful data about your customers value, product and content preferences, behaviours and optimal times and channels to use to connect. When you combine all this information it allows you to build a very accurate picture of your customer and also on an aggregate level begin to make predictions about likely actions and future requirements.

Here are a number of areas in which this can be useful to you:

Next best action	Changes in customer circumstances	Customer attrition
Predicts what a customer is likely to be interested in/purchase next	Detects certain changes in a customer's life that may trigger new needs and wants	Predicts certain behaviours that indicate a customer may churn away from your brand

It's important to develop your capability in this area using a range of different tools such as Teradata (www.teradata.co.uk) or Personyze (www.personyze.com).

Amazon presents a good example[2] of how it is able to use 'next best action' predictive analytics based on recent browsing and purchase history to determine what customers may also prefer and offer it to them both in real time as well as in its CRM communications later on. Furthermore, this also helps when presenting offers, promotions and even rewards as they are more tailored to what a customer's future needs are likely to be.

Permissions and regulations

An increasingly important area for you to consider is regulations when it comes to data storage, processing and how you use this data. Depending on where you are reading this book, you will likely have a set of regulations that you need to adhere to, although there are many commonalities between them. These regulations are aimed at protecting individuals and their privacy, and ensuring you follow them is not only a legal requirement but also leads to a greater amount of trust.

Across the European Union (EU), the General Data Protection Regulation or GDPR is in force that governs how EU citizen data is handled and processed, even outside of the EU. Penalties for mishandling data carry high penalties, with a maximum fine of 20 million euros or 4% of the total annual worldwide turnover in the preceding year, whichever is higher.

It has seven key principles that must be adhered to.

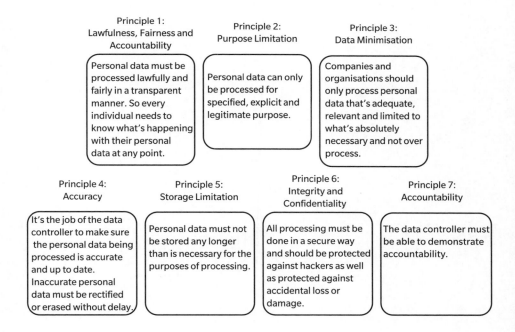

Principle 1:
Lawfulness, Fairness and Accountability

Personal data must be processed lawfully and fairly in a transparent manner. So every individual needs to know what's happening with their personal data at any point.

Principle 2:
Purpose Limitation

Personal data can only be processed for specified, explicit and legitimate purpose.

Principle 3:
Data Minimisation

Companies and organisations should only process personal data that's adequate, relevant and limited to what's absolutely necessary and not over process.

Principle 4:
Accuracy

It's the job of the data controller to make sure the personal data being processed is accurate and up to date. Inaccurate personal data must be rectified or erased without delay.

Principle 5:
Storage Limitation

Personal data must not be stored any longer than is necessary for the purposes of processing.

Principle 6:
Integrity and Confidentiality

All processing must be done in a secure way and should be protected against hackers as well as protected against accidental loss or damage.

Principle 7:
Accountability

The data controller must be able to demonstrate accountability.

For more detailed guidance, it's worth visiting the ICO website: https://ico.org.uk/for-organisations/guide-to-data-protection/guide-to-the-general-data-protection-regulation-gdpr/

chapter 14

The power of smartphone marketing

We will now take a close look at the opportunities that smartphone marketing presents to you and your brand to engage your audiences and expand across markets. We will look at the different ways you can market and advertise your message across this channel using the following methods.

It will probably come as no surprise to you that on average we spend around three hours a day on our mobile devices.[1] The amount of time per day increases when you look at younger demographics, suggesting that this trend towards a mobile-centric world is here to stay and likely to increase over time.

But perhaps more interesting is the way in which these devices are used, with the most popular ways being:[2]

- social media
- music
- gaming
- shopping.

In addition, it's also worth noting that the vast majority of the time is spent on smartphone apps (think Facebook, Spotify or Amazon app), compared to the web browser on the phone. However, interestingly the latter actually gets used more frequently overall but for shorter durations.[3]

In many ways smartphone marketing is the final frontier for marketers allowing them to reach new audiences around the world in a personalised way and even in places that have been hard to reach through conventional marketing channels, with increasing sophistication where certain apps can even determine a user's mood based on artificial intelligence!. There are clearly two major enablers of this. The first is mobile penetration where today over 70%[4] of the world population have access to a mobile phone. The second is access to cost-effective and high-speed mobile data, which is unevenly distributed globally. For instance, the cost of 1GB of data in India is $0.09 the cheapest in the world, compared to say Bermuda at almost $29 being one of the most expensive places.[5] In addition, it is likely that as 5G becomes more ingrained that the potential of mobile marketing will increase significantly as well.

There is a third element to consider: social media mobile marketing, but since it equally applies to other devices as well I have covered it in other chapters (refer to Chapters 7, 8 and 9).It is worth noting that a large part of mobile marketing encompasses many other marketing elements covered throughout this book, so rather than repeat these points I will signpost you to the relevant chapter to learn more.

Information and service app-based marketing

As we have noted, information and service apps are where the majority of people spend their time on their mobile phones and therefore present the greatest opportunity to market through this channel. There are two ways to achieve this.

Own app real estate	Communicate through other third-party apps
Ability to market to your customers through your own app	Place communications in other third-party apps where most people spend their time

Own app real estate

You have the ability to market to your customers through your own app, using a variety of UX and CRM techniques (see Chapters 15 and 13, respectively). In addition, there are a number of channel-specific considerations to maximise the effectiveness of mobile marketing through your app.

The first is the ability to do push notifications that can be relevant information or even time-sensitive offers. For example, Deliveroo regularly gives its customers preferential deals within a limited timeframe.

The second is that you can create reward and loyalty programmes that can be redeemed using the app and therefore store interesting insights and information on your customer's buying habits. For example, Pret launched an industry-first coffee subscription service in the UK where subscribers can order up to five coffees a day all regulated by the app.[6] It records data such as when a customer redeems their coffee, from which store and the frequency of their purchase.

The third is that you can create engaging content and dedicate certain real estate spaces to raise awareness of certain products and services that you offer using banners, pop-ups and text ads. These can even be dynamic at certain times, either when your user is in a certain location (more to come on this), at a certain point in their in-app journey or certain time of day.

Finally, given the rise of voice-activated commands such as Siri and Alexa, it is likely that more people are going to use this technology for tasks such as search and shopping. Being able to use this to your advantage on your app will become increasingly important. You can even build and integrate Alexa Skills into your app – see https://developer.amazon.com

Write down your thoughts on which areas you can adopt.

Communicate through other third-party apps

In order to communicate through other third-party apps you have the ability to use a number of ad networks or exchanges (much like programmatic advertising that we discussed in Chapter 9). In the mobile world, many of the networks differ depending on whether you want to advertise on apps that are on iOS (the Apple operating system) or Android. There are ad networks that also cater for both.

AdColony https://www.adcolony.com/	Admob https://admob.google.com	Airpush https://airpush.com/
With AdColony, publishers can show video ads during in-app usage. Popular with game developers to show ads in-between levels	Owned by Google, it allows you to have four types of ads available: • banner ads • video ads • native ads • full-page interstitials ads	Offers up to 12 different ad formats, some of which include: • push notifications • video ads • overlay ads • rich media ads • post-click landing page ads • in-app banners

Investigate each of these networks and circle the one that you think would be most suited to your brand. These networks enable you to have your adverts on other apps in a highly targeted way. In addition to these exchanges, you can also take advantage of social media mobile advertising, through the mainstream social media platforms such as Facebook and Instagram. We have covered how these work in Chapter 8 so do refer to this chapter for a more detailed understanding of targeting options as well.

Another very highly relevant trend is the rise of podcast marketing. The number of people tuning into podcast is increasing. IAB suggests that around 8 million people listen to podcasts each week in the UK alone.[7] This creates significant opportunities to integrate your brand message into this channel, either within the podcast or around it. It works in the same way as networks described above, and platforms such as Podscribe (www.adswizz.com/) allow you to create highly contextualised marketing opportunities that cut across a variety of podcasts.

Write down the type of advertising formats you think would be most relevant for your brand – banner ads, video ads and so on.

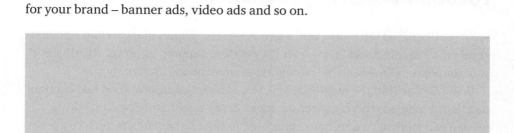

In-game mobile app marketing

The next way to market is through in-game mobile marketing. In fact, e-sports and mobile gaming has seen a considerable increase in recent years, particularly with the rise of virtual and augmented reality games and faster data speeds with the onset of 5G. It is set to exceed a total value of over $166 billion in 2020 and be the largest gaming platform of any.[8] This makes it prime territory to market your brand across this platform to reach new audiences in creative ways. There are a number of specific opportunities to achieve this to consider.

The first is the ability to advertise around the gaming experience, for instance, below the game or in-between the loading of a game. You can do so by using one of the ad exchanges above.

The second is product placement within mobile games which allows people to interact with your brand often in a subtle but effective way. For example, you could create quizzes, banners or other animations in the gaming experience that your users can choose to engage with that have subtle hints, cues and prizes for positive action. This technique is becoming increasingly popular for more immersive experiences such as virtual reality games where players can actually use real money to buy items within the game – just the way they would in the real world.

The third is where the actual key players become influencers and you can partner with them for product endorsements or other promotions (see Chapter 12 on influencer marketing for more details).

Finally, you have the ability to actually create hybrid gaming experiences combining augmented reality (AR) to gamify offline experiences. For example, Pokemon Go is a great example of this where you can integrate the real world with your gaming experience. Using this technique, you can create a buzz by getting people to learn more about your product and services in say the physical environment using AR on your mobile to pick up points and prizes.

Location-based app marketing

We have discussed the merits and a number of techniques of location-based marketing in Chapters 8 and 9; however it's worth re-capping its power to influence your audiences when used in the context of smartphone marketing.

Using GPS within the mobile device, you can service information and communications based on where someone is located, say near a store or even within a section of a store once they have consented to this. To help illustrate, let's use a customer journey analysis framework in the context of a coffee shop to highlight how we can leverage mobile marketing in this way. Let's break the journey down into three stages.

Attracting customers to the coffee shop

In the first stage, you need to get customers into the coffee shop. Using location-based information when they are in close proximity you can:

- send a push notification to their app when they are close to the coffee shop with:
  - time-bound offers
  - specials of the day
  - menu highlighting previous orders
- invite them to pre-order and pay on the app so they do not need to wait to collect, for example, Starbucks allows people to achieve this through their app
- highlight the benefits and rewards of immediate purchases to make it more attractive to get them to want to come in.

In-store interactions and journey

In the second stage, you can use location-based marketing tools such as beacons to determine where someone is in the store so you can determine the types of items that may be of interest. Here are a number of ways you can maximise this opportunity:

- Get your customers to 'check-in' when they enter the coffee shop.

- Send notifications of particular items based on where someone is in the store.
- Offer complimentary suggestions to items that may be of interest.
- Order directly from their table using menus in their app and QR codes to record which table they are on.
- Use augmented reality to present more nutritional information on the items.
- Use QR codes or other technology so people can self-pay using the app, which means they do not have to queue – Amazon Go has no checkouts and allows customers to add things into their shopping basket and walk out as they are charged through the app.

Post-purchase

In the final stage, you can continue the engagement with your customers using location-specific tools once they have left the coffee shop:

- Get them to redeem their points or rewards with partners which they can be notified of when they pass relevant areas.
- Foster a community allowing them to see other 'members' in their local area.
- Determine their behaviours and regular routes and encourage them to pop in.

As you can see from the above, there are so many ways that you can use location-based marketing to really get closer to your customer and add additional value to them. Use the template below to determine how you could use this technique at each stage of the customer journey for your brand.

Attracting customers	In-store interactions and journey	Post-purchase

chapter 15

Conversion rate optimisation and UX design

In this chapter, we are going to explore a range of techniques that you need to consider when developing your conversion rate optimisation and user experience design plan. We are going to cover two critical points in the journey and look at how you can optimise each.

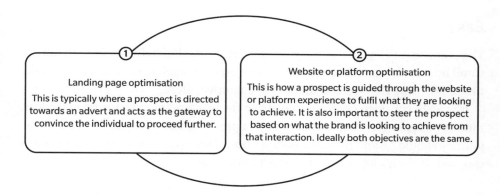

① Landing page optimisation
This is typically where a prospect is directed towards an advert and acts as the gateway to convince the individual to proceed further.

② Website or platform optimisation
This is how a prospect is guided through the website or platform experience to fulfil what they are looking to achieve. It is also important to steer the prospect based on what the brand is looking to achieve from that interaction. Ideally both objectives are the same.

Conversion rate optimisation

Conversion rate optimisation, or CRO for short, is a discipline within marketing that begins once a user has clicked through on to your website. It is the process of 'nudging' them to carry out certain desired actions that can range from filling in a form to purchasing what you have to offer. It forms part of the overall UX design of a website or platform that aims to create a seamless experience for the user.

Before diving into these specific areas, it's worth noting that at the heart of CRO and UX design lies the cross-section of two key disciplines that need to be combined to create what is known as 'design thinking'.

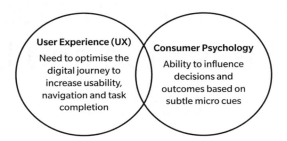

There is an approach developed by the UK government's Behavioural Insights Team known as EAST (easy, attractive, social and timely) that encompasses both these disciplines and is useful to consider when implementing a CRO and UX approach.

Let's take each aspect in turn.

Easy

The premise is to 'make it as easy' as possible for the individual to both understand how to navigate through the website and to complete the tasks they would like to do, using the minimal amount of cognitive effort.

It's worth considering the journey from the user's point of view and make it as intuitive as possible. People tend to have a preconceived expectation of how the journey should be and the more your journey lines up with this, the more at ease they will feel – it's like a form of confirmation bias.

Consider how you can implement these.

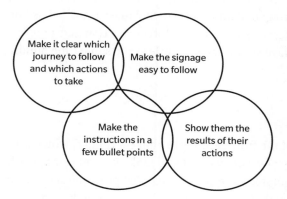

Attractive

Every page has roughly seven seconds to grab attention[1] so you have an incredibly short amount of time to entice and engage a user to want to complete the task. Part of making the experience attractive is to demonstrate the following.

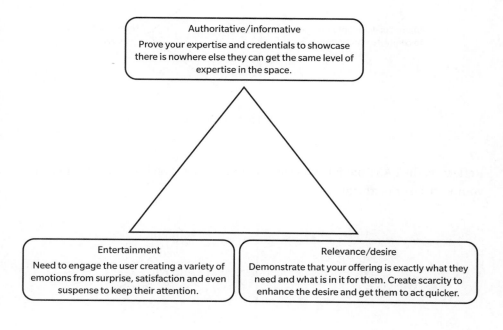

Social

A key technique to influence a change of perception is to use 'other people in your social group or community' to feel like this, which is known as social proofing. This acts as a positive reinforcement that gets people to be influenced by others who have similar needs while at the same time building comfort and trust.

Timely

The final part of the framework is to 'make it timely', which is to consider how to create a sense of urgency to act and make it as quick as possible to go through the journey. A notable example for this CRO principle is posts on booking.com encouraging customers to hasten the decision of making a reservation as it might be booked by another customer if they don't.

Here are four areas for you to track.

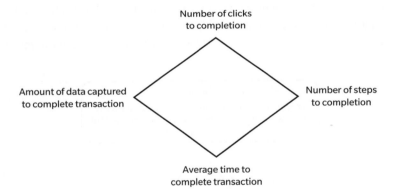

Reflect on the EAST model and write down your notes on how it could apply to your website or platform journey.

Landing page

The first question you may ask is why should I bother having a landing page when I can just direct people to my website? The answer is simple: it leads to better conversion as you can be very specific to answer the exact intent your prospect is looking for. You can also segment these pages more effectively than your main site and have bespoke engagement strategies for different audiences, for example, an offer on a certain landing page versus another.

There are a range of strategies you should adopt when creating your landing pages. Here is a summary:

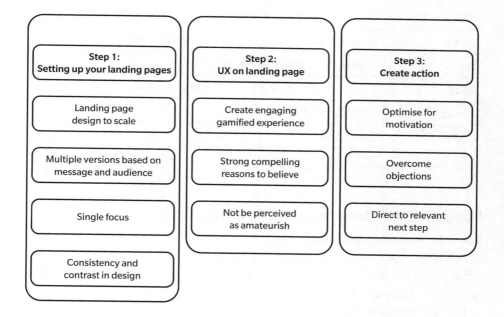

Step 1: Setting up your landing pages

Landing page design to scale

The first thing you need to do is to create your landing page templates in a way that both easily scale but are also mobile optimised. They must also be SEO-friendly to ensure that they rank in for search terms related to the proposition. You can easily create your landing pages using templates from companies such as Unbounce (https://unbounce.com/).

Here is a template structure for a landing page that is useful to adopt.

	Navigational Intent Landing Page Brief
H1 Title	Design, Make or Create [Keyword]
Text	Create [Keyword] with Canva's free [Keyword] Maker
Button	> Start Designing Your [Keyword]
Sentence	Let your personal style shine. Create your own custom [Keyword] for your laptop, desktop and phone
Image	Product showcasing ideal asset
H2 Title	Make a picture-perfect [Keyword] for your phone or computer
Body	2 paragraphs w/3 keyword references
CTA	> Open a New [Keyword] Design
Title	How To Create a Custom [Keyword] in just a few clicks
List	5 Steps or Tips For Creating [Keyword]
Body	2-3 Paragraphs w/ 2 H1s referencing keywords
Accordion	2-3 FAQ in re: [Keyword]
Quote	Testimonial

Source: https://foundationinc.co/lab/canva-seo

Multiple versions based on message and audience

It may seem obvious but it's important to ensure that you match your advert to your landing page. Whatever entices your prospect to click on your ad must be reflected on the landing page they then see. Otherwise it's likely they will leave without paying any further attention.

It is sometimes easier said than done, especially when you have multiple landing pages based on multiple products, a prospects search intent or query and different markets that you serve. For example, Canva has over a hundred different landing pages that each target different keywords and audiences.

It is also important to tailor your landing page based on the advert and/or keywords of the likely search intent of the prospect. This way it will appear on search results as well as be familiar and relevant to the person when they click through to it.

Here is a template that you can use to detail each landing page.

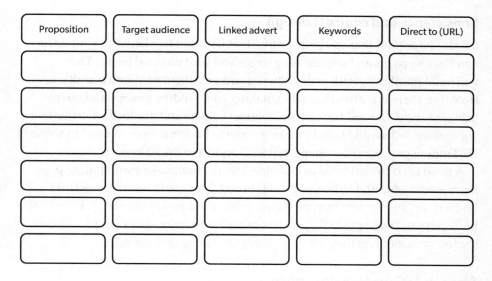

Proposition	Target audience	Linked advert	Keywords	Direct to (URL)

Single focus

A landing page should have a single focus, with one clear action that you would like your prospect to take action on. Oli Gardner from Unbounce calls this 'attention ratio' to mean the number of things you can do on a page versus what you want people to do. For instance, if you include two links to articles, one social media page and an action to fill out a form, the primary purpose for the landing page, in essence you have created a ratio of 4:1. However, the closer to 1:1, the better to ensure you get maximum conversion on the single action you want the person to achieve.

To achieve this, consider the following.

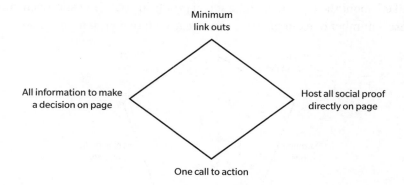

Minimum
link outs

All information to make
a decision on page

Host all social proof
directly on page

One call to action

Consistency and contrast design

It's also important that you gain a consistent look and feel between your advert and landing pages and your landing pages and your directed pages. This will build familiarity with your audience and give them a smooth transition. However, there is nothing wrong in making your landing pages stand out by using eye-catching and fun visuals, contrast colours and gradients. Furthermore, you can use videos and GIFs to make it come to life even more. A good example is the landing page for the Jumanji movie. Google it to take a look.

A good tip is to also build in custom elements that make your landing page more memorable and in line with your brand. This could be anything from imagery to unique fonts or even the way that you develop your copy. Often the more minimalistic approach, perhaps using white space, gives your headlines greater standout and they are more likely they are to get noticed.

Step 2: UX on landing page

Create engaging gamified experiences

As you have learnt at the beginning of this chapter there is a need to combine being authoritative, relevant and entertaining in order to keep your prospect engaged. A good way to achieve this is to combine a high degree of interactivity, in a gamified way, on the landing page. This will help increase the time your prospect spends on your pages, increasing the likelihood of conducting your desired call to action. A good platform for off-the-shelf interactivity you can use is Genially (www.genial.ly). Another good method is to make your data capture forms interactive using the likes of Leadformly (https://leadformly.com).

Strong compelling reasons to believe

We talked about the need to include social proofs in your CRO approach, and here are a number of examples you can integrate into your landing page.

Not to be perceived as amateurish

It's important that the landing pages look professional and therefore extra care must be given to every detail from spelling to image quality. Furthermore, it needs to be compatible with all screen sizes and browsers. You can easily check this using Browserling (www.browserling.com/).

Step 3: Create action

Optimise for motivation

Often we devise actions that we want the prospect to take rather than consider the output. Think about how you can motivate them to act on something immediately by leveraging a range of cognitive bias. Two very popular techniques use these and it leads to much higher conversions, so consider integrating the following:

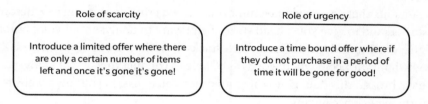

Role of scarcity

Introduce a limited offer where there are only a certain number of items left and once it's gone it's gone!

Role of urgency

Introduce a time bound offer where if they do not purchase in a period of time it will be gone for good!

Overcome objections

A good landing page would have already considered the type of objections that are likely to get typically raised and come up with responses for those. Here are some of the typical type of questions you may get objections on.

Can i return the product?

Can i get a free trial?

What is the warranty?

Can i pay in instalment?

How soon can i have it?

Direct to relevant next step

This last point may seem obvious, but by actually linking to a relevant next page is absolutely key to taking the journey to the next stage. All too often, landing pages have broken links or take the prospect to the homepage of the website when it should really go to the checkout page. Double-checking this each and every time is really important. Finally, do not forget to say thank you to the prospect for each action they complete with you – it will not go unnoticed.

Website or platform optimisation

Once your prospect has landed on your website or platform, it's fundamental that they feel reassured and comfortable as well as that it comes across as intuitive for them to complete their intended task. To achieve this requires constant iteration and testing, using a variety of techniques that we will discuss in the next chapter. For now, I will focus on providing you with a checklist of all the key elements that you need to be mindful of when crafting this journey. Before I get started and to give you a head start, if you want to analyse your competitors' design elements and the different 'tech stacks' that they use to create their UX go to www.builtwith.com where you will be able to conduct this useful analysis.

I have broken this down into three areas for you to assess your own website or platform experience against.

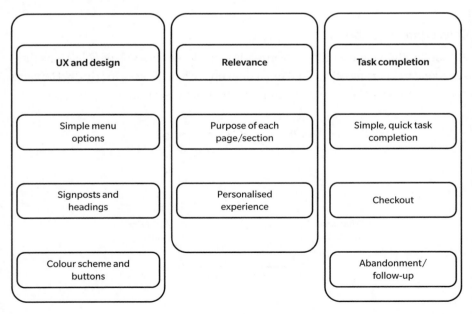

UX and design	Relevance	Task completion
Simple menu options	Purpose of each page/section	Simple, quick task completion
Signposts and headings	Personalised experience	Checkout
Colour scheme and buttons		Abandonment/ follow-up

UX and design

The most effective websites or platforms are those that have a very simple user interface and design. Think about Google's website. The key to its success is that you immediately know the single most important thing you need to do on it – type in what you are searching for. There is no ambiguity. It is obvious and intuitive.

Simple menu options

I cannot overemphasize just how important choosing the right menu structure for your website is, bearing in mind that it may need to dynamically change to fit different screen sizes. A menu is the first thing someone will look for on your site and it will give them a sense of what the site is about, acts as a sitemap and gives people a 'pin' of where they are at as they browse your site.

Here are a range of menu options to choose from and when it's best to apply each.

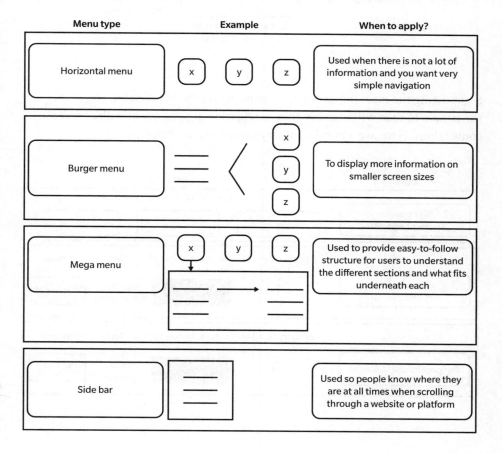

Signposts and headings

The most important signposts are headings. These sit within the website and act as a single port of call to highlight what the page is about. Great headlines require a combination of copywriting and design skills. Here is some of the key considerations when creating your headings:

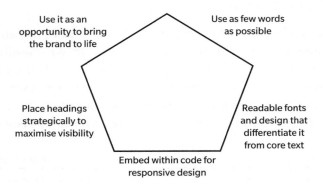

Signposting the most important information and the actions that you would like the person to take will improve their navigation experience and also increase conversions. Here are a number of ways you can use signposts.

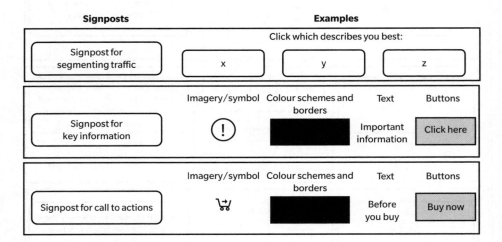

Colour schemes, symmetry and buttons

One way to differentiate the different elements of your website is through the use of a colour scheme to denote different things. There are a variety of ways you can use colour schemes from differentiating between sections, products or to highlight important information. The first thing you need to do is to choose and adopt a consistent colour palette throughout your website that is in line with your brand.

Once you have done this, assign different colours for different purposes. Use this template to help you determine how you can use different colours in different sections of the website to help highlight key pieces of information.

Colour	Section	Rational
Dark blue	Use in all pages relating to product 1	Becomes associated with product 1

It is also important to create symmetry throughout the website, so when someone is clicking from one element to the next there is a sense of familiarity and commonality to the way the navigation works. It's a careful balance between trying to differentiate each element and yet maintaining uniformity so people don't get confused or worried that they have suddenly left the site.

There is certainly both a science and art to creating buttons that people just automatically want to click on. Drawing people towards these buttons and then enticing them to click is perhaps the most important aspect of getting them to take an action. Therefore, button design itself needs to be given careful consideration. There are two aspects of this.

First is button principles.

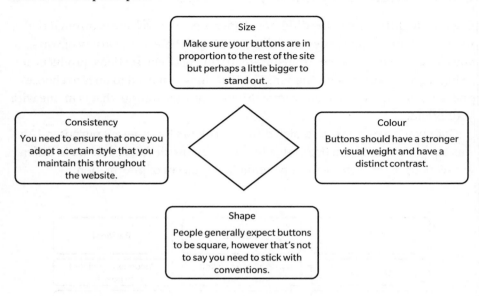

And second is the types of buttons.

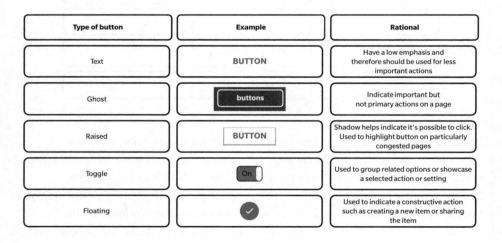

Type of button	Example	Rational
Text	**BUTTON**	Have a low emphasis and therefore should be used for less important actions
Ghost	**buttons**	Indicate important but not primary actions on a page
Raised	BUTTON	Shadow helps indicate it's possible to click. Used to highlight button on particularly congested pages
Toggle	On	Used to group related options or showcase a selected action or setting
Floating	✓	Used to indicate a constructive action such as creating a new item or sharing the item

Relevance and purpose of each page or section

It's important to navigate the user to the relevant pages that may be of interest to them and then focus on bringing that value to life on the page. This can be achieved by using a range of the following elements.

Summary statements	This is where you have short and concise statements about the item and include the benefits to the user. It should be clear and unambiguous, demonstrating the value they get for the price paid.
Infographics	Use a range of visuals such as tables, diagrams and infographics to explain exactly what the proposition is and how it will benefit the individual.
Demonstrations	This is where you can effectively use video demonstrations to bring to life how the item could be used in a real environment. By understanding your target customer you can customise the video to be relevant for them so they know the benefit they would have if they purchased the item.
Case studies	Getting your existing customers or clients to talk about how they are using the item and how much it benefits them will encourage other similar people to want to give it a try as well.
Results	Being able to have proven results, for instance, by conducting studies you can reassure people that this item delivers the value you suggest.

Personalised experience

Taking the previous point one step further, rather than demonstrating the benefits of the item to others, if you can create a level of personalisation on your website or platform to really narrow in on what the user is looking for, you will be on to a winner. Furthermore, you should also consider how you can customise the end-to-end experience to make it more personalised for them.

A good example of an organisation that achieves this level of personalisation is Air Asia (www.airasia.com). If you visit its website it is likely that no two customer experiences will be the same. It uses machine learning to predict your likely product purchases, behaviours and even context from which you entered the site from. Using over 75 million customer data points allows it to deliver you a highly personalised experience and service the most relevant products to you first. So, for example, if you are more likely to buy hotels as compared to activities based on your purchase history, the website will then display the hotels carousel before the activities one.[2]

For those of us who do not have the luxury of such an extensive dataset, do not despair as there are a range of ways that you can achieve a level of personalisation across your experience. Here are a number of ideas to consider:

- Have a log-in section with previous interactions and purchase history logged making it very easy to re-order.
- Create self-help guides and diagnosis tools such as calculator or interactive surveys.
- Allow users to customise items before purchase.

Simple and quick task completion

The faster you can get someone to complete the task you would like them to, the higher the likelihood that they will do so. Therefore, for every step in the way is a potential barrier and should be minimised. Here is an interesting study of the number of clicks you need to open a bank account across the various institutions in the UK.

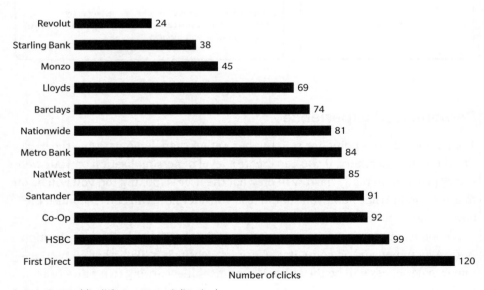

Number of clicks

Source: https://builtformars.co.uk/banks/

Here are a number of ways to get them to complete more efficiently:

- Monitor how many clicks it takes from the start of the journey to the end and remove unnecessary steps.
- Only collect essential information to make it less cumbersome for the user.
- Do not present too many options or the ability to link out.
- Encourage the user to continue through interactivity and gamification.
- Reward them for each step closer to the outcome.

Checkout

Your prospect is almost there and is at the final stage: the checkout. However, despite being so close you need to get them over the line. Here are a number of the most common reasons why people do not follow through with a purchase at this stage.

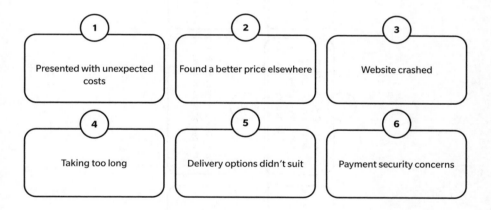

Now you understand why people do not complete, you should put measures in place to mitigate against these. Here are eight approaches you can take to maximise conversion at checkout.

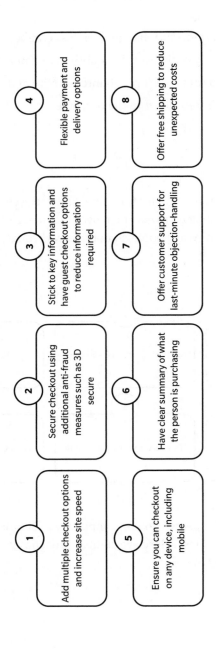

1. Add multiple checkout options and increase site speed

2. Secure checkout using additional anti-fraud measures such as 3D secure

3. Stick to key information and have guest checkout options to reduce information required

4. Flexible payment and delivery options

5. Ensure you can checkout on any device, including mobile

6. Have clear summary of what the person is purchasing

7. Offer customer support for last-minute objection-handling

8. Offer free shipping to reduce unexpected costs

Abandonment follow-up

It is inevitable, for the reasons described above, that some people will abandon completion at the final stages. Since they have shown such high purchase or task completion intent it's certainly worth trying to nudge them into doing so. This is where you can follow up with them as a way to encourage completion. There are a number of ways you can achieve this from subtle reminders that they need to complete the task, to offering additional incentives to do so. For instance, many airlines will send an email to those who abandoned their shopping cart at the last minute with a promise to match the price quoted if they return and complete within 24 hours.

The key is to reinforce the value of the item and also to reassure the customer of the quality of the product. Furthermore, showing the customer that you appreciate them and considering sweetening the deal a little may well help to overcome the original objection and get them to complete the desired action.

part 5

How to check your marketing is working

chapter 16

Measure and improve your marketing

In this chapter, we are going to look at a variety of metrics and measurement tools to determine how your marketing efforts are going, so you can optimise them over time. This will help with key decisions like where to spend your marketing money based on what marketing activities are working. It will be divided into two parts: first, we will look at how to assess your brand-building efforts and then in the second part we assess your sales activation plan. They both come together in what I term the 'cycle of marketing'.

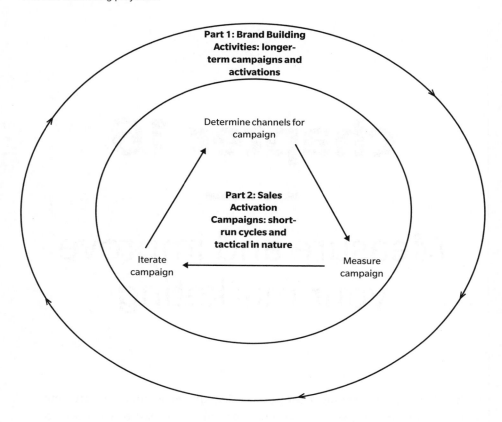

There is a wonderful quote from John Wanamaker proponent of advertising and a 'pioneer in marketing', who once said, "Half the money I spend on advertising is wasted. The trouble is I don't know which half." You'll be happy to note that today it has become much clearer on how we can measure our marketing activities using a variety of metrics and measurement techniques.

Despite the advances in this area, many have argued that our relentless reliance on attrition (how we identify how each marketing channel and advert performs to the nth degree) also has its drawbacks. The wonderful work of Les Binet and Peter Field[1] known as the 'Long and Short of it' illustrates this aptly. Often, in our drive to measure our marketing efforts we turn to short-term tools and tactics that deliver a return on investment quicker and have a more direct link to the communication. However, as a consequence we are seeing overall advertising effectiveness drop[2] as we are not engaging in long-term marketing activities, such as brand-building, since the longer effects are harder to measure given the long tail effects, previously discussed. Yet they can be more impactful as Binet and Field found.

Here is how short-term sales and brand-building play a role in sales growth.

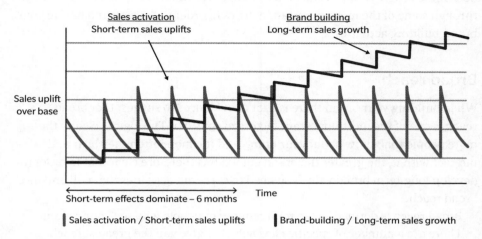

Source: https://effworks.co.uk/wp-content/uploads/2017/10/MEDIA_IN_FOCUS_FINAL_PDF_909.pdf

It's therefore worth remembering that both short-term sales activation and long-term brand-building need to work together to create strong marketing results. For instance, Binet and Field report that strong brands get much higher response rates from their activation campaigns, while companies that do good activation campaigns make more money from their brand. The key therefore when developing your own marketing activities is to recognise that it is not an 'either/or' situation but an 'and' situation and invest in both sides of the coin.

Part 1: Brand building

Brand-building activities enable you to achieve a number of different marketing objectives that include the following.

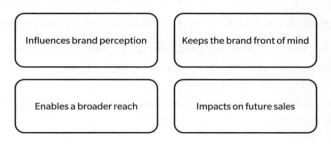

To achieve these objectives, you need to have a number of metrics in place to determine progress so you can be on a path of continuous improvement. Let's go through some of the most important metrics in order to develop and iterate your brand-building activities.

Broad reach

When building your brand there is a lot of evidence[3] to suggest that broad reach is one of the most important factors to consider. The logic is clear – the more people that know about your brand and the more often they hear and interact with it, the greater the brand equity. It is therefore clear that in order to develop long-term brand value you need to carry out activities that will enhance broad reach.

Broad reach is defined as the total number of people who see your content. There are a number of specific channels that give you the greatest reach.

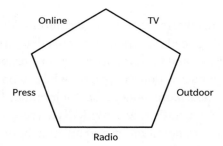

How can you determine broad reach?

Well, it depends on the channel you are using. In channels such as TV, a system known as 'gross rating points' is used based on the reach of channel offers and the frequency at which the viewer sees the ad. The formula used is:

$$\text{Audience reached} \times \text{frequency of exposure} = \text{gross rating}$$

On the other hand, if using online advertising, reach is calculated as the total number of people that see the advert over a period of time.

How can you improve broad reach?

There are a number of key techniques that you can use to improve the broad reach of your marketing activities.

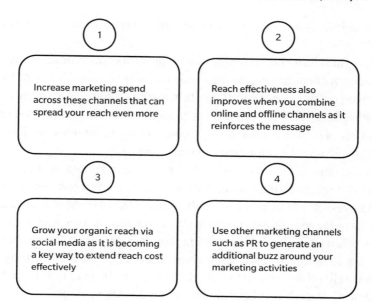

1
Increase marketing spend across these channels that can spread your reach even more

2
Reach effectiveness also improves when you combine online and offline channels as it reinforces the message

3
Grow your organic reach via social media as it is becoming a key way to extend reach cost effectively

4
Use other marketing channels such as PR to generate an additional buzz around your marketing activities

Consider how you can extend the broad reach of your brand.

Share of voice

Share of voice is a relative metric and looks at a brand's media spend and effectiveness compared to the rest of the industry. In essence, it looks at how loud they can shout about their offering relative to all their competitors. It links to the concept of 'repeatability' which is how many times does a consumer hear about the brand relative to others in the market. The higher the share of voice the better. Interestingly, this is where certain traditional channels can still have an extremely important role. For example, studies from Lumen have shown that when broken down into cost per attentive seconds, TV is the most cost-effective and delivers the best reach across certain populations. This is why advertisers still pay such premium rates for media slots such as the Superbowl. Therefore, integrating with these types of channels is still very important in order to hit a range of brand metrics (budgets permitting of course!).[4]

The formula is: Brand's share of category media spend divided by total category media spend

In today's marketing environment you do have the opportunity to increase share of voice without having to constantly increase the overall size of the media budget. Investing in organic social media growth is a key way to improve your share of voice as it gets your community to amplify your messages. You can also use the power of influencer marketing and creativity to increase the level of shareability and amplification (see Chapters 7 and 12).

This also relates to another concept by Bryon Sharp known as 'mental availability'. This is where by improving your share of voice and constantly being in the mind's eye of your customer you will increase the amount of time and recall that they have for your brand relative to the competition. This will be extremely beneficial when it comes to them making purchase decisions. Remember, it is unlikely that they will be ready to purchase a product exactly when they see your advert. Therefore, you need to find ways to stay front of mind so when they do have a need, they think of your brand above all other competitors.

Write down some ways that you can increase share of voice for your brand.

Market share

Byron Sharp in his book *How Brands Grow* found a strong relationship between sales and brand, therefore suggesting that market share is a key driver of brand growth as well. This leads to an interesting point between the relationship between sales activation and brand building and clearly has the dual benefit of generating revenue while building the brand for over the long term. It's therefore essential that you track market share, which can be defined as the percentage of total sales in an industry generated by a particular company. The formula is:

Company sales divided by the total sales of the industry over a period of time.

Brand emotion tracking

There is no doubt that at the heart of any powerful brand is its ability to drive a strong emotional connection with its audience. In fact, the ability to evoke an emotion from the consumer is one of the leading indicators of brand health as it creates relatability and shareability.

It has a range of influences on other brand drivers as well. For example, if you can create an emotional connection with your audience they are far more likely to share your content. This improves your share of voice, reach and hopefully market share.

There are four key brand attributes that are worth tracking.

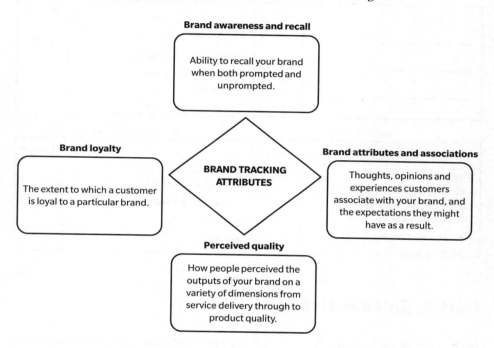

Brand awareness and recall
Ability to recall your brand when both prompted and unprompted.

Brand loyalty
The extent to which a customer is loyal to a particular brand.

BRAND TRACKING ATTRIBUTES

Brand attributes and associations
Thoughts, opinions and experiences customers associate with your brand, and the expectations they might have as a result.

Perceived quality
How people perceived the outputs of your brand on a variety of dimensions from service delivery through to product quality.

It's worth conducting regular research in order to track these over time to see how customer perceptions are evolving in this area. A good way to do this is to have a customer panel that consists of a cross-section of your target audience that you can refer back to at different points in time to determine how their perceptions and responses may have changed of the brand.

Consider how you could implement a similar process to determine how your brand's perceptions are changing over time.

It is worth bringing all of these together in one place so you can see the full brand picture easily and at a glance. You can achieve this by creating a dashboard that includes actual and desired metrics.

Here is a template that you can use.

Broad reach			Market share		
Channels	Actual	Desired		Actual	Desired
_____			Brand market share		
_____			Competitor market share:		
_____			_____		
			_____		
			_____		

Share of voice			Brand emotion tracking		
	Actual	Desired		Actual	Desired
Brand share of media spend			Brand tracking:		
Total category media spend			Awareness and recall		
Competitor media spend:			Brand attributes and associations		
_____			Perceived quality		
_____			Brand loyalty		
_____					

Part 2: Sales activation

In this second part, we will take a look at the popular metrics and measurement techniques you can use in relation to your tactical sales activation campaigns, otherwise known as performance marketing. Typically, this type of activities deliver the following.

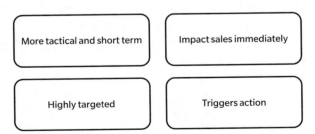

This is where digital marketing channels typically come in to deliver a highly targeted and personalised communication to the customer, with the intention to get them to act quickly to take up an offer.

Let's break this down into three stages.

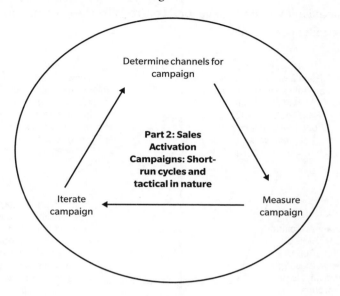

Determine channels for campaign

The first step is to determine the types of channels that you will use. To achieve this it's worth turning to the digital marketing mix that consists of three different types of channels.

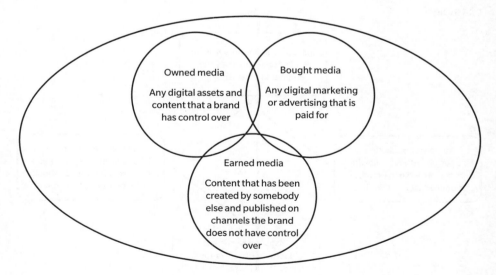

Let's explore some examples from each in a little more detail.

Owned media allows you to have total control over the content and channel. Here are a number of examples.

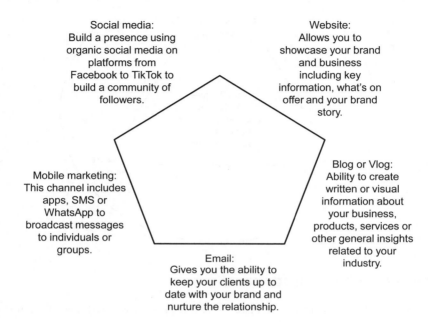

Social media:
Build a presence using organic social media on platforms from Facebook to TikTok to build a community of followers.

Website:
Allows you to showcase your brand and business including key information, what's on offer and your brand story.

Mobile marketing:
This channel includes apps, SMS or WhatsApp to broadcast messages to individuals or groups.

Blog or Vlog:
Ability to create written or visual information about your business, products, services or other general insights related to your industry.

Email:
Gives you the ability to keep your clients up to date with your brand and nurture the relationship.

Bought media is any channel where advertising is paid for. Here are some examples.

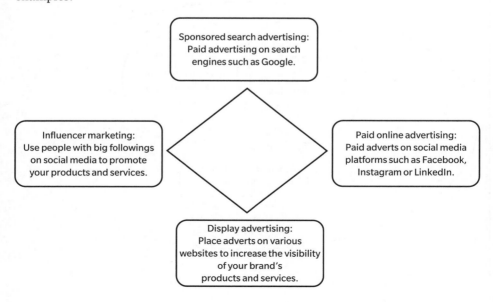

Sponsored search advertising:
Paid advertising on search engines such as Google.

Influencer marketing:
Use people with big followings on social media to promote your products and services.

Paid online advertising:
Paid adverts on social media platforms such as Facebook, Instagram or LinkedIn.

Display advertising:
Place adverts on various websites to increase the visibility of your brand's products and services.

Earned media are positive messages that others say about your brand, products and services. Here are a number of examples.

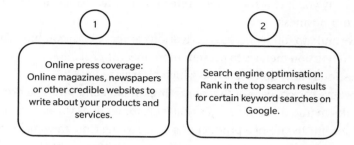

1 Online press coverage: Online magazines, newspapers or other credible websites to write about your products and services.

2 Search engine optimisation: Rank in the top search results for certain keyword searches on Google.

Write down the types of channels you would use for your brand.

Measure campaign

Across these various channels there are typically two types of metrics that get used: engagement and conversion metrics.

Engagement metrics have really erupted at the hands of digital analytics where you are able to measure an almost infinite number of things from each user's keystroke to their end-to-end web journey. But be aware that an engagement metric tends to have a high number on it that makes it sound cool but doesn't really shed light on how the campaign is translating into increased company profit. On the other hand, a conversion metric shows that you have your marketing activities move the dial on business performance.

Most companies will constantly report engagement metrics, but in isolation of conversion metrics it is difficult to derive meaningful commercial insights about campaign performance. A good example is that of the email open rate metric. Often people will proudly talk about high email open rates. This is not a bad thing, it's just not a good thing in isolation. I mean you could have 100% open rate but what does that say about your business? Not a lot. However, say you add in a conversion metric such as conversion rate, it could actually be very revealing. So now say you had a 100% open rate and no conversions, it certainly says a lot about your business.

So the formula to follow in sales activation campaigns is: combine engagement and conversion metrics to present more meaningful data.

The question is how do we choose which metrics to use?

This is where the concept of the marketing funnel comes in. The process can be broken down into different stages that a customer goes through from the time they become aware of a product or service to the time they make a purchase. The aim of sales activation marketing is to drive your customer down the funnel to make a purchase in a narrow range of time, so we can use this framework to determine the metrics and measurement techniques to use. It's worth noting that the marketing funnel can also be used in the context of brand building. You can effectively break the funnel down into three stages.

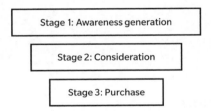

Based on these, you can build up a dashboard of engagement and conversion metrics to report on your various marketing campaigns and activities. Here is a list and description of some of the key engagement and conversion metrics to consider, broken down into the marketing funnel.

Engagement Metrics	Marketing Funnel	Conversion Metrics
Views: total views of communication/page Unique page views: total unique views of communication/page	Awareness Generation	Website traffic: total number of visitors to the website Dwell time: how long they stay for in one session
Followers: number of fans on social media Likes/shares/comments: engagement metrics on social media Open rates: number of email or message opens Pages per visit: number of pages seen in a given session	Consideration	Leads: Total number of leads Bounce rate: percentage of visitors who enter the site and then quickly leave Click-through rate: Number of visitors that click from a marketing message to site Enquiries/trials: Number of people that go on to enquire/trial about the product/service
	Purchase	Revenue: Total sales Profit: Total sales minus expenses Cost per sale: Total marketing spend/number of sales Referrals: Number of recommendations received Attrition: Percentage of people churning

Let's understand the potential insights that these metrics can give you when they are combined. Here are a number of examples.

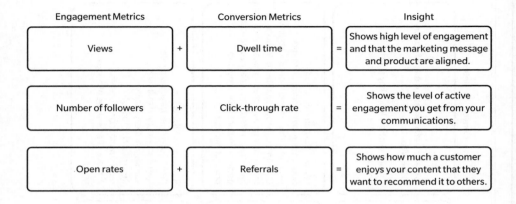

OK, now it's time to create your own dashboard for your sales activation activities. It is worth considering what good looks like and adding in some benchmarks for what you would like to achieve with each metric. Use the template below to do this.

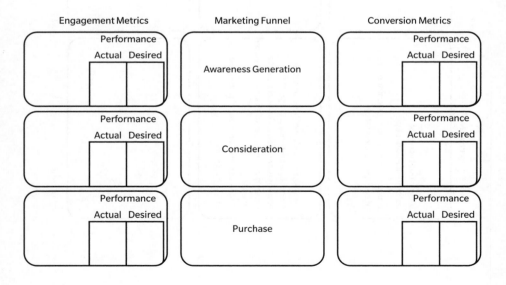

Iterate campaign

The final stage is to understand how to iterate your campaign based on performance. To achieve this, you want to once again revert back to your dashboard to determine your actual versus desired performance. Throughout this book we have talked about a variety of different ways to test and learn to optimise your approach. The key is to set up a test infrastructure and environment where you are able to test one aspect of the campaign at a time to determine if there is an increase in performance. You can then deploy a range of techniques from A/B testing, test and control and even econometrics to determine the incremental uplift.

To help here is a template that you can use when iterating the campaign to achieve a test and learn approach.

Channel Variations	Content Variations	Customer	
		Test	Control

Notes

Introduction

1. https://www.indiatoday.in/mail-today/story/potpourri-of-the-real-and-the-imagined-world-1596774-2019-09-08

2. https://www.mckinsey.com/business-functions/marketing-and-sales/our-insights/marketings-moment-is-now-the-c-suite-partnership-to-deliver-on-growth#

3. https://www.amazon.com/What-Got-Here-Wont-There/dp/0739342231

4. https://www.researchgate.net/figure/Average-company-lifespan-on-S-P-500-Index-each-data-represents-a-rolling-7-year-average_fig9_307560120

5. https://www.qad.com/blog/2019/10/sp-500-companies-over-time?utm_source=newsletter&utm_medium=email&utm_campaign=newsletter_axiosmarkets&stream=business

6. https://www.microsoft.com/en-us/microsoft-365/blog/2020/04/30/2-years-digital-transformation-2-months/

Chapter 1

1. https://www.emarketer.com/content/how-marketers-using-social-listening-right-now

2. https://www.thinkwithgoogle.com/consumer-insights/deal-seeker-path-to-purchase/

Chapter 2

1. https://hbr.org/2011/04/why-most-product-launches-fail

2. https://www.businessinsider.com/amazon-products-services-failed-discontinued-2019-3?r=US&IR=T

3. https://www.lexisclick.com/blog/customer-obsession-the-secret-to-amazons-success#:~:text=Amazon's%20definition%20of%20Customer%20Obsession,competitors%2C%20they%20obsess%20over%20customers.

4. https://www.gminsights.com/pressrelease/video-conferencing-market

5. https://www.youtube.com/watch?v=4sZMHAMN0DQ

6. https://mattfrancois.com/how-to-build-your-saas-platform-prototype-in-one-week

7. https://inc42.com/resources/airbnbs-journey-failing-startup-25-bn-company/

Chapter 3

1. https://hbr.org/sponsored/2018/02/3-principles-disney-uses-to-enhance-customer-experience

2. https://www.qualtrics.com/blog/6-ways-disney-world-delivers-top-customer-experiences/#:~:text=When%20it%20comes%20to%20world,the%20top%20of%20the%20list.&text=Disney%20puts%20value%20on%20the,rate%20for%20first%2Dtime%20visitors.

3. https://www.qualtrics.com/blog/6-ways-disney-world-delivers-top-customer-experiences/#:~:text=When%20it%20comes%20to%20world,the%20top%20of%20the%20list.&text=Disney%20puts%20value%20on%20the,rate%20for%20first%2Dtime%20visitors

4. https://www.qualtrics.com/blog/6-ways-disney-world-delivers-top-customer-experiences/#:~:text=When%20it%20comes%20to%20world,the%20top%20of%20the%20list.&text=Disney%20puts%20value%20on%20the,rate%20for%20first%2Dtime%20visitors

5. https://www.qualtrics.com/blog/6-ways-disney-world-delivers-top-customer-experiences/#:~:text=When%20it%20comes%20to%20world,the%20top%20of%20the%20list.&text=Disney%20puts%20value%20on%20the,rate%20for%20first%2Dtime%20visitors

6. https://www.business2community.com/customer-experience/the-relentless-pursuit-of-the-perfect-customer-experience-a-netflix-story-02240302

7. https://www.kaushik.net/avinash/

8. https://www.business2community.com/customer-experience/the-relentless-pursuit-of-the-perfect-customer-experience-a-netflix-story-02240302

Chapter 4

1. https://www.business2community.com/customer-experience/the-relentless-pursuit-of-the-perfect-customer-experience-a-netflix-story-02240302

2. https://www.amazon.co.uk/Permission-Marketing-Turning-Strangers-Customers/dp/1416526668

3. https://www.edelman.com/trustbarometer

4. https://www.ikea.com/gb/en/this-is-ikea/about-us/vision-and-business-idea-pub9cd02291

5. https://www.youtube.com/watch?v=S1xRJaNiOtU

6. https://about.ads.microsoft.com/en-us/blog/post/january-2020/2020-vision-trends-to-define-the-next-decade?feed=blogposts

7. https://qz.com/1547366/mastercard-has-a-new-sonic-logo/

8. https://www.ipsos.com/sites/default/files/ct/publication/documents/2020-02/power-of-you-ipsos.pdf

9. https://www.campaignlive.co.uk/article/why-just-eat-waited-five-weeks-unleash-its-snoop-dogg-campaign/1682517

10. https://www.campaignlive.co.uk/article/why-just-eat-waited-five-weeks-unleash-its-snoop-dogg-campaign/1682517

11. https://consulting.kantar.com/wp-content/uploads/2019/06/Purpose-2020-PDF-Presentation.pdf

12. https://www.weforum.org/agenda/2020/06/3-ways-companies-build-resilient-society-after-covid-19/

13. https://www.linkedin.com/posts/gordon-stanley-02a1442_discussion-values-leadership-activity-6672464949891088384-_q6p

14. https://www.etftrends.com/smart-beta-channel/blackrock-confirms-resilience-of-esg-during-market-downturn/

15. https://justcapital.com/news/chart-of-the-week-americas-most-just-companies-are-bouncing-back-more-quickly-during-the-current-recession/

Chapter 5

1. https://www.bbc.co.uk/news/business-53257933#:~:text=Tesla%20 has%20become%20the%20world's,%24209.47bn%20(%C2%A3165bn)

2. https://www.thestreet.com/technology/history-of-tesla-15088992#:~:- text=The%20modern%20face%20of%20Tesla,into%20full%20 production%20in%202012

3. https://www.campaignlive.com/article/marketing-times-crisis-master- cards-global-cmo-shares-4-common-traps-better/1688895

4. https://www.businessinsider.com/spacex-boeing-nasa-commercial-crew- program-launch-astronauts-2020-1?r=US&IR=T

5. https://www.linkedin.com/posts/braunbenjamin_new-this-week-catalyst- magazine-issue-3-activity-6691289667238805504-hknZ

6. https://www.adobomagazine.com/global-news/cannes-lions-2019-burger- king-is-named-as-the-first-ever-cannes-lions-creative-brand-of-the-year/

7. https://www.contagious.com/news-and-views/insight-and-strategy-behind- burger-king-moldy-whopper-advert

8. https://metro.co.uk/2020/08/21/terrys-chocolate-orange-launches-new- limited-white-chocolate-edition-13158571/

9. https://www.whowhatwear.co.uk/birkin-bag-prices

10. https://www.thedrinksbusiness.com/2020/08/brewdog-partners-with- ricky-gervais-on-beer-to-help-stray-dogs/

11. http://offthecuffldn.co.uk/blog/mens-lifestyle/haagen-dazs-caramel- royale-cocktail-with-secret-cinemas-secret-sofa/

12. https://www.talkingretail.com/products-news/frozen/haagen-dazs-jack- daniels-collaborate-final-secret-sofa-04-06-2020/

Chapter 7

1. https://www.nielsen.com/us/en/insights/article/2017/when-it-comes-to- advertising-effectiveness-what-is-key/

2. https://www.nielsen.com/us/en/insights/article/2017/when-it-comes-to- advertising-effectiveness-what-is-key/

3. https://www.mckinsey.com/business-functions/mckinsey-digital/ our-insights/creativitys-bottom-line-how-winning-companies-turn- creativity-into-business-value-and-growth

4. The Gunn Report, IPA

5. https://fttoolkit.co.uk/perch/resources/the-board-brand-rift-2.pdf

6. http://bbh-labs.com/the-business-case-for-creativity/

7. https://www.mobilemarketer.com/news/burger-king-whopper-detour-mobile-marketer-awards/566224/

8. https://www.vegansociety.com/news/media/statistics#:~:text=Veganism%20in%20the%20UK,-In%202018%2C%20the&text=The%20number%20of%20vegans%20in,150%2C000%20(0.25%25)%20in%202014

9. https://www.thisismoney.co.uk/money/markets/article-7026795/Greggs-shares-spike-vegan-sausage-rolls-fly-shelves.html

10. https://adage.com/article/opinion/new-research-uncovers-biggest-differentiator-effective-marketing-bravery/2186146

11. http://bbh-labs.com/most-marketing-is-bad-because-it-ignores-the-most-basic-data/#_edn2

12. https://www.thisismoney.co.uk/money/markets/article-7026795/Greggs-shares-spike-vegan-sausage-rolls-fly-shelves.html

13. https://www.amazon.co.uk/Good-Great-Jim-Collins/dp/0712676090

14. https://www.linkedin.com/pulse/time-reset-how-businesses-can-accelerate-out-pandemic-woodward/

15. https://www.oneclub.org/articles/-view/what-does-it-take#.XujrLcgm-VE.twitter

16. https://hbr.org/2017/02/how-spotify-balances-employee-autonomy-and-accountability#:~:text=They%20are%20organized%20into%20a,agile%20coaching%2C%20and%20web%20development

17. https://www.ted.com/talks/steven_johnson_where_good_ideas_come_from?language=en

18. http://significantobjects.com/

19. https://jobadder.com/blog/marketing-no-longer-about#:~:text=%E2%80%9CMarketing%20is%20no%20longer%20about,stories%20you%20tell%E2%80%9D%20%E2%80%93%20Seth%20Godin

20. https://www.ebiquity.com/news-insights/webinars/recording-how-creativity-drives-advertising-effectiveness/

21. https://www.warc.com/content/paywall/article/warc-webinars/fluent_devices_and_the_forgotten_art_of_memorability/117454

22. https://www.clearvoice.com/blog/what-is-freytags-pyramid-dramatic-structure/#:~:text=Devised%20by%2019th%20century%20German,action%2C%20resolution%2C%20and%20denouement

23. https://www.lumen-research.com/blog/p653k3atys5ubp58jcydxoyn0d0wik

24. https://www.lumen-research.com/blog/p653k3atys5ubp58jcydxoyn0d0wik

Chapter 9

1. https://support.google.com/google-ads/answer/140351?hl=en-GB

Chapter 10

1. https://www.bakeryandsnacks.com/Article/2020/05/12/PepsiCo-goes-direct-to-consumer-with-online-snack-sites2#:~:text=To%20capitalise%20on%20this%20trend,of%20snacks%20and%20breakfast%20products.&-text=The%20snack%20giant%20said%20new,customised%20to%20meet%20consumer%20preferences

2. https://www.youtube.com/watch?v=UrbgO2v5tTw

Chapter 11

1. https://www.linkedin.com/posts/grantcardone_my-overnight-success-fired-from-seven-activity-6681677437094424577-b46B/

2. https://www.youtube.com/watch?v=xNgQOHwsIbg

3. https://en.wikipedia.org/wiki/Ben_Franklin_effect

Chapter 12

1. https://www.businessinsider.com/influencer-marketing-report?r=US&IR=T#:~:text=The%20influencer%20marketing%20industry%20is,gold%20standard%20for%20the%20group

2. https://edition.cnn.com/2020/09/25/tech/david-attenborough-instagram-intl-scli-gbr-climate/index.html

3. https://edition.cnn.com/2020/09/25/tech/david-attenborough-instagram-intl-scli-gbr-climate/index.html

4. https://influencermarketinghub.com/growth-of-esports-stats/#:~:text=eSports%20Viewership%20is%20Growing,-Since%202016%2C%20

there&text=Between%202016%20and%202017%2C%20there,the%20 total%20audience%20335%20million.&text=And%20that%20there%20 will%20be,the%20total%20audience%20557%20million

5. https://influencermarketinghub.com/esports-influencers/

6. https://www.adweek.com/brand-marketing/disregard-speculation-influencer-marketing-is-still-a-necessity-in-strategies/

7. https://www.thedrum.com/news/2017/08/02/brands-will-pay-75000-celebrity-influencer-endorsements-despite-confusion-over-fees

Chapter 13

1. https://www.zuora.com/guides/business-logic-ltv-amazon-gives-things-away-free/

2. https://www.sellerapp.com/blog/amazon-predictive-analytics/#:~:text= Amazon%20Predictive%20analytics%20considers%20a,to%20sell%20 a%20better%20experience

Chapter 14

1. https://mindsea.com/app-stats/#:~:text=In%202017%2C%202018%2D%20 to%2024,likely%20to%20use%20a%20desktop

2. https://mindsea.com/app-stats/#:~:text=In%202017%2C%202018%2D%20 to%2024,likely%20to%20use%20a%20desktop

3. https://mindsea.com/app-stats/#:~:text=In%202017%2C%202018%2D%20 to%2024,likely%20to%20use%20a%20desktop

4. https://www.gsma.com/mobilefordevelopment/wp-content/uploads/ 2019/07/GSMA-State-of-Mobile-Internet-Connectivity-Report-2019.pdf

5. https://www.cable.co.uk/mobiles/worldwide-data-pricing/

6. https://www.pret.co.uk/en-GB/your-pret

7. https://mobilemarketingmagazine.com/the-podcast-opportunity

8. https://www.dotcominfoway.com/blog/infographic-mobile-game-market-trends-2020/#gref

Chapter 15

1. https://www.tributemedia.com/blog/you-have-7-seconds-what-a-visitor-should-know-about-your-website-within-moments

2. https://medium.com/@AirAsia.com/the-power-of-you-launch-of-homepagepersonalization-at-airasia-com-part-1-of-3-cb0b6e5edbeb

Chapter 16

1. https://ipa.co.uk/knowledge/publications-reports/the-long-and-the-short-of-it-balancing-short-and-long-term-marketing-strategies
2. http://bbh-labs.com/the-business-case-for-creativity/
3. https://effworks.co.uk/wp-content/uploads/2017/10/MEDIA_IN_FOCUS_FINAL_PDF_909.pdf
4. https://www.lumen-research.com/blog/p653k3atys5ubp58jcydxoyn0d0wik

Index